UNIVERSITY OF NORTH CAROLINA AT CHAPEL HILL

DEPARTMENT OF ROMANCE LANGUAGES

NORTH CAROLINA STUDIES IN THE ROMANCE LANGUAGES AND LITERATURES

Founder: URBAN TIGNER HOLMES

Editor: MARÍA A. SALGADO

Distributed by:

UNIVERSITY OF NORTH CAROLINA PRESS

CHAPEL HILL

North Carolina 27515-2288

U.S.A.

NORTH CAROLINA STUDIES IN THE
ROMANCE LANGUAGES AND LITERATURES
Number 234

A POETICS OF ART CRITICISM

A POETICS OF ART CRITICISM:
THE CASE OF BAUDELAIRE

BY
TIMOTHY RASER

CHAPEL HILL

NORTH CAROLINA STUDIES IN THE ROMANCE LANGUAGES AND LITERATURES
U.N.C. DEPARTMENT OF ROMANCE LANGUAGES
1989

Library of Congress Cataloging-in-Publication Data

Raser, Timothy Bell.
A poetics of art criticism: the case of Baudelaire / by Timothy Raser.

p. – cm. – (North Carolina studies in the Romance languages and literatures; 234).
Bibliography: p.
Includes index.
ISBN 0-8078-9238-6
1. Baudelaire, Charles, 1821-1867 – Knowledge – Art. 2. Baudelaire, Charles, 1821-1867 – Aesthetics. 3. Baudelaire, Charles, 1821-1867 – Prose. 4. Art criticism –France – History – 19th century. 5. Aesthetics, French – 19th century. I. Title. II. Series: North Carolina studies in the Romance languages and literatures; no. 234.

PQ2191.Z5R28 1989.
841'.8 – dc19 88-27319
CIP

ISBN 0-8078-9238-6

DEPÓSITO LEGAL: V. 578 - 1989 I.S.B.N. 84-599-2628-1

ARTES GRÁFICAS SOLER, S. A. - LA OLIVERETA, 28 - 46018 VALENCIA - 1989

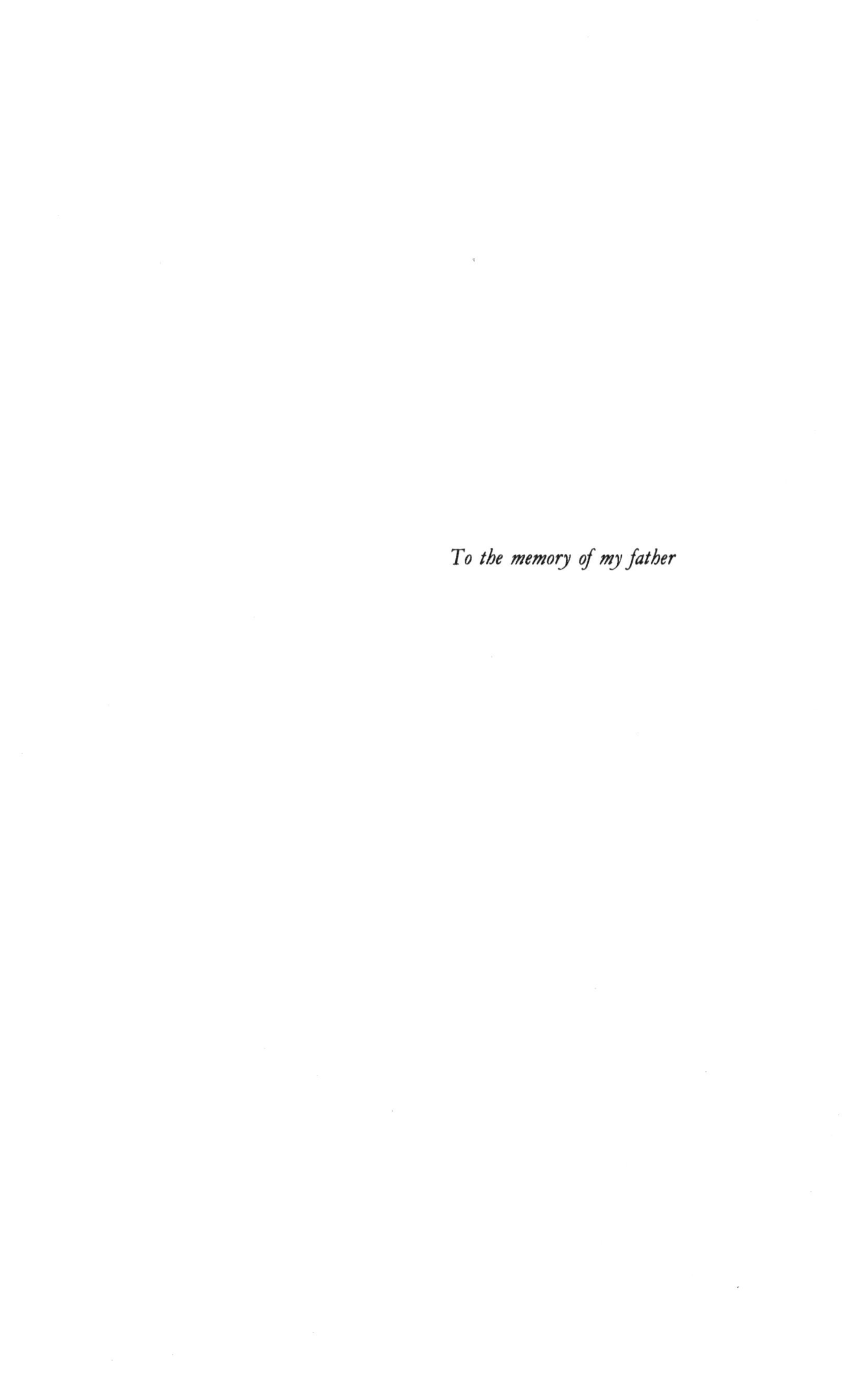

To the memory of my father

TABLE OF CONTENTS

ACKNOWLEDGEMENTS

I would like to express my gratitude here for support received from the University of Tulsa and the University of Georgia which permitted research for this project. The extent of my debt to Claude Pichois becomes more apparent with every reference to his splendid edition of Baudelaire's *Œuvres complètes.* My thanks go also to the editors of *SubStance* and the *Romanic Review* for their permission to reprint chapters 1 and 3, earlier versions of which appeared in their journals. I am grateful to *Editions Gallimard* for their kind permission to use material from editions of the works of Chateaubriand, Hugo, Baudelaire and Proust, appearing the *Bibliothèque de la Pléiade.* M. and Mme R. M. Jourdain of AGRACI also receive an expression of my sincere thanks, for permission to use their photograph of Delacroix's *Pietà.* I wish to express my gratitude to Norman Grabo and to Jean Gaudon, for the invaluable comments they gave on early stages of the manuscript. Special thanks go to Serge Trottein for his readings and support, and whose *Théorie du jeu* is so close to the heart of this work that its presence cannot go unrecognized. Above all I thank my wife Melinda for her patience and love during the most trying moments of this undertaking.

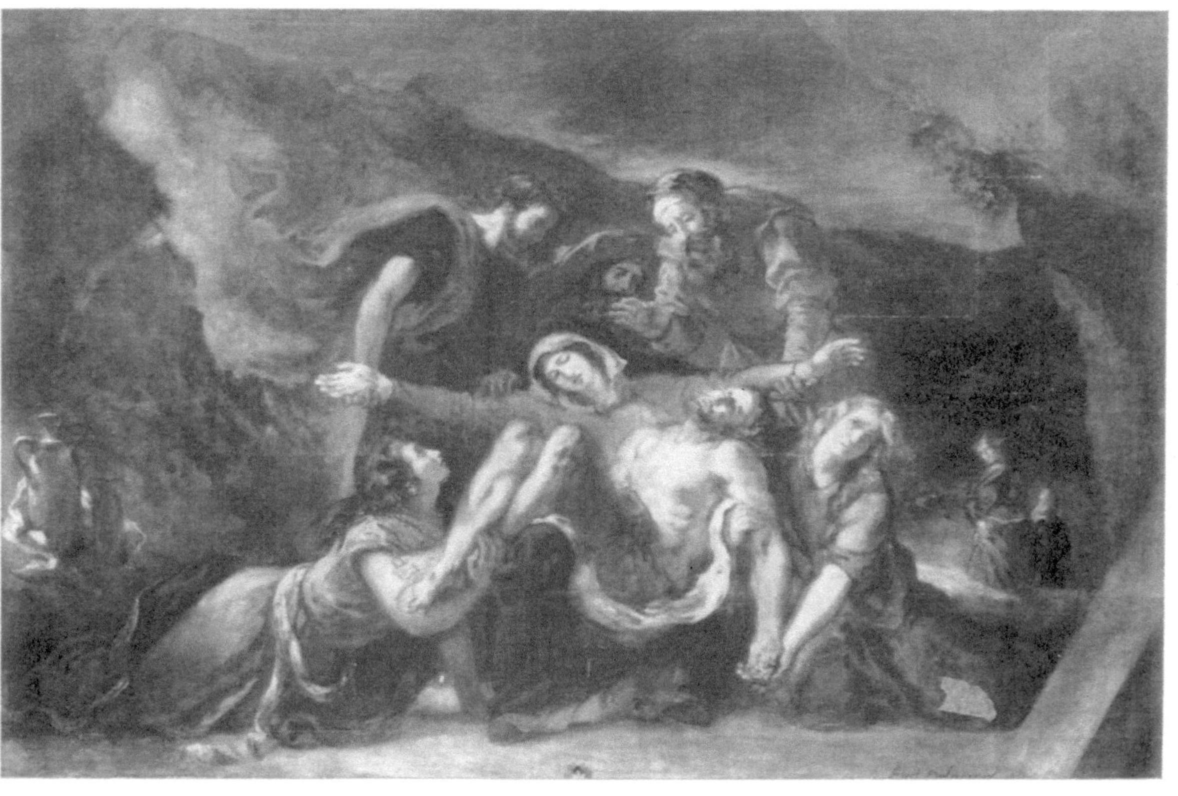

Eugène Delacroix, *Pietà*, 1844. Saint-Denis du Saint Sacrement, Paris.
Photo: AGRACI

INTRODUCTION

A consensus exists that there is something valuable and elusive about Baudelaire's art-criticism: it must be read, its lesson must be learned, even if that lesson has to do with things other than the artists Baudelaire discussed. Anne Coffin Hanson refers to the *Peintre de la vie moderne* to explain Manet's relation to tradition;[1] Timothy Clark uses that title to explain Manet's modernity;[2] Margaret Gilman seeks a general theory of the imagination in the *Salon de 1859;*[3] Christopher Miller invokes the *compte rendu* of the *Exposition universelle* to define Baudelaire's notion of alterity.[4] Michael Fried has demonstrated the significance of a complex theory of memory and precursorship as the criterion of judgment in the *Salon de 1846.*[5] There is a theoretical component to this criticism that extends far beyond its application to painting and sculpture from the mid-nineteenth century.

It is also agreed that this writing is not merely instrumental: Georges Blin has called *Le Peintre de la vie moderne* "le plus grand des poèmes en prose de Baudelaire."[6] Claude Pichois, editor of the *Œuvres complètes,* describes the evocation of Boudin's pastels as

---

[1] Anne Coffin Hanson, *Manet and the Modern Tradition* (New Haven: Yale University Press, 1977).

[2] Timothy Clark, *The Painting of Modern Life* (New York: Knopf, 1984).

[3] Margaret Gilman, *Baudelaire the Critic* (New York: Columbia University Press, 1943), pp. 114-68.

[4] Christopher Miller, *Blank Darkness: Africanist Discourse in French* (Chicago: University of Chicago Press, 1985), pp. 87-93.

[5] Michael Fried, "Painting Memories: On the Containment of the Past in Baudelaire and Manet," *Critical Inquiry* 10, No. 3 (March, 1984), pp. 510-42.

[6] Georges Blin, *Annuaire du Collège de France,* 69ème année (1969-70), *Résumé des cours de 1968-1969,* p. 525.

"comme un poème en prose."[7] Baudelaire himself initiated such comparison of his descriptions with poetry by writing verse descriptions of works of art such as those commented by Jean Prévost: "Les Phares," "Le Masque," "Danse macabre," "Bohémiens en voyage," and so forth.[8]

Finally, Baudelaire's preferences have attracted much attention, and, comparing such preferences, several readers have traced the portrait of the judge. Pierre-Georges Castex has applauded the poet for the strength of his judgments and their accuracy.[9] Certainly this aspect of Baudelaire's criticism is not the least rewarding to study, for he did have an uncanny knack for predicting future taste. And even when Baudelaire chose to praise second-rate artists – Constantin Guys comes to mind – his judgments have tended more to bring about re-evaluation of the artist than re-evaluation of his judgment.

Judgment, explanation, description: these are the elements of art-criticism. The foregoing paragraph will have indicated that much scholarship has been devoted to Baudelaire's criticism: his judgments have been sifted and appraised; the poetic passages of his essays have been noted and related to specific poems; his theories of beauty have been analyzed, applied and employed in many different contexts. However, I can think of no attempt to relate systematically the components of his criticism, to respond to these questions: what is the relation of Baudelaire's theory to his judgment? of description to judgment? of theory to description? Above all of these questions hangs another: what is the nature of the judgment that theory explains and description illustrates? If aesthetic taste were like ordinary taste (taste of the palate), one could use such judgments to describe the judge – his preferences in painting would be similar in nature to preferences of wine or perfume. Determined by early experience, such tastes would open doors onto the judge's development, but by the same token, would only be expressions of psychology, not the fruit of a freely-made judgment. Alternatively, if aesthetic judgment resulted from the

[7] Claude Pichois, ed., *Œuvres complètes,* by Charles Baudelaire (Paris: Editions Gallimard, Bibliothèque de La Pléiade, © 1975-6), II, 1407.

[8] Jean Prévost, *Baudelaire: essai sur l'inspiration et la création poétiques* (Paris: Mercure de France, 1953).

[9] Pierre-Georges Castex, *La Critique d'art en France au* XIX*ème siècle* (Paris: Centre de Documentation Universitaire, 1958), pp. 27-78.

application of a system, all criticism would be entirely predictable, and consequently, uninteresting. Finally, if beauty resided in the object, there would be agreement, even in the absence of aesthetic theories, as to which objects are beautiful. Unfortunately, none of these hypotheses is corroborated by experience, and art criticism remains mysterious.

It is in order to examine such problems, and to gain thereby a synthetic view of Baudelaire's art-criticism that I have written this book. These questions expand very quickly when one considers them, and a theoretical introduction to the study of Baudelaire's critical essays is necessary. The first chapter opposes scientific to aesthetic attitudes in criticism, the better to understand what the implications of aesthetic judgment are. The second looks at the metalanguage used by criticism to frame its descriptions, while the third evaluates the reliability of description in the service of arguments, both narrative and logical.

It is only with the second part of the book that I return to Baudelaire: his *Salon de 1846, Exposition universelle: Beaux-arts – 1855, Salon de 1859, Le Peintre de la vie moderne,* and finally, *L'Œuvre et la vie d'Eugène Delacroix*. While not a comprehensive selection, these essays do offer a wide view of Baudelaire's criticism, and together invoke the essential features of aesthetic judgment. I believe further that there is a logical progression to be discerned behind the chronological sequence of the essays, and this evolution tells the story of Baudelaire's response to the constraints of aesthetic judgment.

Part I

A POETICS OF ART CRITICISM

1

THE FALLACIES OF IMITATION

Juger, toujours juger autrui![1]

Since Zeuxis, the role of painting has been imitative: those canvases or frescoes whose illusion is more convincing have been considered more proficient, more truthful, more artistic. Art criticism has correspondingly been considered easy: it suffices to determine how closely the painting approximates its model, and such determinations, as the fable puts it, can be made by unthinking animals.[2] Imitation is thus an essential part of painting, but it cannot be all of it; there is something more . . . Perhaps a more understanding account of imitation can be found in literary criticism.

Even there however ambiguities persist. The concept of imitation has long received much attention from literary theorists, but since the Romantics, much of that has been unfavorable. Imitation is the doctrine against which very different movements have sought to define themselves; while they all despise imitative theories of art, there is no agreement on what it is exactly that they condemn, or, more importantly, what will be put in its place. Three decades ago, M. Abrams analyzed early nineteenth-century literary theory, and concluded that the Romantics had abandoned an imitative theory in favor of an imaginative theory of art, that they asked art to function as a lamp illuminating the world rather

---

[1] Charles-Augustin Sainte-Beuve, *Mes Poisons* (Paris: Plon, 1926), p. 10.

[2] For an account of the Zeuxian myth, see Norman Bryson, *Vision and Painting: The Logic of the Gaze* (New Haven: Yale University Press, 1983), chap. 1.

than as the mirror that reflects it.[3] Current semiological and ideological analyses are elaborating procedures of literary production, and like the Romantics, oppose a generative theory of literature to an imitative one.[4] While the Romantics, however, put forward a theory of imagination, described with organic metaphors, semiology elaborates a theory of production, described with mechanical metaphors. Earlier, artistic genius avoided the facile way of imitation; currently, the subtle logic of language undermines its own capacity to imitate.

Such efforts to distinguish a representational theory of literature from another are by no means confined to contemporary debate: the distinction of formal reactions to a work from those which look upon it as a transmission of information, is characteristic of most responses to mimetic art. The work is not considered the place to go to learn how someone looked or how an event occurred.

While it is known why imitative theories are rejected, it is less sure why other theories are preferred, and the variety of such theories is matched only by the vehemence of their proponents. Indeed, such vehemence is necessary, for often it is difficult to determine how, precisely, they differ from the imitative theories they replace. A good example of this difficulty occurs in Quatremère de Quincy's *De l'imitation;* I choose this example to start because here, the distinction made is unashamedly evaluative: the preferred mode is preferred because it is better. The distinction Quatremère makes lies between "imitations" and "copies." (I note here that of the two terms, it is "copy," not "imitation" that corresponds to what I am elsewhere calling "imitative" art; "imitation" for Quatremère is more than mere representation.) Both Quatremère's "copy" and current "imitations" are qualified as "servile." As his distinction progresses, however, it becomes less and less evident that it is positive or demonstrable, and more and more obvious that it is entirely arbitrary. When, for example, Quatremère distinguishes literary copies from literary imitations, it

---

[3] M. H. Abrams, *The Mirror and the Lamp* (New York: Oxford University Press, 1953).

[4] See, for example, Jonathan Culler's *Pursuit of Signs* (Ithaca: Cornell University Press, 1981) and Fredric Jameson's *The Political Unconscious* (Ithaca: Cornell University Press, 1981).

appears that an imitation is an imitation, not a copy, by virtue of an elusive quality loaded with associations: it is not "vulgar," "banal," or "servile." That is, an imitation corresponds to some unformulated norms, the failure to correspond to which denies the "copy" any prestige:

> Pour en donner un exemple entre beaucoup d'autres, qu'offrira par la suite de cette théorie . . . , reproduire servilement dans le discours que l'écrivain prête aux personnages qu'il fait parler, les pensées, les formules, les locutions banales, ou les termes d'un langage vulgaire, voilà ce que l'on prétend être la répétition de la réalité, au lieu de la ressemblance imitative. Il est sensible par cet exemple, que la chose à reproduire par l'imitation, c'est-à-dire dans un autre discours, ne se reproduit pas dans une autre chose, c'est-à-dire un autre discours qui en devient l'image. Il est sensible qu'il n'y a plus là deux choses distinctes, mais deux fois la même chose.
>
> C'est ce qu'on appelle *copie;* car copie, *copia,* ne signifie qu'un *double.*[5]

Imitation differs from copy by virtue of an arbitrary valorization; the more valued of the two terms is selected by a judgement which is ultimately undefined. One cannot be sure that there exists a representation which is not a copy, but one does know that copies are "merely" representations. Quatremère distinguishes two representations of an object, and states that one is "only" a representation, while the second merits the epithet "imitation" by being "more" than a representation. "Imitation" lies elsewhere than in representation.

This argument has not been discarded in the subsequent evolution of criticism. It can be found very close to contemporary debates in Abrams's *Mirror and the Lamp,* the subject of a critique by Jonathan Culler, "The Mirror Stage." Culler seeks to determine what separates the "imaginative" from the "imitative" theories distinguished by Abrams, and concludes that the opposition is unfounded. The very mode of writing that describes a change from mimetic to imaginative principles, Culler argues, is itself mimetic

---

[5] Antoine-Chrysostome Quatremère de Quincy, *De l'imitation,* eds. Léon Krier and Demetri Porphyrios (1823; rpt. Brussels: Archives d'Architecture Moderne, 1980), 23-4.

(for it seeks to represent the two modes of writing), and thus calls into doubt the validity of the periodization Abrams bases on this distinction. Abrams proves, unintentionally, the continued existence of a mode of writing he claims was surpassed. Culler pursues to say that Abrams's argument cannot be historical, but must be evaluative: ". . . his distinction, whose historical content is variable and idiosyncratic, is primarily evaluative."[6] Again, the two modes prove to be distinct only in an evaluative sense, and this evaluation serves to prevent positive assessments of imitation.

A last example should suffice to demonstrate that this preference continues to this day, even in the most scientific of discourses. Michael Riffaterre has consistently shown how literature can be intelligently analyzed without reference to any knowledge of "reality," and proves that, in fact, the specificity of the literary text lies in its internal relations rather than in its extra-textual appeals. To pursue this analysis, Riffaterre distinguishes between "mimetic" reading, which looks for relations between the text and reality, and "semiotic" reading, which seeks the internal structure of the text. The two modes of reading differ as multiplicity differs from unity, as enumeration differs from number:

> Now the basic characteristic of mimesis is that it produces a continuously changing semantic sequence, for representation is founded upon the referentiality of language, that is, upon a direct relationship of words to things. . . . Mimesis is thus variation and multiplicity.
>
> Whereas the characteristic feature of the poem is its unity: a unity both formal and semantic. Any component of the poem that points to that 'something else' it means will therefore be a constant, and as such it will be sharply distinguishable from mimesis. . . . From the standpoint of significance, the text is one semantic unit.[7]

It can be objected however that textual unity is a matter of subjective preference: one man's chaos is another's unity. Such is the case, for example, of enumeration, the classic mimetic proce-

[6] Culler, "The Mirror Stage," in *Pursuit*, p. 163.

[7] Michael Riffaterre, *Semiotics of Poetry* (Bloomington: Indiana University Press, 1978), pp. 2-3.

dure: what sometimes appears as a random list, obeying no other constraint than that of naming the features of the object represented, appears elsewhere as a text subordinated to complex and interlocking formal patterns. In Riffaterre's theory, it is the literary status of the text that defines it as structured, and that necessitates and legitimizes the search for structure.[8] The text is thus semiotic if is it poetic. Of course, "poetic" is an evaluative term, as is "literarity," and thus the notion of a mode of reading different from the mimetic mode presupposes a judgment.

In theories both of production and of reception, both at present and in the past, the notion of imitation has been rejected in favor of other theories. It is rarely stated however, just how the other theory differs from imitative theory, and it seems, looking more closely at these distinctions, that they are aesthetic. Qualities of "power," "life" and "poetry" – common figures of beauty – are reserved to these modes, whatever difficulties are encountered when one tries to define them. To produce art, one must go beyond representation.

This assertion is found so often in aesthetics that one may wonder whether it is not presupposed by any discussion of imitation: preliminary to speaking of imitation, one asserts that beauty is its possible product, that although the representation of a beautiful object can be less than beautiful, the representation of an ugly object can be beautiful. Such, for example, is Aristotle's observation in the *Poetics*:

> ... there are some things that distress us when we see them in reality, but the most accurate representations of these same things we view with pleasure – as, for example, the forms of the most despised animals and corpses.[9]

While such assertions serve to distinguish model and imitation, they also serve to identify imitation and beauty.[10] Detaching

---

[8] "... le problème essentiel que l'œuvre d'art pose au linguiste est celui de la *littérarité*." Michael Riffaterre, *La Production du texte* (Paris: Editions du Seuil, 1979), p. 7.

[9] Aristotle, *Aristotle's Poetics*, trans. Leon Golden, ed. O. B. Hardison, Jr. (Tallahassee, University Presses of Florida, 1981), p. 7.

[10] For example, in the first pages of his *Aesthetics*, Hegel refuses to discuss the beauty of nature, asserting his exclusive interest in the beauty of art: "... we may

appreciation of imitation from that of its model, aesthetics attaches itself to representation. Aesthetic reactions to representations replace cognitive reactions.

This distinction prevents one from responding to the object represented instead of to the work, but it also serves to exclude cognitive responses generally from among the possible reactions to art. Something that is recognized – a subject, a form, a sign – can also be imitated, and is thus not to be considered the object of aesthetic judgment. There is agreement that art contains recognizable features, but agreement also that it is not the presence or absence of such features that defines its beauty. One says: "Yes, it does represent a beautiful object; yes, it does display balanced form; yes, it transmits an important truth; yet, is it beautiful?" This distinction serves to conserve the autonomy of the aesthetic judgment, which, as Kant demonstrated in his third *Critique,* demands the assent of its audience while refusing to refer to any concept. The aesthetic judgment is free from obedience to any authority, but is nevertheless tyrannical in its insistence on its own validity. Beauty, as the term is understood, is an attribute, not an essence; it may be lost or acquired in the representation of an object in a work of art. Beauty is not transmissible by representation, but can be produced by it.[11] The accidental status of beauty

---

assert against this view, even at this stage, that the beauty of art is *higher* than nature. The beauty of art is beauty *born of the spirit and born again,* and the higher the spirit and its productions stand above nature and its phenomena, the higher too is the beauty of art above that of nature." Georg Wilhelm Friedrich Hegel, *Hegel's Aesthetics,* trans. T. M. Knox (Oxford: The Clarendon Press, 1975), I, 2. William Gilpin argues the contrary opinion: that a beautiful sight in nature can be less than beautiful in its artistic representation: "We admire the horse, as a *real object*; the elegance of his form; the stateliness of his tread; the spirit of all his motions; and the glossiness of his coat. We admire him also in *representation.* But as an object of picturesque beauty, we admire more the worn-out cart-horse, the cow, the goat, or the ass . . ." William Gilpin, *Essays on Picturesque Beauty* (1917; rpt. Wemstead: Gregg International Publishers Limited, 1972), p. 14.

[11] Some theories do hold that the beauty of a work results essentially from its transmission of the beauty of its subject, and that the degree of the former depends on the faithfulness of that representation. Such, for example, is the case of the Abbé du Bos: "Les Peintres et les Poëtes excitent en nous ces passions artificielles, en présentant les imitations des objets capables d'exciter en nous des passions véritables. Comme l'impression que ces imitations font sur nous est du même genre que l'impression que l'object imité par le Peintre ou par le Poëte ferait sur nous; comme l'impression que l'imitation fait n'est différente de l'impression que l'objet ferait, qu'en ce qu'elle est moins forte, elle doit exciter

is accepted, even if it means that any aesthetic judgment is an act implying the force of the judge rather than the accuracy of his judgment.

Understandably, a formulation which reduces the question of an object's beauty to a question of force, or perhaps more commonly, the stubbornness of the person proposing the judgment, is of some concern to any writer who uses the term "beauty," or, more generally, to any critic whose conceptual systems use oppositions employing the evaluations characteristic of aesthetic judgment. It seems further that literary theory that discusses the problem of representation is led inevitably to use such systems, for they serve to define "imitation."

The stakes of this debate are quite high, for the attribution or withholding of "beauty" can serve several functions. Of course, the application of an aesthetic judgment can express a simple preference: that an imitation is "better" than a copy, or that art is more beautiful than "life." But these "disinterested" evaluations can also be more insidious: that a distinction might awaken an arbitrary preference is a relatively harmless possibility by comparison with the possibility that a preference might legitimate a spurious distinction. The value-laden terms "servility," "banality," and "repetition" contributed the largest share to Quatremère's distinction of imitation and copy, and it can be inferred that if one were to suspend judgment of these categories, one would also have to efface the distinction. When, as is found in Aristotle, a distinction between art and "reality" is judged in aesthetic terms, suspicions arise: if it is possible to distinguish the two, why is that distinction supported with aesthetic judgments?

When the distinction of an object's beauty from that object's representation causes such difficulties – for one can never be sure that the structure used to describe the work is not the toy of an aesthetic preference or the instrument of an ideological prejudice –

dans notre âme une passion qui ressemble à celle que l'objet imité y aurait pû exciter. La copie de l'objet doit, pour ainsi dire, exciter en nous une copie de la passion que l'objet y aurait excitée." Abbé Jean-Baptiste du Bos, *Réflexions critiques sur la poésie et sur la peinture* (1770; rpt. Geneva: Slatkine Reprints, 1982), p. 14. Such theories, however, lead to the conclusion rejected by most theorists: that the representation of a beautiful object must be beautiful, while the representation of an object that is not beautiful cannot be beautiful.

it is prudent to investigate its implications. An unfinished article by Marcel Proust addresses the problem directly, and furnishes an unexpected answer to the question: "What is the relation between the beauty of an object and the beauty of its artistic representation?"

Pierre Clarac has entitled the article "Chardin et Rembrandt"; it dates from the mid-nineties, and discusses the alternative to an aesthetic view of the world.[12] Proust analyzes principally the art of Chardin, who was known, since Diderot, as the most truthful of painters.[13] Characteristically, his paintings are described in terms of referential exactitude, of illusionism. Chardin has caught the play of light over objects of different textures so exactly that one feels as if one could touch, taste, or smell the object. Furthermore, these paintings are often of objects – such as fresh seafood, or half-eaten fruits – which are not considered beautiful, thus exemplifying Aristotle's adage about imitation, and suggesting, paradoxically, that it is the faithfulness of his depiction of ugly objects that produces the beauty of his paintings.

Proust frames his comments about these paintings with a scenario which indicates plainly that he seeks to overcome the distinction between represented and representation. He describes a young man before an uncleared table who, viewing this disorder and this decomposition, becomes aware of ugliness in his life, and seeks solace in the beauty of art, notably in splendid representations of a luxurious world very different from his own: a world of palaces, princes and seaports. Proust states that such a search is misdirected, for the contrast between the ugliness of life and the beauty of art will only exacerbate the first feeling, which is of more importance, for the young man must live his life amidst this ugliness, and can only occasionally escape to the museum.

---

[12] Marcel Proust, "Chardin et Rembrandt," in *Contre Sainte-Beuve*, ed. Pierre Clarac (Paris: Editions Gallimard, Bibliothèque de la Pléiade, © 1971), 372-382. All further citations from works by Proust, whether from this article or from the preface of *La Bible d'Amiens* will be from this edition, and are used by permission. References to them will be included in the text.

[13] For example, Diderot writes: "Il y a au Salon plusieurs petits tableaux de Chardin; ils représentent presque tous des fruits avec les accessoires d'un repas. C'est la nature même; les objets sont hors de la toile et d'une vérité à tromper les yeux." Denis Diderot, *Œuvres esthétiques*, ed. Paul Vernière (Paris: Garnier, 1968), p. 483.

> . . . il se lève et, s'il ne peut pas prendre le train pour la Hollande ou pour l'Italie, va chercher au Louvre des visions de palais à la Véronèse, de princes à la Van Dyck, de ports à la Claude Lorrain, que, ce soir, viendra de nouveau ternir et exaspérer le retour dans leur cadre familier des scènes journalières. (373)

What he needs instead is to find an art closer to his life, and which will teach him the beauty of that life. The beauty of art, Proust asserts, Aristotle to the contrary, can imply the beauty of life, and Chardin is the painter whose works do just that:

> Si je connaissais ce jeune homme, je ne le détournerais pas d'aller au Louvre et je l'y accompagnerais plutôt; mais le menant dans la galerie Lacaze et dans la galerie des peintres français du XVIIIème siècle, ou dans telle autre galerie française, je l'arrêterais devant les Chardin. (373)

How does one question a distinction which has informed so many aesthetic analyses? Proust's first argument is an argument from authority: that an artist would not have represented an object unless he considered it beautiful, and his opinion is a guarantee of its beauty:

> Si tout cela (the subjects of Chardin's paintings) vous semble maintenant beau à voir, c'est que Chardin l'a trouvé beau à peindre. Et il l'a trouvé beau à peindre parce qu'il l'a trouvé beau à voir. Le plaisir que vous donne sa peinture d'une chambre où l'on coud, d'une office, d'une cuisine, d'un buffet, c'est, saisi au passage, dégagé de l'instant, approfondi, éternisé, le plaisir que lui donnait la vue d'un buffet, d'une cuisine, d'une office, d'une chambre où l'on coud. Ils sont si inséparables l'un de l'autre que, s'il n'a pas su s'en tenir au premier et qu'il a voulu se donner et donner aux autres le second, vous ne pourrez pas vous en tenir au second et vous reviendrez forcément au premier. (373-4)

This argument presupposes that nothing comes from nothing, and that a beautiful representation implies a beautiful subject. If we fail to detect the beauty of certain objects until Chardin's pictures have taught their lesson, the reason is that Chardin sees better than we do.

> Vous l'éprouviez déjà inconsciemment, ce plaisir que donne le spectacle de la vie humble et de la nature morte, sans cela il ne se serait (pas) levé dans votre cœur, quand Chardin avec son langage impératif et brillant est venu l'appeler. Votre conscience était trop inerte pour descendre jusqu'à lui. Il a dû attendre que Chardin vînt le prendre en vous pour l'élever jusqu'à elle. (374)

Chardin's pictures serve as a sort of road sign to the beauties of the world: the painter has been this way before, and can direct the traveller towards beauty. Thus Chardin points at things in the world which his paintings in turn represent. The guarantees of this system's truth are the reputation of Chardin and the prestige of art: if Chardin thought it was beautiful, it must be beautiful, and one must agree with him.

The faith such a system requires in things like reputation and prestige is not as widespread as Proust would like, and he elaborates a second argument to prove that the beauty of the work implies the beauty of the thing it represents. The second argument is more insidious and more difficult to reject. Summarized, it is this: the life of beauty implies the beauty of life: ". . . pour avoir compris la vie de sa peinture vous aurez conquis la beauté de la vie." (374) Proust argues that "beauty" and "life" are overlapping concepts: they are inseparable from each other, touching and communicating. To demonstrate that beauty is "alive," Proust reads stories, indicative of human passions and desires, into the static paintings called still-lives. Before a Chardin, one discovers a story, and this story is its life:

> Comme la Princesse réveillée, chacun est rendu à la vie, reprend ses couleurs, se met à causer avec vous, à vivre, à durer. Ce buffet où, depuis les plis rapides de la nappe à demi relevée jusqu'au couteau posé de côté, dépassant de toute la lame, tout garde le souvenir de la hâte des domestiques, tout porte le témoignage de la gourmandise des invités. (374-5)

Proust proves that beauty can be found by giving the narrative description of the painting; he postulates antecedents and consequences of the situation represented. But the proof of the converse – that life is beautiful – is left unarticulated, as though the logic uniting the two terms were so strong that it sufficed simply to demonstrate how A implies B for one to understand how B implies A.

There is a certain truth to this demonstration. When one says that "beauty" is "alive," and explains by indicating that by "beauty," a work of art is meant, and by "life," a narrative, one concludes that works of beauty are like life by virtue of their ability to imply the temporal structures characteristic of life. With such definitions, one must accept that B implies A: that life is beautiful, for, if one defines life as narrative, one describes it as – in its essence – a work of art, and thus, it is beautiful.

As soon then as temporal structures are taken into consideration, Aristotle's distinction of the beauty of an object and the beauty of its representation is troubled, for both works of art and "reality" share those structures that make the former beautiful, and the latter real. Beauty and life are two names for a single thing: time. Within this framework, Proust reverses the traditional formulation: beauty is not an accident of imitation, but its essence.

It is easy to understand how this theory of art would work in drama or narrative, but then again, painting is the example Proust proposes, and when one considers that he uses painting as an example of narrative fiction, it seems that he has employed a fiction to advance a theory of fiction, where one would have expected him to use description to advance a theory of description. The distance between Proust's theory and its nominal object is apparent in a very small detail: he uses the word "vie" to describe works whose name in French is *nature morte,* and the theme of movement to describe what in English are called "still-lives." The meaning of the word "vie" shifts in the formulation in question: ". . . pour avoir compris la vie de sa peinture vous aurez conquis la beauté de la vie." Why is his account of visual representation so obstinately at odds with the works he describes?

It would not advance any understanding of Proust or of art to accuse him of a deceptive use of a single word in different contexts, but one has much to learn by asking why even a writer as brilliant as Proust allows the meaning of an important word to stray so far. First, it should be pointed out, following Paul Ricoeur, that Aristotelian "mimesis" refers principally to narratives: "Ce concept n'est défini que contextuellement et dans un seul de ses emplois, celui qui nous intéresse ici, l'imitation ou la représentation d'une action."[14] Further, the considerations of fiction, the figures of new-found life, the value of reality all spring from the many senses of the word "vie." "Life" is existence taken as duration, as possibility, and as what is known. These senses come to life, as it were, in the sentence around which the article turns; they come to life when the relation of the two words is reversed, when beauty is no longer an attribute of art, but the substance of which art is the attribute.

When Proust writes that in order see the beauty of life it is necessary to see the life of Chardin's paintings, he reverses the common relation: that of substance and attribute is subject to tropological play, and the meanings of words shift as they are used as substances or as attributes. The attribute of those paintings, beauty, becomes the substance of another beauty. Beauty is both an attribute (of paintings) and a substance (of another beauty); it is the attribute of an attribute and the substance of a substance. Proust thus designates mimesis as subject to beauty's figural play, play which corrupts the very opposition distinguishing representation and beauty, that of substance and attribute.

By relegating beauty to the status of a trope, Proust has questioned its reliability as a criterion for distinguishing one work of art from another. Further, he has presented this argument in a fictional frame which generates fictions: identifying beauty with "life" he has equated criticism with fiction. Fictions are essentially beautiful, and beauty is essentially fictitious. He has fictionalized that proposition by advancing it in the narrative of the young man searching for an alternative to "life": just as Proust formulates beauty not as the attribute of a substance, but as the attribute of an attribute, he formulates his criticism not as the truth of a fiction but as the fiction of a fiction, inaccessible to refutation or verification. Such criticism differs from any criticism that considers imitation a stable basis for structural distinctions.

When one says that an imaginative work is more beautiful than a merely imitative one, not simply does one fail to find positive traces that distinguish the two works, but one also fails to find beauty different from either of the two works compared. The alternative to mimetic art springs forth fully formed, more beauti-

---

[14] Paul Ricœur, *Temps et récit* (Paris: Editions du Seuil, 1983), p. 58.

ful than mimetic art before it is judged, and different from mimetic art before the latter is defined. The fate of the aesthetic judgment is to be put to use even before it has been made. More importantly, however, such judgments are inevitable in criticism, for they are profoundly imbedded in the very notion of representation. If so, aesthetic criticism, which allows notions of beauty to enter critical consciousness, will always be more lucid than that which pretends such judgments can be avoided.

2

MAKING PICTURES TALK

> Simonides, however, calls painting inarticulate poetry and poetry articulate painting: for the actions which painters portray as taking place at the moment literature narrates and records after they have taken place.[1]

There is no form of writing that insists on the problems of representation more strongly than art criticism. The art critic writes about plastic works which represent a recognizable reality; the critic's work seeks, at some point, to represent those representations, and because the works the critic discusses are frequently identifiable, the reader often compares object and description in order to assess the accuracy of the latter. However, one quickly concludes that accuracy is an illusory aspiration for art criticism: what word accurately names an image? How many words are necessary to produce a sufficient or an exhaustive account of it? What order of words can hope to correspond to an image which is perceived at once in its totality?

Nevertheless, art criticism does exist, and one can neither dismiss such efforts as futile returns to a naive conception of language, nor can one celebrate them as supreme mystifications: art criticism always demands the formulation of a relation between a specific reality and a specific text, and both of these responses fail to meet that demand. Art criticism includes an act of reference to a

---

[1] Plutarch, *Plutarch's Moralia,* trans, F. C. Babbit (Cambridge: Harvard University Press, 1957), IV, 501.

work of art, and at the same time, a coherent internal structure that dispenses with the need to appeal to the work.

Thus, if one cannot ask criticism accurately to transmit an equivalent of its object, one can ask what it does with that pretext: if it does not seek to reflect the image of a work of art, what is its aim? The effects a commentary produces should indicate its aim: I can think of no other way of determining function. An example of such an effect can be found in a famous painting by J. M. W. Turner, *Slavers throwing overboard the Dead and Dying-Typhon coming on,* currently hanging in the Boston Museum of Fine Arts. [2] Like many of Turner's works, this painting has two titles, the first telling a story, the second describing a condition. The painting itself depicts a lurid seascape in heavy weather: the sky and waves are deep red and brilliant yellow. Near the horizon, the masts of a sailing ship are visible; the ship is small by comparison with the waves. In the foreground, sharks, bodies and debris appear on the water's surface.

The descriptive title – *Typhon coming on* identifies what is visible on the canvas: a storm at sea is represented, with strong winds and dangerous waves; the ship is low in the water. This title gives the picture an immediate content, organizing it about a central idea: peril. The anecdotal title indicates the antecedents and context of the scene represented: the slave trade, the profit motive, the cheapness of human life. This title adds terms orienting the reading

---

[2] The painting, also known as *The Slave Ship,* was first exhibited in 1840. Ruskin owned it between 1844 and 1869. For its further history, see M. Butlin and E. Joll, *The Paintings of J. M. W. Turner* (New Haven: Yale University Press, 1975), I, 214. Ruskin's own famous description of the painting insists on the prevailing meteorological and maritime conditions, accounting for waves, clouds, sun and sky. At one moment, however, the narrative of the slave trade breaks the surface of this description, giving it a far more pathetic sense. Ruskin chooses to use "gold" and "blood" to describe Turner's yellows and reds:

> The whole surface of the sea included in the picture is divided into two ridges of enormous swell, not high, nor local, but a broad low heaving of the whole ocean, like the lifting of its bosom by deep-drawn breath after the torture of the storm. Between these two ridges the fire of sunset falls along the trough of the sea, dyeing it with awful but glorious light, the intense and lurid splendour which burns like gold and bathes like blood.

See John Ruskin, *The Works of John Ruskin* (Library Edition), eds. E. T. Cook and A. Wedderburn (London: George Allen, 1903-12), III, 571. Further references to Ruskin's works will be to this edition, and will be included in the text.

of the first: "well-deserved peril," perhaps, or "man's cruelty compounding nature's violence." The difference between the two titles becomes apparent when they are considered in combination: the narrative title confers an ethical edge to an image which otherwise would be a statement of fact. The narrative title transforms a painting whose initial structure is "Here is . . ." into a proposition whose structure is "We must. . . ." To recall Aristotle's example: the death of a man crushed by a statue has one effect; if, however, the statue that crushes him is the effigy of the man he murdered, the effect is quite different.[3] The antecedents of an image orient its meaning. Turner's double title exemplifies two options available to the art critic: he may identify the elements of a painting, and even assign to it a static meaning, or he may relate the work to another term, implying a larger narrative context, and deriving a narrative signification; criticism may name or relate. However, the distinction of naming and relating is difficult to formulate with rigor: isn't relating just naming a relation, while naming is nothing more than relating one sign to another? Is a real alternative available to the art critic?

In order to examine in greater detail the problem under discussion, I turn to two passages of criticism describing similar pictures. The critics are Ruskin and Baudelaire, defenders of colorist painters at the same historical moment. In the two passages, they describe pictures of clouds – a preferred subject of colorist painting – a subject particularly appropriate to this question, for these forms have always been associated with the problem of legibility.

---

[3] It is those actions whose interrelations reveal a hidden design or cause that form the best plots:

> Since the imitation is not only a complete action but is also of fearful and pitiable incidents, we must note that these are intensified when they occur unexpectedly, yet because of one another. For there is more of the marvelous in them if they occur this way than if they occurred spontaneously and by chance. Even in regard to coincidences, those seem to be most astonishing that appear to have some design associated with them. We have an example of this in the story of the statue of Mitys in Argos killing the man who caused Mitys's death by falling upon him as he was a spectator at a festival. The occurrence of such an event, we feel, is not without meaning and thus we must consider plots that incorporate incidents of this type to be superior ones.

See Aristotle, p. 18.

The passage by Ruskin concludes his account of the rain-cloud in *Modern Painters I*: the moderns alone, he contends, have observed clouds and painted them accurately, and of them, Turner has painted this subject best. Confronted, however, with the argument that Claude Lorrain was Turner's model, Ruskin denies that the former ever achieved the accuracy he attributes to the latter, and to support this assertion, he describes a sequence of scenes visible over the course of a day from a hilltop location. The description is punctuated with the refrain "Has Claude given this?" and each part of it is referred to a specific vignette or engraved illustration. Ruskin affirms finally that Turner's watercolors are so accurate that they are interchangeable with on-the-spot observations. Later, Ruskin describes this passage asserting accuracy as itself accurate: it is ". . . perhaps the best and truest piece of work done in the first volume." (VII, 175) The chapter culminates with a flourish:

> And then wait yet for one hour, until the east again becomes purple, and the heaving mountains, rolling against it in darkness, like waves of a wild sea, are drowned one by one in the glory of its burning: watch the white glaciers blaze in their winding paths about the mountains, like mighty serpents with scales of fire: watch the columnar peaks of solitary snow, kindling downwards, chasm by chasm, each in itself a new morning; their long avalanches cast down in keen streams brighter than the lightning, sending each his tribute of driven snow, like altar-smoke, up to the heaven; the rose-light of their silent domes flushing that heaven about them and above them, piercing with purer light through its purple lines of lifted cloud, casting a new glory on every wreath as it passes by, until the whole heaven, one scarlet canopy, is interwoven with a roof of waving flame, and tossing, vault beyond vault, as with the drifted wings of many companies of angels: and then, when you can look no more for gladness, and when you are bowed down with fear and love of the Maker and Doer of this, tell me who has best delivered His message unto men! (VII, 418)

Turner and God are interchangeable: they both "make" and "do." The effect of the red light of sunrise on the snow and ice-covered mountains is so strong in both scene and representation that it does not matter what the referent is: the Alps or their illustration.

Instead of describing any specific scene or picture, Ruskin asks the reader to accept Turner's supremacy on the strength of the significance of the scene represented. We should admire Turner because of the joy with which the *idea* of sunrise fills us; he assigns signifieds to the pictures, and among them, this one: "the presence of the divinity."

This signified appears also in Ruskin's own use of signifiers: echo effects, for example, are so prevalent that one wonders whether individual words were chosen for sound or content: "k*een* str*eams*," "br*ight*er than the l*ight*ning," "r*o*se *li*ght of their s*il*ent d*o*mes," "*ab*out *them* and *ab*ove *them*," "*pur*er *li*ght through its *pur*ple *li*nes." If one effect of rhyme is to establish similarities between words whose meanings differ, one should ask what differences such rhymes and echoes serve to hide.

The passage is no doubt breathtaking, but is so because it stands the world on its head. Antithetical elements combine to form oxymorons: mountains, resembling waves, are "drowned" in the "fires" of sunrise. Natural relations are reversed: the "fires" of the peaks kindle downwards; it is the mountains that light the sky. That these reversals do not strike the reader as wrong, but as miraculous, is proof of the effectiveness of the echoes in making them appear motivated. The internal rhymes serve to confer a spurious authority by attributing to them a formal, if not semantic source. Such miracles in turn imply the presence of a divinity, a sense which is corroborated by the religious vocabulary, dominant in the last lines: "heaven," "vault" (as in a cathedral), "angels," and so forth. It is the presence of the divinity that confers significance on the otherwise banal moment of sunrise: sunrise is only of interest when its repetitive nature is forgotten, and it acquires the status of an event. In the present case, Ruskin implies that sunrise repeats creation; it is the moment when the intervention of a divinity in the world becomes visible. The passage describes a sunrise, but signifies its creator.

Different from Ruskin, Baudelaire does not attach an abstract meaning to the pictures he describes. Rather, he frames them in a narrative which draws out their meaning. The passage in question comes from Baudelaire's comments on pastels by landscape painter Eugène Boudin, found in the *Salon de 1859.* I note that these pastels were not even exhibited at the Salon, and that Baudelaire's insertion of this discussion is in accordance with what he calls the rule of Imagination: what is absent is of more significance than what is present.

> . . . mais pourquoi l'imagination fuit-elle l'atelier du paysagiste? Peut-être les artistes qui cultivent ce genre se défient-ils beaucoup trop de leur mémoire et adoptent-ils une méthode de copie immédiate, qui s'accommode parfaitement à la paresse de leur esprit. S'ils avaient vu comme j'ai vu récemment, chez M. Boudin, qui, soit dit en passant, a exposé un fort bon et fort sage tableau (le *Pardon de sainte Anne Palud*), plusieurs centaines d'études au pastel improvisées en face de la mer et du ciel, ils comprendraient ce qu'ils n'ont pas l'air de comprendre, c'est-à-dire la différence qui sépare une étude d'un tableau. Mais M. Boudin, qui pourrait s'enorgueillir de son dévouement à son art, montre très modestement sa curieuse collection. Il sait bien qu'il faut que tout cela devienne tableau par le moyen de l'impression poétique rappelée à volonté; et il n'a pas la prétention de donner ses notes pour des tableaux. Plus tard, sans aucun doute, il nous étalera dans des peintures achevées les prodigieuses magies de l'air et de l'eau. Ces études si rapidement et si fidèlement croquées d'après ce qu'il y a de plus inconstant, de plus insaisissable dans sa forme et dans sa couleur, d'après des vagues et des nuages, portent toujours, écrit en marge, la date, l'heure et le vent; ainsi, par exemple: *8 octobre, midi, vent de nord-ouest.* Si vous avez eu quelque fois le loisir de faire connaissance avec ces beautés météorologiques, vous pourriez vérifier par mémoire l'exactitude des observations de M. Boudin. La légende cachée avec la main, vous devineriez la saison, l'heure et le vent. Je n'exagère rien. J'ai vu. A la fin tous ces nuages aux formes fantastiques et lumineuses, ces ténèbres chaotiques, ces immensités vertes et roses, suspendues et ajoutées les unes aux autres, ces fournaises béantes, ces firmaments de satin noir ou violet, fripé, roulé ou déchiré, ces horizons en deuil ou ruisselants de métal fondu, toutes ces profondeurs, toutes ces splendeurs me montèrent au cerveau comme une boisson capiteuse ou comme l'éloquence de l'opium. Chose assez curieuse, il ne m'arriva pas une seule fois, devant ces magies liquides ou aériennes, de me plaindre de l'absence de l'homme.[4]

---

[4] Charles Baudelaire, *Œuvres complètes,* ed. Claude Pichois (Paris: Editions Gallimard, Bibliothèque de La Pléiade, © 1975-6), II, 665-6. All further

Initially, Baudelaire seems to be proposing a theory of referential accuracy: Boudin's virtue lies in the resemblance between his studies and their models. Further, these studies are evidence of his memory: Boudin will use them to recall details in his studio and will thus transform these "notes" into finished works. Boudin's exactitude thus indicates a power Baudelaire denies to other painters.

Despite the reverence Baudelaire claims for accuracy, the passage continually shifts its focus, as though the poet were unable to consider a single object for any length of time: a discussion of pastel studies replaces that of Boudin's oils; landscape replaces pictures of people; *je* replaces *vous*; a theory of intoxication – implying altered perceptions – replaces assertions of exact observation. And more tellingly, the past tense replaces the future as the passage concludes: ". . . il ne m'arriva pas, devant ces magies liquides ou aériennes . . ." The passage itself suffices to turn a deferred vision into a finished spectacle, to transform the studies into completed works.

What Baudelaire has done is to turn description into a narrative possessing beginning, middle and end: from initial subject, the pastels become preliminary studies and finally finished works. Within the description, all is in turbulent movement. As it opens, Baudelaire employs accumulation: the conjunction *et* unites pairs of qualifiers to produce larger units. As the passage closes, however, the conjunction *ou* distinguishes alternative interpretations, as though the writer were unable to synthesize his impressions. The movement from accumulation of details to their dispersal resembles nothing so much as the continual process of condensation and evaporation constantly going on in the seemingly stable things called clouds.[5]

Introducing the description with a rudimentary narrative, Baudelaire has endowed it with a purpose: like a story, it aims at

---

references to works by Baudelaire will be taken from this edition, are used by permission, and will be included in the text.

[5] The metaphor is central to Baudelaire's poetics: "De la vaporisation et de la centralisation du *Moi.* Tout est là." (I, 676) For an admirable gloss on this aphorism, see Leo Bersani, *Baudelaire and Freud* (Berkeley: University of California Press, 1977).

an ending.[6] The paintings strive to alter perceptions, to intoxicate the viewer, and are instruments, just as wine, hashish, and opium are. Grammatically too, intoxication is the aim of the passage. The long enumeration, introduced by "A la fin . . . ," constitutes a huge subject in search of a predicate. Each demonstrative *ces,* each *tout,* reminds the reader that even after several lines, the sentence is no closer to resolution. The description imposes labels on the pastels, repeatedly naming them; their movement sketches a brief narrative: from sobriety to intoxication, from certainty to doubt. The very names imply fictions. Specifically, the fiction the passage produces is the illusion of man: by putting the description into motion, Baudelaire implies that its real focus is Boudin the creator, rather than his pastels. This illusion is so strong that as the passage ends, he no longer regrets man's absence from the pictures. While Ruskin assigned meaning directly to the pictures he described, Baudelaire employs narrative, and if the former discovered "divinity" in Turner's watercolors, Baudelaire derives "humanity" from Boudin's pastels.

But what is at stake in this opposition? Is there a fundamental difference between the procedures of the two critics? In the case of Baudelaire, examinations of art-critical texts have largely addressed such issues as the critic's accuracy, or his theory of beauty. Only one – Michael Fried – has examined the dymamics of judgment of judgment in these texts: what is the criterion, and what are the implications of its use? At a more general level, there do exist several important contributions to the field. An article by Roland Barthes from 1964 goes very far in its examination of at least one side of the question. In "Rhétorique de l'image," Barthes distinguishes two kinds of pictorial signs, denotation and connotation. In the former, a signifier signifies a signified directly, neither element of the sign being itself a sign. Denotation is, as it were, the dream of language: simple, unproblematic, univocal. In connotation, by contrast, the signifier is an entire sign, signifier and signified. In photography, the two signs function differently: a photograph's denotations are trivial, slavish representations of real

[6] The "sense of an ending" is one of the features that distinguishes fiction from description and from discursive prose; to attribute an aim to a description is thus to assimilate fiction and description. See Frank Kermode, *The Sense of an Ending* (New York: Oxford University Press, 1967).

objects, while its connotations, are significant. Requiring interpretation, connotations are part of a larger cultural system, while denotations admit of immediate deciphering. Saussure's *arbor* exemplifies denotation: "Nous appelons *signe* la combinaison du concept et de l'image acoustique . . ."[7] A set of phonemes signify a certain idea. However, an entire denotative sign can itself function as signifer of a further signified, and this higher-order sign is connotative: in the present case, the use of *arbor* signifies acquaintance with a basic text of semiology.

To explain the relation of the two signs, Barthes analyzes a pictorial advertisement, a color photograph in which the advertiser's canned sauce and packaged cheese are seen in a shopping *filet* overflowing with peppers, tomatoes, onions, and spaghetti. The photograph *denotes* the items enumerated through conventions of shape and color, but the choice and juxtaposition of yellow, green and red objects *connote* what Barthes calls "italianness," while the proximity of fresh goods to the packaged products *connotes* discriminating shopping. Further, the spilling of all the foods from the shopping bag *connotes* abundance.

It is of course easy to assign connotations to advertisements; publicity is loaded in this respect, for its meanings must be unequivocal. At this stage of his exposition, Barthes points out that denotative signs differ importantly from connotative signs: while the former assist in the reading of other signs, denotative or connotative, the deciphering of a connotative sign will not help in reading another. Once it has been decided that the reddish round form represents a tomato, it is easier to deduce that the whitish one represents an onion. Such reciprocal reinforcement is not characteristic of connotations. Barthes qualifies connotative meaning as "erratic": ". . . ils constituent dans l'image totale des *traits discontinus* ou mieux encore: *erratiques.*"[8] Connotative meaning arrives in a flash, possessing no history and no future. "Italianness" is either perceived in the red, white and yellow objects, or is is not: it cannot be argued, nor does the determination of one connota-

---

[7] Ferdinand de Saussure, *Cours de linguistique générale,* ed. Tulio de Mauro (Paris: Payot, 1972), p. 99.

[8] Roland Barthes, "Rhétorique de l'image," in *L'Obvie et l'obtus* (Paris: Editions du Seuil, 1982), p. 41.

tion aid in the discovery of a second. There is no necessary or even conventional relation between such meanings.

At this point, Barthes advances his most suggestive hypothesis: of the two systems, it is the infallible one that serves the other – denotation is the servant of connotation. Specifically, denotation serves to "naturalize" connotation. Ordinarily, significations as arbitrary and as erratic as connotative meaning are resisted, and, in order to mask their arbitrariness, motivation is sought. Disaster is naturalized by invoking fate; similarly, the arbitrariness of connotation is diminished by relating it to a denotation, by saying that its arbitrary meaning is derived from the analogical (or, at least, accepted) meaning of denotation. Pictures use their denotative signs to disguise the inherent arbitrariness of their connotations.

Pictures possess then a certain resemblance to the things they represent, but this resemblance is not so much their aim as their ploy: a way to introduce meanings which otherwise would be resisted. In advertising, of course, such meanings are manipulative, but there is no reason to believe that a comparable manipulative finality does not exist also in painting or in other mimetic arts: that, for example, the impressionist use of light, however realistic it might have been, did not seek also to brighten a dreary urban environment and attentuate social discontent, merely by representing ordinary life.[9] Further, connotative reading, attaching meaning to a sign, is an inevitable response to the uncertainties of aesthetic experience.

Barthes asserts then that in order to interpret a picture, meanings are attached to complete signs, which are thus relegated to the status of signifiers for new signifieds. Criticism thus constructs higher-level languages which employ the signs pictures furnish, and is essentially connotative. Can criticism however

---

[9] Boudin himself, for example, attributes such an ideological aim to his painting in a letter to his friend M. Martin (September 3, 1868):

> . . . mais entre nous, ces bourgeois qui se promènent sur la jetée vers le coucher du soleil, n'ont-ils aucun droit d'être fixés sur la toile, *d'être amenés à la lumière?*
> Entre nous, ils se reposent souvent d'un rude labeur, ces gens qui sortent de leurs bureaux, et de leurs cabinets.

See Georges Jean-Aubry, *Eugène Boudin d'après des documents inédits* (Paris: Editions Bernheim-Jeune, 1922), p. 70.

construct only connotative languages? There is no reason to assume that criticism, a second-order signifying system, can impose only meanings; it can also name. Such systems have been described: if connotation consists in imposing a meaning on a sign, imposing a name on a sign is called metalanguage.[10]

Ruskin's description of clouds exemplifies connotation: he searches for the meaning of the pictures at the expense of their signifying structure. The passage confuses picture and referent, as though one could forget its materiality. The meaning Ruskin assigns to the pictures – Turner's divinity – is of the greatest generality, and is only with difficulty related to their subject. By contrast, Baudelaire's description is metalinguistic: the variety of names he attaches to the pastels insists on those names as signifiers, not signifieds, for they imply uncertainty, not certainty, i.e., language, not meaning.

Is one of these procedures more proper to criticism than the other? Is it possible really to distinguish the two? I consider Ruskin's text a derivation of meaning, while considering Baudelaire a derivation of language. But both texts, are, of course, linguistic: can criticism be split in this fashion?

In order to examine this question, I turn to another passage by Ruskin, and to the commentary it engenders by his disciple, Marcel Proust. In *The Seven Lamps of Architecture,* Ruskin argues that the beauty of a work of art stems from the "love" with which it was executed, and that the presence of "thought" in a work betrays this "love." In support of this claim, he describes a small stone figure on the north portal of Rouen Cathedral:

> The plan of his head, and the nod of the cap over its brow, are fine; but there is a little touch above the hand especially well meant: the fellow is vexed and puzzled in his malice; and his hand is pressed hard on his cheek bone, and the flesh of the cheek is *wrinkled* under the eye by the pressure. (VIII, 218)

Perhaps because Ruskin drew a picture which, engraved, accompanies the text, his account of the figure is far more interpretive than descriptive. He characterizes the expression of the

[10] Roland Barthes, *Eléments de sémiologie,* in *Le Degré zéro de l'écriture* (Paris: Gonthier, 1971), pp. 163-8.

figure far more than he analyzes or enumerates its elements. He finds a single word – "malice" – to account for the various features that constitute his expression. Ruskin thus writes a psychological portrait of the figure which is in fact a set of conclusions derived from unstated observations, and, so doing, adds an emotional intention to the figure: he recognizes its meaning.

This account elicited Proust's enthusiastic praise. In the introduction to his translation, *La Bible d'Amiens,* Proust attributes tremendous power to Ruskin's text, and, by inference, to criticism generally: it brings the work of art "back to life"; it ressuscitates and resurrects dead meaning. And the passage he singles out as exemplary of this capacity is the account from *The Seven Lamps.* Proust embeds his account of the figure in two stories, one within the other. In the first, Ruskin comes to Rouen, finds, and saves the little figure for later generations. This discovery makes possible a second one, analogous to it: the writer, seeking to understand Ruskin by visiting objects the latter described, goes to the cathedral, searches for, and finally finds the little figure. The passage – quite long – runs thus:

> J'avoue qu'en relisant cette page au moment de la mort de Ruskin, je fus pris du désir de voir le petit homme dont il parle. Et j'allai à Rouen comme obéissant à une pensée testamentaire, et comme si Ruskin en mourant avait en quelque sorte confié à ses lecteurs la pauvre créature à qui il avait en parlant d'elle rendu la vie et qui venait, sans le savoir, de perdre à tout jamais celui qui avait fait autant pour elle que son premier sculpteur. Mais quand j'arrivai près de l'immense cathédrale et devant la porte où les saints se chauffaient au soleil, plus haut, des galeries où rayonnaient les rois jusqu'à ces suprêmes altitudes de pierre que je croyais inhabitées et où, ici, un ermite sculpté vivait, isolé, laissant les oiseaux demeurer sur son front, tandis que là, un cénacle d'apôtres écoutit le message d'un ange qui se posait près d'eux, repliant ses ailes, sous un vol de pigeons qui ouvraient les leurs et non loin d'un personnage qui, recevant un enfant sur le dos, tournait la tête d'un geste brusque et séculaire; quand je vis, rangés devant ses porches ou penchés au balcon de ses tours, tous les hôtes de pierre de la cité mystique respirer le soleil ou l'ombre matinale, je compris qu'il serait impossible de trouver parmi ce peuple surhumain une figure de quelques centimètres. J'allai pourtant au portail des Libraires.

Mais comment reconnaître la petite figure entre des centaines d'autres? Tout à coup, un jeune sculpteur de talent et d'avenir, Mme. L. Yeatman, me dit: 'En voici une qui lui ressemble.' Nous regardons un peu plus bas, et . . . la voici. Elle ne mesure pas dix centimètres. Elle est effritée, et pourtant c'est son regard encore, la pierre garde le trou qui relève la pupille et lui donne cette expression qui me l'a fait reconnaître. L'artiste mort depuis des siècles a laissé là, entre des milliers d'autres, cette petite personne qui meurt un peu chaque jour, et qui était morte depuis bien longtemps, perdue au milieu de la foule des autres, à jamais. Mais il l'avait mise là. Un jour, un homme pour qui il n'y a pas de mort, pour qui il n'y a pas d'infini matériel, pas d'oubli, un homme qui jetant loin de lui ce néant qui nous opprime pour aller à des buts qui dominent sa vie, si nombreux qu'il ne pourra pas tous les atteindre alors que nous paraissons en manquer, cet homme est venu, et dans ces vagues de pierre où chaque écume dentelée paraissait ressembler aux autres, voyant là toutes les lois de la vie, toutes les pensées de l'âme, les nommant de leur nom, il dit: 'Voyez, c'est ceci, c'est cela.' Tel qu'au jour de Jugement, qui non loin de là est figuré, il fait entendre en ses paroles comme la trompette de l'archange et il dit: 'Ceux qui ont vécu vivront, la matière n'est rien.' Et, en effet, telle que les morts que non loin le tympan figure, réveillés à la trompette de l'archange, soulevés, ayant repris leur forme, reconnaissables, vivants, voici que la petite figure a revécu et retrouvé son regard, et le Juge a dit: 'Tu as vécu, tu vivras.' Pour lui, il n'est pas un juge immortel, son corps mourra; mais qu'importe! comme s'il ne devait jamais mourir il accomplit sa tâche immortelle, ne s'occupant pas de la grandeur de la chose qui occupe son temps et n'ayant qu'une vie humaine à vivre, il passe plusieurs jours devant l'une des dix mille figures d'une église. Il l'a dessinée. Elle correspondait pour lui à ces idées qui agitaient sa cervelle, insoucieuse de la vieillesse prochaine. Il l'a dessinée, il en a parlé. Et la petite figure inoffensive et monstrueuse aura ressuscité, contre toute espérance, de cette mort qui semble plus totale que les autres, qui est la disparition au sein de l'infini du nombre et sous le nivellement des ressemblances, mais d'où le génie a tôt fait de nous tirer aussi. En la retrouvant là, on ne peut s'empêcher d'être touché. Elle semble vivre et regarder, ou plutôt d'être prise par la mort dans son regard même, comme les Pompéiens dont le geste demeure interrompu. Et c'est une pensée du sculpteur, en effet, qui a été saisie dans son geste par l'immobilité de la

> pierre. J'ai été touché en la retrouvant là; rien ne meurt donc de ce qui a vécu, pas plus la pensée du sculpteur que la pensée de Ruskin. (125-6)

The passage is considerably more complex than either Ruskin's or Baudelaire's. It can be analyzed from two points of view: as an account of Ruskin's commentary of the figure, or as a commentary on Ruskin's commentary, but in both cases, it should be considered as criticism, i.e., as signs whose referents are signs.

Immediately, however, a difficulty arises: it is impossible to classify either commentary as connotative or metalinguistic. There is a curious ambivalence in the account of Ruskin's commentary. On one hand, Proust treats it as accurate: Ruskin correctly recognizes meaning; he discovers the *pensée du sculpteur,* the *regard* of the stone figure, and the figure consequently returns to "life," to the condition of intelligibility it once possessed. Such an interpretation is "true," for it corresponds to the lost intention of the sculptor. Further, just as Ruskin discovers the creature's meaning, so, later does the narrator discover the creature itself: Proust analogizes concrete and abstract recognition, and attributes the empirical verifiability of the former to the latter, while the analogy between critical judgment and Last Judgment confers the finality of the latter to the former. In Proust's account, Ruskin's commentary assigns meaning to the stone figure, and this meaning dominates the signifiers that transmit it. Proust reads Ruskin's criticism for the connotations the latter discovers.

But at the same time, Ruskin's criticism is metalinguistic: he has attached signifiers to the figure. He "named it with its name"; he drew it; he spoke about it. He has not so much recognized it as baptized it; his commentary is not so much in the service of truth as in that of power. This motive appears in the hyperbolic characterization of the critic as Christ presiding over the Last Judgment, consigning some works to oblivion, while raising others from the dead. Such prestige is invested in the act of judgment that it will occur even when recognition does not, and criticism will become an act of power with no antecedent. It will attach labels referring to no prior meaning; it will give names to objects which had none.

Proust's commentary manifests the same ambivalence: both connotative and metalinguistic, it simultaneously serves principles of truth and of power. It recognizes and baptizes. In a first moment, Proust attributes a connotative meaning to Ruskin's passage: "generosity." The text and drawing characterize a figure and signify the critic's charity: he has given his time to the figure; he has given it a name and a plastic representation; he has endowed it with expression and intention; it has regained through Ruskin the life it had lost.

However, the passage is embedded in a system of signifiers to such an extent that those signifiers serve to label the passage by framing it. There are two signifiers of this kind, a narrative and an analogy. A story precedes the passage: Ruskin's trip to Rouen, his naming and his drawing of the figure, his description of it. Ruskin's description culminates and concludes a search; it is also the starting point of an afterlife, the guarantee of the figure's immortality. The description is the result of a story, the conclusion of an adventure. The "sense of an ending" permeates the passage. The presence of this conclusion is inscribed in every element of the story; each step of the anecdote points to its aim. Just as Roquentin was to say, "La phrase est jetée négligemment, elle a l'air superflue; mais nous ne nous y laissons pas prendre et nous la mettons de côté: c'est un renseignement dont nous comprendrons la valeur par la suite."[11] The reader knows that Proust's and Ruskin's searches succeed: otherwise, the account would not exist. The passage thus aims at the descriptions, which serve as its purpose. It is however the mere existence of the passage that confirms this purposiveness, for nothing more specific is necessary. The passage thus aims at the descriptions, but when the reader arrives, he finds he was always already there: the passages possess purposiveness without purpose, or, as Kant had said a century earlier, they possess *beauty*. Proust baptizes the passage as *beautiful*.

In short, the passage is both connotative and metalinguistic, for it attaches meaning to signs – "charity," "immortality" – and it also attaches a signifier: "beauty." In principle, these ambitions are mutually exclusive: either one names or one interprets, one cannot do both. When a critic undertakes to recognize the object's meaning, he accepts it as already named; when he labels it, he does so without reference to its meaning. One cannot "name things

[11] Jean-Paul Sartre, *La Nausée* (Paris: Gallimard, 1938), p. 63.

with their names." They are either to be named, in which case they have no name, nor they are to be recognized, in which case they are not to be named.[12]

The problem lies in the status of the second-order sign, fundamental to criticism, but perhaps exemplary also of other signs. Criticism attaches the signifier "beauty" to the signs it comments, but those signs also demand connotative signifieds. Is beauty then discovered or imposed? It is impossible to say. Ruskin's "name," for example, is a signifier: he "recognizes" the expression of the figure, and finds the word that corresponds to it. It meaning was already there. But simultaneously, he gives it its life: it owes its meaning, its expression, its *regard* to him. Has he found a meaning or imposed a name? Proust says, in fact, that he found the name that he gave: Ruskin has imposed an interpretation, only to turn around and refer to it as a truth. Criticism is simultaneously an act of power and a gesture of reference, both a vehicle of meaning and an instrument of arbitrary force. It is a language which accomplishes the paradoxical feat of recognizing the appropriateness of the name it has just imposed.

Pictures are often used in discussions of linguistics: it is fairly easy to distinguish signifier from signified when, as in painting, it is possible to specify a medium of signification. But even these signs are not unproblematic, and if so, art criticism forces a reflection on the sign, and specifically, on its connotative and metalinguistic aspects. In principle, the two aspects are easily distinguished, but in art criticism, and in particular, when aesthetics comes into question, this distinction fails. When it judges, art criticism uses some version of the term "beauty": it imposes this epithet on some works, and imposes its contrary on others. However, the term behaves less like a name than like a concept: it demands recognition, and Baudelaire, Ruskin, and Proust testify to the force of this demand. Producing fictions, generating narratives, beauty bridges the gap between metalinguistics and connotations, between names and meanings, and so doing, makes dumb pictures talk.

---

[12] What is in question is the "positing power of language," analyzed by Paul de Man in "Shelley Disfigured," in *Deconstruction and Criticism*, ed. H. Bloom (New York: Seabury Press, 1979): "... language posits and language means (since it articulates) but language cannot posit meaning; it can only reiterate its reconfirmed falsehood." (p. 64).

3

REFERENCE AND ALLEGORY IN ROMANTIC DESCRIPTION

> La description est tout naturellement *ancilla narrationis,* esclave toujours nécessaire, mais toujours soumise, jamais émancipée.[1]

For many years, description was considered the literary homolog of painting; its relation to its referent was considered simple. Description designated a reality which it also represented with some degree of accuracy; recent discussions of it however have sidestepped the question of reference. Whether a text refers to something "beyond" itself or not has been replaced by another question: "How is such an effect of reference produced?" By treating reference as an effect like another (such as pathos or comedy) the analysis of description has passed from the assessment of its accuracy or verifiability to one of technique, and this passage serves to assimilate the problems of description to those of narration. Formulations of such problems have been proposed recently by Roland Barthes and Michael Riffaterre under the title *effet de réel.*[2] Both writers treat reference as an illusion or an effect, traceable to specific textual mechanisms. Barthes argues that any element that serves no function in the narrative where it is found is automatically interpreted as indicative of the text's referential

---

[1] Gérard Genette, "Frontières du récit," in *Figures II* (Paris: Editions du Seuil, 1969), p. 57.

[2] Barthes's formulation occurs in the article "L'Effet de réel," in *Le Bruissement de la langue* (Paris: Editions du Seuil, 1984), pp. 167-74; Riffaterre uses the term in his *Semiotics of Poetry,* p. 167.

exactitude: the gratuitous detail serves to disarm the question "Is this true?" Riffaterre argues, to the contrary, that the demonstrable illusion of reference produced by certain details results not from a gratuitous presence in the text, but from a detail's strongly motivated presence there. When such a detail fills several narrative functions, participating in several formal patterns, it seems "real." Riffaterre pursues to conclude that the text does not refer to something outside of itself, but to itself: that its inner patterns are so many references to signifiers, not to signifieds.

This debate, however, for all its contemporary resonances, is a modern phrasing of one which has a long history; it was born with Romanticism, if not several times before, and earlier resolutions have failed to put it to rest. Like Pater's *Gioconda,* it attracts the reader with the mystery particular to a woman with a "past," but when its enigma has been solved, it haunts him like the ghost of the father he has killed.[3] But it is not so much the *Gioconda* that should be invoked, as Jocasta: like the queen of Thebes, description is both familiar and unrecognized, and its attraction lies in the reader's inability to recognize it. The very model of description is the Sphinx's riddle, but while solutions to description's enigma might provide a sense of accomplishment, do they tell the whole story?

Historically, description has been relegated to a secondary role in literature. It has been studied essentially in the context of narrative, and when studied there, it has been attributed the status of plot's "handmaiden": it serves only to amplify elements which are themselves of narrative importance. This subordinate role is surprising, and indicates if need be that description poses a problem which one would prefer to forget. Gérard Genette has pointed out that of description and narration, it is only the former that is indispensable, for one can describe without narrating, but never narrate without describing.[4] Discussion of description has not so much been neglected as avoided.

But in order to avoid this discussion one must overlook the very considerable importance early theorists of description granted the form at the time when it began to occupy a larger place in

---

[3] See Walter Pater, *The Renaissance,* ed. Donald L. Hill (Berkeley: University of California Press, 1980), pp. 97-9.

[4] Genette, p. 57.

literature. These theoreticians are writers of significance and analytic ability. Chateaubriand, for example, grants description a central place in the poetics of the 19th century; it is the use of description, among other things,[5] that distinguishes contemporary writing from ancient, and description defines a kind of poetry which achieved its greatest expression in France of the late 18th century. Description is a defining feature of Romanticism, yet, a generation later, Sainte-Beuve still attributes great importance to it, asserting that the principal achievement of the new school lies in developing a style which "paints" truthfully, i.e., which describes accurately.[6]

These early analysts detect great promise in description, saying that Romanticism lies there, if anywhere. But present modes of reading tend to reduce description's importance by subordinating it to other structures. When description is considered the handmaiden of narration, is it not misread? Does description bring on its own neglect, by systematically deflecting attention away from itself? One might ask whether description possesses any features that would give it a linguistic identity.

During the pre-romantic period, the genre of descriptive poetry developed; its chief exponents were Delille and Saint-Lambert. While the importance of this poetry is debatable,[7] it is

[5] The features that Chateaubriand qualifies as distinctive of modern writing are its use of *le merveilleux* (the fantastic), *les épisodes* (incidental action), and description. Each of these features was considered secondary by classical theorists; Chateaubriand's selection of these features indicates that he is reevaluating the importance of principal and secondary aspects of literature, and that his own aesthetics is more explicitly anti-classical than his writing implies. See François-René de Chateaubriand, *Essai sur les révolutions - Génie du Christianisme*, ed. M. Regard (Paris: Editions Gallimard, Bibliothèque de la Pléiade, © 1978), p. 628. All further references to the works of Chateaubriand are taken from this edition, and are used by permission.

[6] Charles-Augustin Sainte-Beuve, *Vie, poésies et pensées de Joseph Delorme*, ed. Gérald Antoine (Paris: Nouvelles Editions Latines, 1956), p. 148. The metaphor of painting is a catchword for referential interpretation of description: analogizing description to painting allows the introduction of a notion of accurary, the meaning of which diminishes considerably when applied to writing.

[7] Chateaubriand and Sainte-Beuve attributed great importance to descriptive poetry because it refused to vehicle an abstract content; Hegel condemned its German version for just the same reason. Hegel categorizes descriptive poetry as a form of conscious symbolic art, arbitrary rather than essential in its relating of form to content. The complement of didactic poetry, which artificially relates a form to the idea it communicates, descriptive poetry is all form and no idea. See

plain that these versified accounts of nature did express the hope that such descriptions would find an audience, and I would ask how they intended to derive beauty from the representation of nature. Jean-François de Saint-Lambert, author of *Les Saisons,* prefaces his poem with an apology of descriptive poetry, and sketches its characteristic tensions and aspirations. He opposes the poetry of a golden age to that of modern times, and shows thus what poetry must do if it wishes to be beautiful. Once, the beauty of poetry was the beauty of its object: description was transparent, a window through which its referent appeared.

> La poésie est plus naturelle à tous les hommes qu'on ne le pense, elle est commune chez les peuples sauvages qui sont plus près que nous de la Nature. . . . La mémoire du plaisir est une des consolations que nous donne la nature; plusieurs Poëtes ont chanté leurs plaisirs, parce que les chanter c'étoit en jouir encore: dans l'enthousiasme que leur inspiroit le Printems après un long Hiver, une récolte abondante après la disette, la vie douce & paisible après les dangers, les habitants de la campagne ont célébré leur bonheur, ou dans les tems moins heureux, ils se sont consolés par des fictions agréables.[8]

Now however it is necessary mechanically to produce the beauty that once was immediately present; nature is no longer as beautiful as it once was, and reference no longer suffices to produce beauty. Saint-Lambert thus elaborates the devices that produce the effect of natural beauty, and correlatively, produce the effect of its presence. Certain aspects of nature work infallibly:

> Le spectacle de la Nature peut donner différentes émotions. Elle est sublime dans l'immensité des cieux et des mers. . . . Elle est grande & belle, lorsqu'elle nous présente un espace étendu,

Hegel, I, 421-6. For Riffaterre, description is a major literary effect which different genres realize differently. It is produced, for example, in didactic poetry by referring to the device specific to this genre: the transformation of nature into miracle. This suggests that description is not a form, but a variety of forms, or perhaps better, a response to a variety of intertextual devices. See Michael Riffaterre, "Système d'un genre descriptif," *Poétique* 9, 1972.

[8] Jean-François de Saint-Lambert, *Les Saisons,* 3ème éd. (Amsterdam, 1771), p. xi.

> mais que l'imagination peut terminer. . . . Elle est aimable & riante dans un espace fertile & borné. . . .

But in the absence of natural phenomena, it is necessary to produce these effects by artifice, and Saint-Lambert lists several equivalent devices:

> Vous aggrandirez la Nature, si vous la montrez de tems en tems dans le moment où elle est sublime. . . . Vous embellirez la Nature, si vous rassemblez dans un espace étendu, mais limité, ses beautés et ses richesses. . . . Vous rendrez la Nature intéressante, si vous la peignez toujours dans ses rapports avec les êtres sensibles. . . [9]

If a beautiful object once implied a beautiful description, a beautiful description now only implies the illusion of a beautiful object. These recommendations have two implications: they derive an illusion from specific procedures, and thus relegate reference to the status of an effect, but they also propose a very humanized concept of natural beauty. If the interest of a natural scene depends on its resemblance to human forms, or if its formal unity inevitably produces a feeling or a sentiment, one may say that for Saint-Lambert, modern description is the vehicle of human content, and that its function is expressive. In the golden age, nature was of interest; now man interests readers. Description produces its effect when it carries another meaning more important than its literal sense; its truth lies elsewhere, and it produces its effect only at the price of this internal division.

That a description should express a specific proposition different from its own literal meaning is only one possibility; there are others, and Saint-Lambert suggests as much when he indicates a referential mode of reading, if only in a golden age. But for Chateaubriand, such a mode of reading is still feasible. In *Le Génie du Christianisme,* he elaborates a conception of description much different from Saint-Lambert's. The latter attributes a human content to descriptions of nature; Chateaubriand discovers divine signification in such descriptions, and this content requires a different mode of reading.

---

[9] Saint-Lambert, pp. xvii-xxi.

Chateaubriand argues that the art of the Christian epoch is at least the equal of the art of antiquity. Making this assertion, he refers to three features particular to modern art, and which give it this ascendancy: *le merveilleux, les descriptions, les épisodes.* Of the three, the first and last can be found in Christian writing from many periods; but the second, description, only becomes dominant during the Romantic period:

> D'Angleterre elle revint en France, avec les ouvrages de Pope et du chantre des *Saisons.* Elle eut de la peine à s'y introduire; car elle fut combattue par l'ancien genre italique, que Dorat et quelques autres avaient fait revivre; elle triompha pourtant, et ce fut à Delille et à Saint-Lambert qu'elle dut la victoire. Elle se perfectionna sous la Muse française, se soumit aux règles du goût, et atteignit sa troisième époque.[10]

By contrast, ". . . les anciens n'avaient point de poésie proprement dite descriptive."[11] Chateaubriand does not mean to imply that there are no accounts of nature in antiquity; rather, antiquity accounted for nature with myth, while Christianity employs description. Description is thus an alternative to mythology, and must be read differently.

Mythology, Chateaubriand explains, requires the allegorization or personification of natural phenomena: antiquity considered a wood or a stream the representation of a divinity, postulating a dryad behind the former, a naiad behind the latter. These divinities were related to each other in eminently human ways: blood relations, love affairs, commercial exchanges (e.g. Demeter's blackmail of Hades) and social hierarchies. The ancients thus interpreted the nature they perceived according to the structures provided by mythology; these structures, Chateaubriand claims, tended to reduce the importance of nature itself in favor of the narratives used to explain it. Nature was "small" for the ancients; Christianity has enlarged it:

> Oh! que le poète chrétien est plus favorisé dans la solitude où Dieu se promène avec lui! Libres de ce troupeau de dieux

[10] Chateaubriand, p. 725.
[11] Chateaubriand, p. 717.

> ridicules qui les bornaient de toutes parts, les bois se sont remplis d'une Divinité immense. Le don de la prophétie et de sagesse, le mystère et la religion semblent résider éternellement dans leurs profondeurs sacrées.[12]

The Christian author no longer mythologizes nature, but describes it. Instead of using the multiple terms of the mythological narratives, Chateaubriand proposes that the poet relate the elements of his description to a single term, and that each element of the description reflect that idea:

> Le spectacle de l'univers ne pouvait faire sentir aux Grecs et aux Romains les émotions qu'il porte à notre âme. Au lieu de ce soleil couchant, dont le rayon allongé, tantôt illumine une forêt, tantôt forme une tangente d'or sur l'arc roulant des mers; au lieu de ces accidents de lumière, qui nous retracent chaque matin le miracle de la création, les anciens ne voyaient partout qu'une uniforme machine d'opéra.[13]

Using the names of divinities instead of nature's implies that the latter has been subordinated to a narrative as trivial and as stylized as that of opera: mythology does not allow the complexity or wonder of creation to appear. Description, by contrast, produces an effect akin to painting's: a description's every item implies a single idea, just as the different colors of a painting, differently nuancing each of its elements, imply a single source of light. To organize its elements, mythology employs a narrative apparatus, while description employs an idea.

Very early in its development, then, a divergence appears in interpretations of description: Saint-Lambert proposes that description produces its effect when it transmits human elements or expresses a sentiment, when it figures another proposition. Chateaubriand, although he refers to Saint-Lambert, claims description expresses not a human content, but a divine one: it implies a single, central idea, one which unifies its different elements. When the latter are so varied that they can only be subsumed under the rubric "God's creation," description produces its effect. For Saint-

[12] Chateaubriand, p. 720.
[13] Chateaubriand, p. 719.

Lambert, description is best when it is structurally irreducible to another proposition, and when, lexically, its components do not encode familiar notions. It is one thing to designate a better world with the word "Arcadia"; it is another to use the word "Florida."

Description resurrects an ancient problem; it is an enigma in search of a solution. While Oedipus, however, found the solution to the Sphinx's riddle, and thus reduced its status to that of an allegory, it is not plain whether the enigma posed by description has a solution. Perhaps, instead, it will remain a mystery, forever generating efforts to devise its solution. And perhaps, like Oedipus, in his efforts to resolve its mystery, the reader will fail to see its relation to himself, and to understand its past.

This debate, as to whether a finite structure or an indefinite one produces description's effect, comes to a head in the year 1829, when two theories of Romantic poetry are put forward, both of which concentrate on the problem of description, but which are nevertheless diametrically opposed in their interpretations of it. The two writers are Pierre Leroux and Sainte-Beuve. Leroux argues that Romantic description is always the vehicle of an abstract proposition; Sainte-Beuve claims that description's effect is strongest when it is most literal.

Leroux's argument is found in his article "Littérature du style symbolique" from *Le Globe* of April 8, 1829.[14] There he asserts that Romantic poetry differs from earlier poetry in its use of symbolic imagery. He draws his examples from Chateaubriand's canon: both writers, for example, cite Bernardin de Saint-Pierre as typical of "modern" writing. What Leroux finds new in Romantic writing is its use of abridged comparisons: while earlier, poetry took pains to state both the tenor and the vehicle that figured it, modern poetry tends to abbreviate this relation, and to state only the vehicle:

> L'artifice de cette forme de langage consiste à ne pas développer l'idée que l'on veut comparer à une autre, mais à développer uniquement cette seconde idée, c'est-à-dire l'image. C'est donc une forme intermédiaire entre la comparaison et

[14] The article is reprinted in Pierre Leroux, *Œuvres,* (1850; rpt. Genève: Slatkine, 1978), I, 328-38.

> l'allégorie proprement dites, plus rapide que la comparaison et moins obscure que l'allégorie. C'est un véritable emblème.[15]

It is its abbreviation that defines what Leroux calls the "symbolic style," and he asserts that it is proper to modern writing.

Leroux attributes greater "speed" and concision to this style. Although he concedes that the propositions it is best fit to transmit are of the moral order, it is not restricted to such a use. Pierre Albouy, editor of Victor Hugo's poetry, has suggested the poem "Dicté en présence du glacier du Rhône" as an example of Leroux's conception.[16]

The poem compares at length the movement of thought to the circulation of water in nature. Just as the sun warms the sea, producing a mist which rises into the sky, God illuminates the poet's mind, and produces thought which rises to higher things. Just as mist becomes a cloud which moves in the sky, thought becomes poetry which moves from subject to subject. Just as the cloud strikes some places with thunderbolts, poetry strikes certain subject with its judgments. Hugo clearly equates idea and image,

---

[15] Leroux, I, 331. Leroux's use of the words *symbole* and *allégorie* might recall more famous theories of the symbol, Hegel's, for example, or Schelling's: see Tzvetan Todorov, *Théories du symbole* (Paris: Editions du Seuil, 1977), pp. 219-25. Hegel qualifies the terseness characteristic of symbolic representation as a "hint." (I, 351) The content of the symbol is disproportionately large, and the signifier, relatively small, and thus, the symbol merely alludes to the signified. Comparing the relative "adequacy" of the signifier and signified, he concludes that symbolic art is allusive. This analysis differs considerably from Leroux's: when the latter states that the symbol is a truncated comparison, he means that the vehicle alone is present: the tenor is absent. The symbol is abridged, not in the sense that the vehicle is an elliptical statement of an idea, but rather, that one element of the comparison is not present. Leroux's definition does not imply any judgment as to the adequacy of the sign. His is an algebraic conception: ". . . le poëte, dans ses inventions, suit la même loi que Napier inventant les logarithmes ou Descartes l'analyse géométrique. . . . Le poëte rend l'abstrait par le sensible, le géomètre le sensible par l'abstrait; mais tous deux ne font que substituer des rapports à d'autres rapports, ou plutôt reproduire sous des termes différents des rapports identiques." (p. 330) Put differently, Leroux's symbol is an extended metaphor, that is to say, it is an allegory.

[16] "Ce poème-ci offre un nouvel exemple de la manière symbolique de Hugo telle que la définit Pierre Leroux. . . . Il donne, avant 'l'écho sonore' du poème initial, une image et une définition de la poésie hugolienne." Pierre Albouy, ed., *Œuvres poétiques*, by Victor Hugo (Paris: Editions Gallimard, Bibliothèque de La Pléiade, © 1964), I, 1358. All further references to the works of Hugo are taken from this edition, and are used by permission.

suggesting that every image he employs has an exact equivalent in the order of ideas.

But with the fourth stanza, Hugo abandons this parallel structure: he presents the next state of the image – the cloud has turned to snow, which becomes a glacier – without stating what the correlate of this image is in terms of poetry. The verses that concern the glacier are particularly elaborate:

> Enfin sur un vieux mont, colosse à tête grise,
> Sur des Alpes de neige un vent jaloux la brise.
> Qu'importe! Suspendu sur l'abîme béant
> Le nuage se change en un glacier sublime,
> Et des mille fleurons qui hérissent sa cime,
> Fait une couronne de géant!
>
> Comme le haut cimier du mont inabordable,
> Alors il dress au loin sa crête formidable.
> L'arc-en-ciel vacillant joue à son flanc d'acier;
> Et, chaque soir, tandis que l'ombre en bas l'assiège,
> Le soleil, ruisselant, en lave sur sa neige,
> Change en cratère le glacier.
>
> Son front blanc dans la nuit semble une aube éternelle;
> Le chamois effaré, dont le pied vaut une aile,
> L'aigle même le craint, sombre et silencieux;
> La tempête à ses pieds tourbillonne et se traîne;
> L'œil ose à peine atteindre à sa face sereine,
> Tant il est avant dans les cieux! [17]

In Leroux's words, such an image is a "symbol": the reader must translate the "glacier" into terms descriptive of poetry. Thus, just as the glacier transforms ephemeral snow into enduring ice, poetry transforms experience into art; just as the glacier combines extremes of color and temperature, poetry uses antithesis to bring together moral and logical contraries. Just as the glacier seems always to reflect the dawn, poetry seems constantly new. The glacier is a symbol, and effective as such, because it stands alone in the poem, requiring an effort to re-establish the comparison, and thus, to attribute to it its content.

---

[17] Hugo, I, 731-2.

But this "symbol" is also something else, and I would locate the limits of Leroux's analysis here. If the glacier is an abbreviated comparison, it is shorthand for an idea. Thus every element of such an image must imply a homolog in the order of ideas. It is plain however that several elements of the "symbol" serve more to fill out the image than to nuance the idea: what, for example, is the poetic equivalent of the *chamois?* This term only refers with difficulty to a coherent notion of poetry. It would of course be possible to inflect Hugo's thesis and to attribute poetic translations to such terms; such after-the-fact modifications are always possible.[18] However, if one asks whether these terms stand in metonymic relation to the glacier, or in metaphoric relation to poetry, it must be answered that the former is of importance, and is stronger than the latter. The glacier thus figures an aspect of poetry, and to this extent, this image codes another meaning, but at the same time, the elaborateness of the image exceeds what is necessary for the operation of a code. The image of the glacier expands according to internal motivations rather than according to the external requirements of its "idea." Behind the *chamois* can be detected the possibility of an indefinite elaboration of the image, which threatens to become hypotyposis. To the extent that this elaboration does not contribute to its coded meaning we call it description and not allegory.

The difference between a coded reading of elaborate passages, and a descriptive reading appears in *Vie, poésies et pensées de Joseph Delorme,* where Sainte-Beuve attributes some reflections on contemporary poetry to the figure of Delorme, who embodies the very problem under consideration, the failure to reconcile reference and allegory. Delorme distinguishes between pre-Romantic and Romantic poets, claiming that the latter differ from their predecessors in their use of a plainly descriptive language. While earlier poets used expressions such as *lac mélancolique,* the Romantics now say *lac*

---

[18] In *The Queen of the Air,* where he analyzes myth, Ruskin rejects such rewriting of an image, saying that past a certain point, the inclusion of detail detracts from the myth's significance, for the abstraction it vehicles must be made too complicated to be understood: "Only in proportion as I mean more, I shall certainly appear more absurd in my statement; and at last, when I get unendurably significant, all practical persons will agree that I was talking nonsense from the beginning, and never meant anything at all." (XIX, 297)

bleu. Bleu is an example of what Delorme calls *le mot propre,* which possesses the qualities of directness and intensity:

> Depuis que nos poètes se sont avisés de regarder la nature pour mieux la peindre, et qu'ils ont employé dans leurs tableaux des couleurs sensibles aux yeux, qu'ainsi, au lieu de dire un *bocage romantique,* un *lac mélancolique,* ils disent un *bocage vert* et un *lac bleu,* l'alarme s'est répandue parmi les disciples de Madame de Staël et dans l'école genevoise; et l'on se récrie déjà comme à l'invasion d'un matérialisme nouveau. La splendeur de cette peinture inaccoutumée offense tous ces yeux ternes et ces imaginations blafardes.[19]

It is difficult however to understand just how the word *bleu* can be more "intense" than another, and Delorme's comparison of *pittoresque* poetry to landscape painting glides over many problems: while, in painting, the use of local color can contribute to intensity and variety, in poetry, the use of common nouns does not necessarily contribute to such an effect. Rather, the aesthetic value Delorme attaches to *le mot propre* lies in its distance from earlier practice: he finds it beautiful because it is not figural or periphrastic. It is not so much its translatibility into an abstract language that he values, as its opposition to such a language. Specifically, Delorme defines Romantic writing against metaphysical or sentimental writing, which strove to endow each expression with an added dimension: an abstract, as well as a concrete meaning. The innovation brought by Chénier, in this respect, was, Delorme writes, to eliminate such layered significations.

> Le procédé de couleur dans le style d'André Chénier et de ses successeurs roule presque en entier sur deux points. 1° Au lieu du mot vaguement abstrait, métaphysique et sentimental, employer le mot propre et pittoresque; ainsi, par exemple, au lieu de *ciel en courroux,* mettre *ciel noir et brumeux;* au lieu de *lac mélancolique* mettre *lac bleu;* préférer aux *doigts délicats* les *doigts blancs et longs.*[20]

[19] Sainte-Beuve, *Vie,* p. 147.
[20] Sainte-Beuve, *Vie,* p. 146.

When Delorme rejects figural language in favor of an ill-defined proper language, he rejects the aesthetics advocated by Leroux: while the latter valued "symbolic" writing for its concision in transmitting abstract meaning, Delorme values "proper" meaning for its concreteness. While for Leroux, description was effective to the extent it was allegorical, for Sainte-Beuve, description is effective to the extent it is literal. The "color" of a description becomes brighter when the description, in "proper" vocabulary, is punctuated by abstract terms:

> 2° Tout en usant habituellement du mot propre et pittoresque, tout en rejetant sévèrement le mot vague et général, employer à l'occasion et placer à propos quelques-uns de ces mots indéfinis, inexpliqués, flottants, qui laissent deviner la pensée sous leur ampleur; ainsi des *extases* CHOISIES, des *attraits* DÉSIRÉS, un *langage sonore aux douceurs* SOUVERAINES. . . .

The alternation between the two registers makes the abstract terms appear more abstract, the concrete more real. It is the tension rather than harmony between the two that produces the effect of reference:

> Le style d'André Chénier réunit ces ceux sortes d'expressions et les relève l'une par l'autre. C'est comme une grande et verte forêt dans laquelle on se promène; à chaque pas, des fleurs, des fruits, des feuillages nouveaux; des herbes de toutes formes et de toutes couleurs; des oiseaux chanteurs aux mille plumages; et çà et là de soudaines échappées de vue, de larges clairières ouvrant des perspectives mystèrieuses et montrant à nu le ciel.

If words are chosen because of their appropriateness to an object, their enumeration is theoretically indefinite: any real object possesses an inexhaustible supply of properties. But conversely, and more importantly, when a passage resists, by virtue of its richness, its complexity, or even its length, subordination to an allegorical model which would allow one to read it as a code, the reader is dealing with hypotyposis, and must postulate a referent whose simple existence will explain the proliferation of the object's properties. Reference marks the failure of the reader's capacity to allegorize a passage.

In order to illustrate the difference between the two interpretations, let me propose a passage from the preface of *Les Orientales:* both Leroux and Sainte-Beuve consider Hugo to exemplify the new school's writing. Leroux proposes this passage as typical of *le style symbolique.* Hugo uses the image of a city to illustrate a proposition concerning poetry, but this passage, in its use of technical terms,[21] tends to move away from allegory, and into description. It is of some length, but the inevitability of this length is the point of this argument:

> Et puis, pourquoi n'en serait-il pas d'une littérature dans son ensemble, et en particulier de l'œuvre d'un poëte, comme de ces belles vieilles villes d'Espagne, par exemple, où vous trouvez tout: fraîches promenades d'orangers le long d'une rivière, larges places ouvertes au grand soleil pour les fêtes, rues étroites, tortueuses, quelquefois obscures, où se lient les unes aux autres mille maisons de toute forme, de tout âge, hautes, basses, noires, blanches, peintes, sculptées; labyrinthes d'édifices dressés côte à côte, pêle-mêle, palais, hospices, couvents, casernes, tous divers, tous portant leur destination écrite dans leur architecture; marchés pleins de peuple et de bruit; cimetières où les vivants se taisent comme les morts; ici, le théâtre avec ses clinquants, sa fanfare et ses oripeaux; là-bas, le vieux gibet permanent, dont la pierre est vermoulue, dont le fer est rouillé, avec quelque squelette qui craque au vent; – au centre la grande cathédrale gothique avec ses hautes flèches tailladées en scies, sa large tour de bourdon, ses cinq portails brodés en bas-reliefs, sa frise à jour comme une collerette, ses solides arc-boutants, si frêles à l'œil; et puis ses cavités profondes, sa forêt de piliers à chapiteaux bizarres, ses chapelles ardentes, ses myriades de saints et de châsses, ses colonnettes en gerbes, ses rosaces, ses ogives, ses lancettes qui se touchent à l'abside et en font comme une cage de vitraux, son maître-autel aux mille cierges; merveilleux édifice, imposant par sa masse, curieux par ses détails, beau à deux lieux et beau à deux pas; – et enfin, à l'autre bout de la ville, cachée dans les sycomores et les palmiers, la mosquée orientale, aux dômes de cuivre et d'étain, aux portes peintes, aux parois vernissées, avec son jour d'en

---

[21] Technical terms are instances of *le mot propre,* for they are chosen for their referential accuracy, rather than for their possible allegorical uses.

> haut, ses grêles arcades, ses cassolettes qui fument jour et nuit, ses versets du Koran sur chaque porte, ses sanctuaires éblouissants, et la mosaïque de son pavé et la mosaïque de ses murailles; épanouie au soleil comme une fleur pleine de parfums.[22]

Leroux reads the passage thus:

> Et il (Hugo) part de là pour décrire en deux ou trois pages une ville espagnole, avec ses promenades d'oranger le long d'une rivière, ses églises chrétiennes, ses minarets arabes, sa prison, son cimetière, et tout ce qui la compose. Et dans ce long symbole, chaque trait a un sens. Les églises chrétiennes veulent dire des sujets du moyen âge; les minarets, des orientales; et ainsi du reste. On sent combien cette manière, qui est le dernier degré du symbolisme de style, est compréhensive, poétique, précisément parce qu'elle est indéfinie, mais en même temps vague et obscure.[23]

In order to implement the coded reading he advocates, Leroux proposes a reductive paraphrase which considers only a few terms of the comparison, those for which there is an evident correlate in the vocabulary of poetry. One wonders though what to do with the expansion of the terms *cathédrale* and *mosquée,* expansions which today, Michael Riffaterre qualifies as the "descriptive system" of the images.[24] Because of their insertion into this analogical structure, these terms too beg description in the code of poetry, but because they, like the earlier *chamois,* derive from the image, not the idea, the interpretation they demand is open, not closed. The cathedral stands for medieval subjects: so much is plain. But that the mass of the cathedral should correspond to the length of *Notre-Dame de Paris* rather than to its historical pretentions is a matter of conjecture, not certainty. The elements of description are not a code which imposes a definite meaning but an array of terms of sufficient specific gravity to resist such immediate

---

22 Hugo, pp. 578-9.

23 Leroux, I, 335.

24 A "descriptive system" is ". . . a network of words associated with one another around a kernel word, in accordance with the sememe of that nucleus. Each component of the system functions as a metonym of the nucleus." (Riffaterre, *Semiotics,* p. 39.)

translation. At the same time, they invite efforts to devise meaning.

In the debate between Leroux and Sainte-Beuve, both writers attribute specific meanings to descriptive passages: Leroux claims that description is symbolic, but by this, he means that a definite meaning can be attached to it; Sainte-Beuve claims that description is literal, producing its effect when its allegorical (Leroux would say: symbolic) dimension is diminished. It would appear that the descriptiveness of description lies somewhere between the two propositions: that description is inevitably more ample than it need be if it were to function uniquely as a code, but that it just as inevitably appeals to a coded reading, for it must have a term against which to define its referential aspirations.

Until now, I have treated the problem of description as though it were particular to the Romantic period: this is the claim of the writers I have proposed; they seek in description a definition of their own practice. It should be clear however that the problem of description is a problem of language, not of literary history. Put differently, it is a problem of reading, not of writing. Chateaubriand, Sainte-Beuve, and, in England, Ruskin all present description not simply as a reaction against neo-Classicism, but as an effort to rid literary language of clichés, and such efforts are particular to no period. Description, Chateaubriand claims, was only able to develop when the poetry of nature abandoned its use of the stock epithet; Sainte-Beuve proposed *le mot propre et pittoresque* as an alternative to the sentimental cliché; Ruskin's attach on the pathetic fallacy is, in part, an attack on cliché.[25] In each case, the writer makes a claim for description's "accuracy," but the use of cliché erodes whatever plausibility that claim possessed.

Recently, the accuracy of description has become the focus of still another debate, between Roland Barthes and Michael Riffaterre. The two semioticians, whose works overlap in certain areas, offer substantially different explanations for the impression of

---

[25] "There is no greater baseness in literature than the habit of using these metaphorical expressions in cold blood . . . it is only the basest writer who cannot speak of the sea without talking of 'raging waves,' 'remorseless floods,' 'ravenous billows,' &c.; and it is one of the signs of the highest power in a writer to check all such habits of thought, and to keep his eyes fixed firmly on the *pure fact,* out of which if any feeling comes to him or his reader, he knows it must be a true one." (V, 210)

accuracy some descriptions convey. Both writers refer to this impression under the name *effet de réel,* both treat accuracy as a text-produced illusion, whose mechanisms, should they be isolated, would enable one to understand what is at stake in the debate whose earlier stages I have traced.

Barthes and Riffaterre have translated the debate into a more familiar theoretical language. While Sainte-Beuve and Leroux argued over what procedures were responsible for the novelty of descriptive poetry and for its concomittant beauty, Barthes and Riffaterre argue over description's efficacy. The contemporary argument, like its earlier versions, turns on the question: "Is description the allegory of another proposition?"

Riffaterre answers "yes" to this question, arguing that the illusion of accurate representation is attributable to specific textual procedures which obviate the need to refer to reality.[26] A text is read as accurate representation not because of some faithfulness to a referent, but because it employs "overdetermination":

> La représentation est efficace, non parce qu'elle est 'ressemblante,' mais parce que, chaque mot étant surdéterminé par la combinaison des structures et perçu en fonction de leurs modèles préétablis, tout se passe comme si l'arbitraire du signe était annulé.[27]

A word is "overdetermined" when it functions in several formal patterns operating simultaneously in a text. Such participation in different structures confers a kind of necessity on the presence of a word, and the reader, sensing this necessity, interprets it as resemblance or accuracy. For example, when the presence of a particular word is dictated by metrical, rhythmic, and especially, semantic patterns, it tends to be accepted as "realistic." Realism is thus a text-produced illusion, but further, this illusion is best produced by allegory: when the description figures a proposition found in its context, it is allegorical and realistic. Such repetition is a form of motivation: words and their arrangement serve to echo another group of words. This supplementary motivation is a major

---

[26] Riffaterre, "Le Poème comme représentation: une lecture de Hugo," in *Production,* pp. 175-98.

[27] Riffaterre, *Production,* p. 180.

device of realism. The semiotic aspects of the text – its use of different patterns – produce the illusion of mimesis:

> Description, like all literary discourse, is a verbal detour so contrived that reader understands something else than the object ostensibly represented. Description translates this something else into the idiolect of the apparent object. The mimesis is thus subordinated to the significance, rather than the other way around – hence the ungrammaticalities, hence the imagery. The mimesis still presupposes a reality, but uses the descriptive system of that reality only as a conventional code for the semiosis. [28]

Description is essentially a code in figural language for another proposition which is to be found in its context. Description's meaning is thus the abstract proposition that it figures in concrete language, and it can have as many meanings as there are propositions.

By contrast, Roland Barthes restricts the meaning of description to a single general statement: "This is real." If Riffaterre prolongs Leroux's side of the debate, the continuator of Sainte-Beuve's is Barthes. The argument I have been tracing becomes more focussed at this point than at any earlier moment: the two adversaries disagree specifically on the way in which the *effet de réel* produces the illusion of resemblance to an exterior object. Riffaterre traces this effect to overdetermination; for Barthes the contrary is true: an element appears realistic only if, by contrast with its context, its presence is gratuitous.

Barthes analyzes only description in narrative, and relies on an economic model for his interpretation. It is possible to interpret narrative according to a principle of economy: a story will only introduce those elements needed by the plot, and thus, an element's importance can be deduced from its mere presence in the text. But on occasion, one encounters elements, so-called gratuitous details (like the *chamois*) that serve no apparent purpose in the text. It is these elements, Barthes argues, that produce the illusion of reference; they, not larger groups, constitute description. Thus,

---

[28] Michael Riffaterre, "Descriptive Imagery," *Yale French Studies,* 61 1981, p. 125.

in *Madame Bovary*, the truly descriptive passages are not "pertinent" to the plot:

> De la sorte, bien que la description de Rouen soit parfaitement 'impertinente' par rapport à la structure narrative de *Madame Bovary* (on ne peut la rattacher à aucune séquence fonctionnelle ni à aucun signifié caractériel, atmosphériel ou sapientiel), elle n'est nullement scandaleuse, elle se trouve justifiée, sinon par la logique de l'œuvre, du moins par les lois de la littérature: son 'sens' existe, il dépend de la conformité, non au modèle, mais aux règles culturelles de la représentation. [29]

This effect is in fact the product of ideology, which tells us that words are inadequate to signify concrete reality. It is also assumed however that concrete reality possesses a truthfulness inaccessible to language:

> La 'representation' pure et simple du 'réel,' la relation nue de 'ce qui est' (ou a été) apparaît ainsi comme une résistance au sens; cette résistance confirme la grande opposition mythique du vécu (du vivant) et de l'intelligible; il suffit de rappeler que dans l'idéologie de notre temps, la référence obsessionnelle au 'concret' (dans ce que l'on demande rhétoriquement au sciences humaines, à la littérature, aux conduites) est toujours armée comme une machine de guerre contre le sens, comme si, par une exclusion de droit, ce qui vit ne pouvait signifier – et réciproquement. [30]

In argument, one is driven at crucial moments to abandon logic and to resort to pointing at reality, saying, in effect, in support of the proposition just advanced: "Look, see for yourself." In history, photographs serve to "prove" the text's assertions:

> Tout cela dit que le 'réel' est réputé se suffire à lui-même, qu'il est assez fort pour démentir toute idée de 'fonction,' que son énonciation n'a nul besoin d'être intégrée dans une structure et que l'*avoir-été-là* des choses est un principe suffisant de la parole. [31]

---

[29] Barthes, "Effet," p. 171.
[30] Barthes, "Effet," p. 172.
[31] Barthes, "Effet," p. 173.

By a continuation of this procedure, any abandoning of logical argument takes on the status of reference to the concrete. Thus, in novels, gratuitous details and unmotivated descriptions are interpreted as concrete. These indications say: "This proves what I say," and lend their authority to the narrative context.

For the semiologist, such an interpretation is scandalous. Semiology presupposes that signification results from the play of the elements of a system, but here, the "gratuitous" detail is plainly excluded from that system: it is the residue of functional analysis, and to attribute meaning to such detail is to say that there is signification where there is no system. Or rather, to mitigate this scandal, the semiologist invents a larger system that plays off the smaller system and its residue. This larger system is a connotative system:

> La vérité de cette illusion est celle-ci: supprimé de l'énonciation réaliste à titre de signifié de dénotation, le réel y revient à titre de signifieé de connotation; car dans le moment même où ces détails sont réputés dénoter directement le réel, ils ne font rien d'autre, sans le dire, que le signifier: le baromètre de Flaubert, la petite porte de Michelet ne disent finalement rien d'autre que ceci: *nous sommes le réel;* c'est la catégorie du 'réel' (et non ses contenus contingents) qui est alors signifiée; autrement dit, la carence même du signifié au profit du seul référent devient le signifiant même du réalisme: il se produit un *effet de réel,* fondement de ce vraisemblable inavoué qui forme l'esthétique de toutes les œuvres courantes de la modernité.

Signification thus attaches to description, but it is of the greatest generality: "This is real."

Barthes's analysis differs from Riffaterre's in two respects: for Barthes, it is the residue rather than a variant of a narrative system that constitutes description. Consequently, the meaning he attributes to description is not an echo of its context, but something far more vast, discernible in all descriptions: it indicates "reality."

Both Barthes's and Riffaterre's analyses of descriptions leave me dissatisfied, but I believe that, taken together, their contradictory accounts point to a solution of the problem of description. Barthes's economic model has an obvious shortcoming: if description becomes realistic only when it cannot be integrated into its narrative context, realism is inversely proportional to the allegorical persistence of the reader: the more motivation one finds, the less realistic a text appears, conversely, the reader who stops early will discover a more realistic text. But Riffaterre's model also has a shortcoming, for if description is the code in concrete language of another textual device, we will always find some detail which is excessive with respect to that abstraction: a gratuitous detail, which should destroy the illusion.

The illusion, however, does endure, whether "gratuitous details" are encoded or not, and it is perhaps the attractiveness of these features that should be considered if one wishes to explain the illusion: the analyses of both Riffaterre and Barthes testify to this aspect of the *effet de réel.* Both readers assert too that the illusion results from an interpretive effort: to determine the function or purpose of the detail in the text. For Barthes, the effort leads to failure: the detail has no purpose. But does Riffaterre say anything different? The very number of determinations inherent in overdetermination implies that *a* purpose cannot be specified: there are always many. In both cases, then, the *effet de réel* results from a detail's lack of purpose in the text, or the failure of the imagination to ascribe a purpose to it.

An element that acquires interest or attractiveness because it cannot be subordinated to a rule: what I want to suggest is that a homology exists between the *effet de réel,* as defined by Barthes and Riffaterre, and "beauty," as defined by Kant in the *Critique of Judgment.* I shall be discussing the third *Critique* in greater depth in the coming chapter, but for the moment wish to insist on one aspect only of the Kantian analysis of beauty: that "beauty" refers to a sensation that arises when a perception cannot be subordinated to purpose, concept, interest or desire. Beauty, as it has been said many times, has no function, and this theory would explain the attention the *effet de réel* has received: realism is beautiful.

More significantly, though, the analyses of Barthes and Riffaterre rewrite the Kantian definition. According to Kant, an object can be declared beautiful if and only if it fails to refer to a purpose, concept or interest. This condition is part of the definition of the *effet de réel* advanced by the two modern theorists. Nevertheless, they both pursue to ascribe meaning to those details that so evade functional definition: "reality." In other words, the exclusion or play that characterize the *effet de réel* with regard to its context is intolerable: the realistic detail demands (and receives) further interpretation, reinscription into a larger context where it acquires a function. Not simply then does the *effet de réel* exemplify the Kantian definition of beauty, but it also allegorizes the fate of the aesthetic judgment.

Part II

THE POETRY OF BAUDELAIRE'S ART CRITICISM

4

BAUDELAIRE AND THE SALON

> Comme on dit beauté poétique on devrait aussi dire beauté géométrique et beauté médicinale, mais on ne le dit pas et la raison en est qu'on sait bien quel est l'objet de la géométrie et qu'il consiste en preuve et quel est l'objet de la médecine et qu'il consiste en la guérison; mais on ne sait pas en quoi consiste l'agrément qui est l'objet de la poésie.[1]

> . . . an aesthetic judgement is quite unique, and affords absolutely no, (not even a confused,) knowledge of the Object.[2]

Baudelaire's lifetime coincided with the period of greatest importance of the annual Salon, and of the *comptes rendus* of those expositions known as the *Salons.* Before the French revolution, these shows had been much smaller, consisting essentially in the exhibition of the Académie's own works.[3] After 1870, the Salon, too large and too conservative, lost its significance as an exposition of new talent, being superceded in 1884 by Salon des Indépendants, and in 1903 by the Salon d'Automne.[4] The very real importance of the Salon in its heyday can be attributed to its role in educating the French public in the plastic arts. The revolution had opened museums to the public, and had opened the door of

---

[1] Blaise Pascal, *Œuvres complètes,* ed. Louis Lafuma (Paris: Editions du Seuil, 1963), p. 583. (Pensée No. 586)

[2] Immanuel Kant, *Kant's Critique of Judgement,* trans. James Creed Meredith (New York: Oxford University Press, 1952), p. 71.

[3] George Heard Hamilton, *Manet and his Critics* (New Haven: Yale University Press, 1954), p. 9.

[4] Hamilton, p. 11.

the Salons to a large number of artists. The Salon served then to place those artists' works before that public, and required an education in taste if this meeting was to be instructive. During this period of apprenticeship, the number of artists exhibiting increased enormously,[5] as did the number of critical assessments of their work. The Salon, housed initially in the Louvre, was moved in 1857 to the Palais de l'Industrie, site of the 1855 Exposition Universelle.

The history of the Salon is inseparable from that of the Académie des Beaux-Arts, whose members were often in the majority on the juries that selected works for display:[6] from its inception in 1663 to its abolition in 1791, Académiciens and Salon were synonymous. In 1791, Quatremère de Quincy presented a proposal to found a new Institut des arts du Dessin,[7] and in 1795, the Institut des Beaux-Arts replaced the Académie. In 1816, the title of Académie was restored, but the Académie des Beaux-Arts, the honorific and administrative branch of the institution, was distinguished from the Ecole des Beaux-Arts, its pedagogical arm.[8] Its members decided upon eligibility for the Salon, and their influence was profoundly conservative. Quatremère de Quincy, *Secrétaire Perpétuelle de l'Ecole des Beaux-Arts,* decided in 1830 that innovation had gone too far, and strove for the next decade to reverse that trend. This influence was naturally resented by artists, and in 1848, the jury system was abolished, the number of entries rising accordingly. In 1849 a jury elected by the exhibitors themselves was used. In 1850, the government reclaimed the right to appoint a part of the jury.

The effect of the Ecole des Beaux-Arts on the Salon cannot be overestimated: contingent upon success at the Salon were of course large projects such as the decoration of public buildings and

---

[5] Sloane gives these statistics: 1806: 707 pictures; 1848: 5,180 pictures; 1810: 303 artists; 1850: 1,664 artists. See Joseph Sloane, *French Painting between Past and Present* (Princeton: Princeton University Press, 1951), p. 23.

[6] The path to membership in the Académie was patterned after that followed in the medieval corporation: the *élève* who showed promise was made an *agréé;* upon the strength of a specific work commissioned for that purpose, the *agréé* was accepted or refused as *académicien.* See Albert Boime, *The Academy and French Painting in the Nineteenth Century* (London: Phaidon, 1971), p. 4.

[7] Antoine-Chrysostome Quatremère de Quincy, *Considérations sur les arts du dessin en France* (Paris: Devaux, 1791).

[8] Boime, p. 7.

churches, but reception at the Salon also determined the sale of smaller works. At all levels, the buying public took its cue from Salon juries, and melodramatic, academic work correspondingly abounded.[9] As early as 1834, even Ingres was distressed by this tendency, and, having received harsh treatment at the hands of that year's critics, he ceased to send works to the show. Another result of this structure of selection was to exclude increasing numbers of works from exhibition, and it became necessary in 1863 and 1864 to establish a Salon des Refusés where rejected works were shown.

A large number of *comptes rendus* of the Salons served to guide the public among their numerous offerings. Shown in inadequate facilities, physical placement had an inordinate effect on the reception of a work: smaller works were often "skied," and had to be pointed out specially in order to be seen at all; immense *machines,* too large to be placed anywhere but at eye level, occupied spots whose importance corresponded more to their size than to their merit. The writers of *Salons* included professional art critics, members of the government, novelists and poets, as well as artists themselves.[10] Their accounts were as varied as their origins, ranging from quick evaluations of each entry to extended analyses of a small number of works.

Like the Salons they claimed to describe, the *Salons* were a recent development: over the course of the eighteenth century, writing on the arts had become increasingly more abundant, culminating in the explosion of *Salons* of the 40's and 50's.[11] Diderot, whose *Salons* appeared in 1759-67, was of course the

---

[9] John Rewald relates, on p. 16 of his *History of Impressionism* (New York: The Museum of Modern Art, 1973), that the painters now considered the strongest from the second half of the century received very little reward for their work: "Pissaro must have observed with some surprise that all the medals and prizes of the exhibition went to men who followed more or less closely Ingres' lead. Among them were Gérôme and Cabanel, both of whom received the red ribbon of the Legion of Honor; Meissonier, whose precious little genre scenes were rewarded with a *Grande Médaille d'Honneur;* Lehmann, a pupil of Ingres, and Couture, both teachers at the *Ecole des Beaux-Arts* to whom went the first-class medals . . . ; and Bouguereau, who for the time being had to content himself with a second-class medal. Daubigny's medal was third-class; Jonkind and Millet did not receive any, nor did Courbet."

[10] For an excellent description of this writing generally, see Sloane, pp. 24-32.

[11] Sloane states that no fewer than two hundred thirty writers were engaged in art criticism during that period. Sloane, p. 24.

model emulated by nineteenth-century critics, not the least of whom was Baudelaire, who, on the occasion of the publication of his *Salon de 1845,* wrote to Champfleury: "Mais, *si vous voulez me faire plaisir,* faites quelques lignes sérieuses et PARLEZ des *Salons de Diderot.*"[12] While many of the *Salon* writers, a majority in fact, contented themselves with summary judgments of the "quality" of the works displayed, there had been developing since 1719 a series of questions relating to the plastic arts, the answers to which by Baudelaire's time defined what could be called the "philosophy" of art criticism: a set of presuppositions concerning the nature of the plastic arts and the statements that could be made about individual works.

In large part, this "philosophy" strove to refute the famous Horatian dictum: "Ut pictura poesis . . . ," misinterpreted to mean that painting and poetry were essentially similar.[13] The theory was still of great currency in the eighteenth century; it was exemplified in such works as the Abbé Batteux's *Les Beaux-Arts réduits à un même principe,* where the author sought to demonstrate how all the arts, painting and poetry included, achieved their end through the representation of *la belle nature:* ". . . si les Arts sont imitateurs de la Nature, ce doit être une imitation sage & éclairée qui ne la copie pas servilement, mais qui choisissant les objets & les traits, les présente avec toute la perfection dont ils sont susceptibles . . ."[14]

Batteux, however, did not represent the later evolution of eighteenth century thought; that future was predicted by the Abbé du Bos, formulated by Lessing and exemplified by Diderot. In his *Réflexions critiques sur la poésie et sur la peinture* from 1719, du Bos argued that while both poetry and painting are arts of imitation, enjoying the benefits and suffering the drawbacks of that imitative

[12] Baudelaire, *Correspondance,* Claude Pichois, ed., (Paris: Gallimard, 1973), I, 123.

[13] ". . . Horace's famous simile *ut pictura poesis* – as is painting so is poetry – which the writers on art expected one to read 'as is poetry so is painting,' was invoked more and more as final sanction for a much closer relationship between the sister arts than Horace himself would probably have approved." Rensselaer Lee, *Ut Pictura Poesis: The Humanistic Theory of Painting* (New York: W. W. Norton, Inc., 1967), p. 3.

[14] Charles Batteux, *Les Beaux-Arts réduits à un même principe* (1773; rpt. Geneva: Slatkine Reprints, 1969), p. 45.

status,[15] they are also to be distinguished by substantial differences. Poetry is better suited to narrative, the imitation of an action, while painting is better suited to depiction, the description of a scene. Poetry's efforts to describe fully are tedious: ". . . on ne conçoit point comment un Poëte Epique, par exemple, viendroit à bout d'orner son poeme par cette variété, sans s'embarrasser dans des descriptions qui rendroient son ouvrage ennuyeux." Painting is similarly unable to depict variety of emotion: "Un Peintre ne sçauroit exprimer la plûpart de ces sentiments; il ne peut encore peindre dans chaque tableau qu'un des sentiments qu'il lui est possible d'exprimer."[16] There are subjects appropriate to each of the two arts, and evaluation of them must correspondingly take into account the nature of the art.

Diderot's comments on painting and on the arts generally exemplify the conclusions to which du Bos and Lessing also came. To an extent rivalled only by Ruskin, Diderot's criticism took into account the material constraints of painting: the interactions of color, the effect of line and of chiaroscuro, the role of distance in perception, the need for study of anatomy. These considerations converge in his discussion of Chardin's *Raie dépouillée* which Proust was later to evoke:

> C'est celui-ci qui entend l'harmonie des couleurs et des reflets. O Chardin! ce n'est pas du blanc, du rouge, du noir que tu broies sur ta palette: c'est la substance même des objets, c'est l'air et la lumière que tu prends à la pointe de ton pinceau et que tu attaches sur la toile.
>
> Après que mon enfant aurait copié et recopié ce morceau, je l'occuperais sur la *Raie dépouillée* du même maître. L'objet est dégoûtant, mais c'est la chair même du poisson, c'est sa peau, c'est son sang; l'aspect même de la chose n'affecterait pas autrement. Monsieur Pierre, regardez bien ce morceau, quand vous irez à l'Académie, et apprenez, si vous pouvez, le secret de sauver par le talent le dégoût de certaines natures.
>
> On n'entend rien á cette magie.[17]

---

[15] du Bos, p. 20: "L'imitation agit toujours plus foiblement que l'objet imité. . . . L'imitation ne sçauroit donc nous émouvoir quand la chose imitée n'est point capable de le faire."

[16] du Bos, pp. 31 and 29.

[17] Diderot, p. 484.

Judging the painting as an illusion, Diderot implies that its beauty results from his inability to distinguish model and representation; the two are the same: "c'est la substance même . . ." Further, the success with which Chardin achieves this illusion defies comprehension: "On n'entend rien à cette magie."

To a degree far greater than these limited examples suggest there was consistent agreement that painting is somehow simpler to appreciate than poetry: seen, not read; sensed, not deciphered. When Diderot assimilates picture and model, when du Bos denies to painting the ability to distinguish emotions, they imply such simplicity. At the same time, both recognize a need to judge paintings, and invoke a notion of "taste" to do so. Du Bos writes: "Ce goût se forme en nous mêmes, & sans que nous y pensions. A force de voir des tableaux durant la jeunesse, l'idée, l'image d'une douzaine d'excellens tableaux se grave & s'imprime profondément dans notre cerveau encore tendre."[18] Diderot for his part defines taste as a faculty added to talent: "Le talent imite la nature; le goût en inspire le choix . . ."[19] A century later, Emile Littré was to define *goût* thus: "Faculté toute spontanée, qui précède la réflexion, que tout le monde possède, mais qui est différente chez chacun, et qui fait apprécier les beautés et les défauts dans les ouvrages d'esprit et dans les productions des arts . . ."[20] What I shall be arguing is this: that the removal of painting from the domain of poetry increased the importance for art criticism of the faculty of taste. Diderot's use of the verb *entendre* summarizes this evolution: freed from dependence on a linguistic model, the plastic arts are also removed from field of understanding. Taste, not knowledge, is necessary to appreciate them. As long as painting was the handmaiden of poetry, it would be judged in terms of literary accuracy; once its autonomy was recognized, it had to be judged differently, and the notion of taste permitted such judgments. In support of this argument, I would point to the slow but irresistible decline, after the eighteenth century, of history painting, and to the corresponding decline in mythological painting. However, the strongest support of this contention comes from Lessing, who

---

[18] du Bos, p. 245.

[19] Diderot, p. 749.

[20] Emile Littré, *Dictionnaire de la langue française* (Paris: Gallimard/Hachette, 1967), IV, 170.

asserts in his *Laocoön* that the evaluation of painting depends on the "first glance": "The greatest effect depends on the first glance, but if this forces us into laborious reflection and guessing, our desire to be moved is immediately cooled."[21] Judgment is determined by an immediate impression, not "laborious reflection": by taste, not by understanding. If painting is going to be removed from poetry's shadow, it must be judged by a new standard.

It might seem strange at this moment to appeal to Kant's *Critique of Judgment:* Baudelaire almost certainly did not read this work; the only reference to the philosopher in Baudelaire's writings is incidental. However, through Benjamin Constant, Mme de Staël, Poe and Gautier it would have been easy to acquire a vague *kantisme,* if not an actual knowledge of the third *Critique.* This possibility has been explored at some length by John Wilcox, who examines the versions of Kant's aesthetics presented to the French public between 1800 and 1850, and assesses the debt of the proponents of *l'art pour l'art* to the philosopher.[22] Wilcox concludes, however, that any debt was a light one, and the *kantisme* of this movement was so vague as to be non-existent:

> This "school" derived its thought directly from the philosophers of the Sorbonne, Cousin and Jouffroy, and indirectly from Kant. . . . By the mid-century it reached its maturity as the basic aesthetic doctrine of many creative artists. From the beginning of its introduction all essentially Kantian thought had been lost.[23]

Wilcox does however indicate the immense popularity of Victor Cousin, whose course at the Sorbonne in 1816-7 attracted huge crowds, and was republished in 1853, substantially altered, under the title *Du vrai, du beau, et du bien.* In 1846, a disciple of Cousin's, J. Barni published the first French translation of the *Critique of Judgment.* Cousin, although his command of the subject was marginal at best, presented himself as Kant's chief importer,

---

[21] Gotthold Ephraïm Lessing, *Laocoön: An Essay on the Limits of Painting and Poetry,* Edward Allen McCormick, trans. (Baltimore: The Johns Hopkins University Press, 1984), p. 64.

[22] See John Wilcox, "The Beginnings of *l'Art pour l'Art,*" *Journal of Aesthetics and Art Criticism* XI (1953), pp. 360-77.

[23] Wilcox, p. 377.

and took it upon himself to mark out the limits of Kant's theory.[24] For example, in *Du vrai,...*, Cousin presents an undeniably Kantian formulation of the aesthetic judgment:

> Si une personne me dit, en présence de l'Apollon du Belvédère, qu'elle n'éprouve rien de plus agréable qu'en présence de toute autre statue, que celle-là ne lui plaît pas, et qu'elle n'en sent pas la beauté, je ne puis contester son impression; mais si cette personne conclut de là que l'Apollon n'est pas beau, je la contredis hautement, et je prononce qu'elle se trompe.[25]

However, later, diverging from Kant's argument, Cousin insists that the beautiful contains a moral element:

> La forme ne peut être une forme toute seule, elle doit être la forme de quelque chose. La beauté physique est donc le signe d'une beauté intérieure qui est la beauté spirituelle et morale, et c'est là qu'est le fond, le principe, l'unité du beau.[26]

Transforming beauty from a sensation to a sign, Cousin ascribes to it a moral function, and assimilates it to the Good and the True, and this is precisely the kind of aesthetic legislation that Baudelaire cannot abide.

I would submit further that Baudelaire's aesthetics are a continuous refutation of Cousin's. In 1851, in his first article on the poet Pierre Dupont, Baudelaire qualifies Cousin as a advocate of "la rhétorique et la grammaire classique." (II, 30) More significantly, it is almost certainly Cousin who is targeted in the account of the "Exposition universelle" (two years after *Du vrai, ...*) as "un de ces *modernes professeurs-jurés* d'esthétique ... dont les doigts, crispés, paralysés par la plume, ne peuvent plus courir avec agilité sur l'immense clavier des *correspondances!*" (II, 577) More directly, in the 1859 article on Gautier, he writes: "La fameuse doctrine de l'indissolubilité du Beau, du Vrai et du Bien est une invention de la

---

[24] Wilcox's opinion of Cousin is low: "When this brilliant, illprepared youth began to teach philosophy in 1815, he smothered his ignorance with eloquence. He even made jejune efforts to refute Kant before he was able to read him." See Wilcox, pp. 366-7.

[25] Victor Cousin, *Du vrai, du beau, et du bien,* Paris: Didier, 1853, pp. 148-9.

[26] Cousin, p. 178.

philosophaillerie moderne. . . ." (II, 111) As he denies Cousin's assertions, Baudelaire returns to more rigorously Kantian formulations.

In order to demonstrate how Baudelaire's aesthetics tend in this direction, I shall rehearse the four moments of the "Analytic of the Beautiful," in which Kant distinguishes the contradictory requirements and presuppositions of the aesthetic judgment.

The "Analytic of the Beautiful" enumerates four conditions which characterize the aesthetic judgment: 1) it must be disinterested (an object is not beautiful because it satisfies a need); 2) it must refer to no concept of beauty (reference to rules is the correlate of cognitive, not aesthetic judgments); 3) it must express no purpose (beauty is not the attribute of an aim fulfilled); 4) it must be necessary (when an object is qualified as beautiful, the listener is expected to agree).[27] With the exception of the fourth characteristic, these conditions are more or less commonsensical: beauty's independance from interest, rules and purpose is inscribed in our proverbs and received ideas about it. The fourth characteristic is somewhat more difficult to accept, in view of other received ideas concerning beauty's existence in the eye of the beholder: suffice it to say that while one doesn't argue about the taste of cheese, for example, nothing is more common than to argue about the beauty of a painting, a building, or a statue, and if so, the conceptions of beauty held by such disputants must be universal, and one of beauty's attributes is thus necessity. The effect of these conditions in combination is well known, but is perhaps less well-understood: the aesthetic judgment is free, referring neither to rules, nor to needs, nor to aims, and yet it is peremptory, demanding the assent of its listener. Indeed this formulation is necessary if one is to explain the vehemence of aesthetic arguments, on one hand, and their inconclusive character on the other.

However, even the most rigorous of aesthetic judgments is unstable. Kant defined the judgment as a paradox, for it claims universality but is unable to put forward a concept of beauty in support of that claim. In paragraph 16 of the "Analytic," Kant, having defined free beauty, goes on to define another beauty,

---

[27] These four conditions paraphrase the conclusions of the four "moments" of the "Analytic of the Beautiful." See Kant, pp. 41-89.

"dependent beauty," "ideal beauty," which does refer to a concept. Pure beauty would be that of an ornament or a musical improvisation: representing nothing, it is free. Dependent beauty would be that of a house, a horse, or a man: notions of such beauty are strongly influenced by ideas of shelter, transportation, or virtue. Even if the former is pure, Kant seems to incline towards the latter, and we may infer from this inclination that there exists a tension within the aesthetic judgment which causes even those who assert the freedom of beauty to ground individual aesthetic judgments in rules and concepts.[28]

The appeal to Kant is in fact less implausible than it at first seemed. "Le beau est toujours *bizarre*" (II, 578), Baudelaire wrote in 1855. While the precise sense of this statement has been vigorously debated, it certainly does mean that beauty cannot be reduced to a set of rules: that there is no concept of beauty as such. On this point, Baudelaire and Kant agree, the latter having concluded the second moment of the "Analytic" with the assertion "The *beautiful* is that which, *apart from a concept,* pleases universally."[29] In the third moment, Kant distinguishes beauty from purpose: beauty cannot be defined in terms of finality. Baudelaire's rejection of utilitarianism, and his refutation of the assimilation of beauty and progress bring him close to Kant on this point: beauty cannot be defined in terms of an aim, internal or external. In 1859, Baudelaire distinguishes the imaginative artist from the interested one, asserting that only the former can make works of beauty; this statement corroborates Kant's conclusion to the first moment of the "Analytic": beauty is judged apart from any interest. In practice, there are other significant similarities: both argue that ornament can be beautiful; both allow that nature can be beautiful, but prefer to say so when some mark of human activity can be ascribed to the scene in question.

In addition to seeking indications of humanity, many other ways exist to avoid the free play of the pure aesthetic judgment; strictly speaking, any effort to relate one's judgment to any criteria whatsoever denies the essential freedom of that judgment. Aesthet-

---

[28] This argument is more fully developed in my "Fate of Beauty in Romantic Criticism," *Nineteenth-Century French Studies,* 14 (1986), Nos. 3 & 4, 251-259.

[29] Kant, p. 60.

ic debates are often disagreements over just this point, and at the moment Baudelaire was writing, the debate over line and color sought a solution to the problem of recognition in aesthetics.

As at no other period of history, perhaps, this debate had succeeded in subordinating to itself all other critical considerations. Earlier, Poussin and Rubens had been used to exemplify the two schools,[30] but in the second quarter of the nineteenth century, Delacroix and Ingres were at the center of the controversy. The former's *Massacre at Scio* (1824) and his *Death of Sardanapalus* (1827) had polarized discussion of painting;[31] in turn, by 1834, Ingres had withdrawn from participation at the Salon because of unfavorable criticism. This debate was to last an extraordinarily long time: when, in 1855, Camille Pissarro came to France, it was still strong: students arriving in Paris were asked to which of the two schools they belonged; *Le Charivari* still carried caricatures depicting the debate between the two schools.[32] And traces of this debate are to be found in all of Baudelaire's art-critical writings.

While there were disciples on both sides, the debate was argued in very large part by its two protagonists: Ingres, elected early to the Académie, worked during his tenure to block the appointment of his rival to that position;[33] Delacroix was only received in 1857, six years before his death. Linear painting became the painting of the Ecole des Beaux-Arts; colorists learned their trade elsewhere, and were denied the recognition given to Ingres's disciples. Delacroix never had the following such institutionalized recognition can bring, even if many of the impressionists were to indicate him as a precursor and to trace their color theory to his.[34]

---

[30] Roger de Piles, *Conversations sur la connoissance de la peinture* (Paris: Langlois, 1677), esp. pp. 91-103.

[31] Delacroix's *Massacre* competed with Ingres's *Vow* in 1824; the former's *Sardanapalus* competed with the latter's *Apotheosis of Homer* in 1827. For further discussion of this question, see pp. 35-7 of Robert Rosenblum's *Jean-August-Dominique Ingres* (New York: Abrams, no date); pp. 83-90 of Frank Anderson Trapp's *The Attainment of Delacroix* (Baltimore: The John's Hopkins University Press, 1971) and pp. 126-130 of Tom Prideaux's *The World of Delacroix* (New York: Time-Life Books, 1966).

[32] Rewald, pp. 20-1. See also the illustration, p. 29.

[33] See Rewald, p. 21.

[34] As in Paul Signac's *D'Eugène Delacroix au néo-impressionnisme* (Paris: Hermann, 1978).

But, as it tends to be the case, the conflict of personalities overlies others, and that of Ingres and Delacroix conceals important oppositions; chief among them is that of classical and romantic art.[35] Daumier's caricature, mentioned earlier, assimilates line and classical art by personifying the former as nude male wearing a helmet, and brandishing an oversized paintbrush as a spear; by contrast, his romantic opponent is a much less beautiful man in modern dress, in a peasant's wooden shoes, crouched in an animal position. The colorists appealed to a notion of perceptual realism; the linearists qualified their use of classical models as idealism.[36] Another of the oppositions implicated in the debate is that of finish and sketch: one of the criticisms levelled against the colorists was that their works were not finished, that they were indistinguishable from sketches.[37]

It would be easy to dismiss this debate as a conflict between its two masters which attained its mid-century dimensions through excessive eagerness on the part of their disciples. The existence of similar debates at other moments in history indicates however that this one has a more enduring foundation than the strength of individual personalities: it overlies the aesthetic question that Kant had formulated: is beauty, properly speaking, recognized? Does one, in the aesthetic experience, compare a present sensation to an

---

[35] "The violent antagonism between these two masters . . . reinstated the traditional French controversy between the apostles of Poussin and those of Rubens, between the *anciens* and the *modernes:* and one heard again the familiar aesthetic oppositions of drawing versus color, intellect versus feeling, deliberation versus impulse, finished paintings versus sketches, classical beauty versus modern aberrations of the ugly and the morbid. Rosenblum, pp. 37-9.

[36] For example, Ingres maintained that all beauty was founded on the model used by antiquity: "Il n'y a pas deux arts, il n'y en a qu'un: c'est celui qui a pour fondement le beau éternel et naturel. Ceux qui cherchent ailleurs se trompent . . ." (Henri Delaborde, *Ingres, sa vie, ses travaux, sa doctrine* (Paris: Plon, 1870), p. 112). Delacroix, on the other hand, maintained that beauty was perceptual: "Ce fameux beau que les uns voient dans la ligne serpentine, les autres dans la ligne droite, ils se sont obstinés à ne le jamais voir que dans les lignes. Je suis à ma fenêtre et je vois le plus beau paysage: l'idée d'une ligne ne me vient pas à l'esprit. L'alouette chante, la rivière réfléchit mille diamants, le feuillage murmure; où sont les lignes qui produisent ces charmantes sensations? Ils ne veulent voir proportion, harmonie, qu'entre des lignes: le reste pour eux est chaos, et le compas seul est juge." Eugène Delacroix, *Journal 1822-1863* (Paris: Plon, 1980), p. 199 (7/15/49).

[37] See Boime on the aesthetics of the sketch, pp. 79-132.

idea of beauty, and consequently *re*-cognize it, or does one simply sense it?

The notion of recognition permeates the values advanced by Ingres in his teaching: one recognizes the subjects of history painting, the authority of classical art, and the perfection of the finished work. Ingres's own pronouncements insist on the notions of model, imitation, and recognition:

> Dessine, peins, imite surtout, fût-ce de la nature morte. Toute chose imitée de la nature est une œuvre, et cette imitation mène à l'art.[38]

> Il faut trouver le secret du beau par le vrai. Les anciens n'ont pas créé, ils n'ont pas fait: ils ont reconnu.[39]

> N'étudiez le beau qu'à genoux.[40]

By contrast, the notion of recognition is repudiated by the colorist school. Even the most banal of received ideas typifies the colorist as disobedient, refusing to recognize authority, whether that of the Academy or that of tradition. A common objection to colorist work was that one could not recognize its subject. In 1822, for example, Delécluze criticized Delacroix's brushwork for lack of coherence: "Vu de près, la touche en est si hachée, si incohérente, quoique exempte de timidité, qu'on ne saurait se persuader qu'au point où le talent d'exécution est parvenu dans notre école, aucun artiste ait pu adopter cette singulière façon d'opérer qu'on retrouve dans quelques peintres à la détrempe."[41] Gustave Planche accused Delacroix of sending undecipherable sketches to the Salon in 1846: his admiration for the painter's work did not go so far as to ". . . lui pardonner d'envoyer au Louvre des esquisses à peine ébauchées, obscures, confuses."[42] More importantly, Delacroix conceived of colorist painting as a dis-habituation to received ideas of color: local color does not

---

[38] See Delaborde, p. 115.
[39] Delaborde, p. 117.
[40] Delaborde, p. 114.
[41] André Ferran, *L'Esthétique de Baudelaire* (Paris: Hachette, 1933), p. 123.
[42] A. Tabarant, *La Vie artistique en France au temps de Baudelaire* (Paris: Mercure de France, 1942), p. 99.

exist, but is an effect of the relation of two other colors.[43] The model also loses its prestige:

> . . . si l'emploi du modèle donnait au tableau quelque chose de frappant, ce ne pouvait être que chez des hommes très intelligents: en d'autres termes, qu'il n'y avait que ceux qui savent faire de l'effet, en se passant du modèle, qui puissent véritablement en tirer parti, quand ils le consultent.[44]

The notion of accuracy falls to that of imagination: "Le réalisme devrait être défini l'antipode de l'art. Il est peut-être plus odieux dans la peinture et dans la sculpture que dans l'histoire et le roman . . ."[45] Ingres and Delacroix fall on either side of the single most important aesthetic question: Ingres argues that recognition is essential to the aesthetic experience; Delacroix asserts that it is not.

When in 1845 Baudelaire entered the field of art criticism, he found himself required to make aesthetic judgments, an obligation he readily embraced. Echoes of these judgments are found everywhere in his writings;[46] the words *beau* and *beauté,* for example, recur 126 times in *Les Fleurs du mal* and 87 times in the *Petits poèmes en prose,* as often, that is to say, as the words *amour* and *aimer,* more frequently than *mort* and *mourir.* The word for the organ of criticism, *œil* is found as often as *cœur.*[47]

---

[43] Charles Blanc, "Eugène Delacroix," *La Gazette des Beaux-Arts* XVI (1885), pp. 5-27 and 97-129: "'. . . je disais que les grands coloristes ne font pas le ton local, et avec vous je n'ai pas besoin sans doute d'aller plus loin.' Eugène Delacroix fit deux pas en arrière, selon son habitude, et clignant les yeux: 'Cela est parfaitement vrai, dit-il: voilà un ton, par exemple (il montrait du doigt le ton gris et sale du pavé); eh bien, si l'on disait à Paul Véronèse: peignez-moi une belle femme blonde, dont la chair soit de ce ton là, il la peindrait, et la femme serait une belle blonde dans son tableau.'"

[44] Delacroix, p. 366 (10/12/1853).

[45] Delacroix, p. 765 (2/22/1860).

[46] Lucie Horner advances this thesis in her *Baudelaire critique de Delacroix* (Geneva: Droz, 1956) as does Armand Moss in his *Baudelaire et Delacroix* (Paris: Nizet, 1973). It can also be argued that Baudelaire's criticism is the search for modernity announced on the last page of the *Salon de 1845,* and in this case, the painter Baudelaire seeks is not Delacroix, but Constantin Guys. For this position, see Anne Coffin Hanson, *Manet and the Modern Tradition.*

[47] See Robert T. Cargo, *A Concordance to Baudelaire's* Les Fleurs du mal (Chapel Hill: University of North Carolina Press, 1965) and *Concordance to*

However, for Baudelaire as for Kant, a pressure exists which requires him to support his aesthetic judgments, even if inherently, such support is impossible. There is no concept of beauty, Kant wrote, and this assertion is corroborated by proverbial qualifications of beauty. But very deeply, this truth is resisted, and can only be resisted: if beauty has no concept, it is of course inconceivable, and the desire to understand is slow to admit such a defeat. Thus Baudelaire, like Kant, Ruskin and others, advances theories of beauty, the main burden of which is to justify his aesthetic judgments, but it must be understood that no matter how elaborate such a theory – imagination, color/line, dominance – might be, its claim to justify the use of an a-conceptual epithet, which by definition eludes all argument, is unfounded.

Baudelaire's art criticism shares many features of the different *Salons* written at the period. His *Salon de 1845,* for example, arranges discussion of the Salon's offerings according to the hierarchies of the day: painting comes first, sculpture last; within painting, historical works precede genre painting and landscape. Such a comprehensive arrangement implies summary treatment of individual artists and works, and while Baudelaire's comments are much more detailed than the single sentence meted out by other critics to each work, they rarely approach the length of the longer analyses he was to write later. An exception is his analysis of William Haussouillier's *Fontaine de Jouvence,* which, in its detail and in its lyricism approaches his later comments on Delacroix and Guys. His aesthetic writings quickly become more theoretical. In 1846, for example, Baudelaire alternates general considerations (on criticism, on color, on portraiture, on modernity) and detailed analyses, subordinating description to the theory advanced. And in 1859, Baudelaire admits in a letter to Nadar that he made only one visit to the Salon,[48] concentrating accordingly on a very small number of works – by Delacroix, Fromentin, Gérome – presenting at the exposition, and on some others – by Boudin, Meryon, Christophe – which he saw elsewhere. This *Salon* is justly famous for the extensive theory of imagination which Baudelaire advances in its first four chapters. The opposition of line and color,

---

Baudelaire's Petits poèmes en prose (University: University of Alabama Press, 1971).

[48] See his letter to Nadar, from May 16, 1859 (*Correspondance,* I, 578).

employed in his *Exposition universelle* and his *L'Œuvre et la vie d'Eugène Delacroix,* organizing painting into two camps, is also an essential part of his theoretical contribution.

If there is no concept of beauty, however, such theories can only be fictions, hypotheses regarding what might cause the sensation of beauty to arise, but hypotheses which are forever barred from verification: only conceptual propositions can be proven true or false. Just as judgments of beauty before them, theories of beauty are precarious, also appealing for support, but finding their support in description. I argued in chapter 3 that description serves to guarantee the truth of a text by producing a reality-effect, telling the skeptical reader in effect: "Just look, see for yourself." Such a device is crucial in aesthetic texts, for it effectively blocks the questions unsupported aesthetic pronouncements necessarily raise. The illusion of reference, *l'effet de réel,* has been divergently interpreted, as the result of an allegorical echo (Riffaterre), or as the result of the reader's inability to integrate a particular element into a narrative system (Barthes). Whatever the cause of the *effet de réel,* it is understood as symbolic, uniting divergent interpretations, and achieving its effect through its very ability to respond to those interpretations.

Descriptions, symbols, and theory's fictions succeed in exemplifying or illustrating aesthetic judgments: they meet its requirements by defining a pleasure without interest, an understanding with no concept, a purposiveness without a purpose. More importantly, only devices such as these can meet the requirements of aesthetic judgment; these are the devices of literature. The only exemplification or illustration of the true aesthetic judgment is poetic. The burden of theory and description in art criticism is to prove the unprovable, to put the inconceivable in conceptual terms, and this is also the burden of art. Description and theory can only fail to justify art criticism's judgments, and the story of Baudelaire's art criticism is the story of this failure.

5

THE UNIVERSAL VOICE: *LE SALON DE 1846*

> . . . le *je* couvre un *nous, nous* immense, *nous* silencieux et invisible. . . (II, 471)

The public expression of a private reaction is perhaps the most paradoxical aspect of the aesthetic judgment, and is certainly the one that Baudelaire develops at greatest length in his *Salon de 1846*. Written two years prior to the revolution in which Baudelaire is said to have participated,[1] the public aspect of the *Salon* – its soon-to-be-abandoned use of political metaphors – has been commented several times.[2] Whatever the sincerity of these images or their later use, one can say that they also serve a purpose in the *Salon,* which, after all, is primarily a work of aesthetics: they express the aesthetic judgment's tendency to demand the assent of its audience, even it if furnishes no basis for such assent.

It is of course difficult to maintain that Baudelaire subscribes to Kantian aesthetics: evidence that the poet read the philosopher lacks, and Baudelaire's criticism does not employ the categorical analysis characteristic of Kant's *Critiques.* Baudelaire does however refer quite explicitly to Diderot, whose *Origine et la nature du beau* Kant read attentively,[3] and the echoes of Kant's aesthetics heard in Baudelaire's criticism might indicate a common source.

---

[1] See Enid Starkie, *Baudelaire* (Middlesex: Penguin Books, 1957), pp. 193-221.

[2] See David Kelley, ed., *Salon de 1846,* by Charles Baudelaire (Oxford: The Clarendon Press, 1976), pp. 15, 34.

[3] P. Vernière, ed., *Œuvres esthétiques,* by Denis Diderot (Paris: Garnier, 1968), p. 389.

Diderot's article appeared anonymously in the *Encyclopédie* in 1752; it was republished separately and attributed to him in 1759, and again in 1772 under the title *Traité du beau.*[4] Diderot seeks in this essay, as Kant was to do in 1790, to account on one hand for the objective structure of the aesthetic judgment, and on the other, for the variety of judgments this apparent absolute elicits. Language ascribes beauty to the object of judgment, not to the judge:

> *Beau* est le terme que nous appliquons à une infinité d'êtres; mais quelque différence qu'il y ait entre ces êtres, il faut ou que nous fassions une fausse application du terme *beau,* ou qu'il y ait dans tous ces êtres une qualité dont le terme *beau* soit le signe.[5]

If this is so, however, the lack of uniformity among the judgments made of a single object requires explanation:

> Après avoir tenté d'exposer en quoi consiste l'origine du *beau,* il ne nous reste plus qu'à rechercher celle des opinions différentes que les hommes ont de la beauté: cette recherche achèvera de donner de la certitude à nos principes. . . .[6]

Thus the question Diderot persistently poses is this: ". . . cela est-il *beau* parce qu'il plaît? ou cela plaît-il parce qu'il est *beau?*"[7] Is "beauty" the term that designates a subjective pleasure or an objective fact? The paradox Diderot explains here was to be treated again by Kant forty years later; it is also the paradox that dominates the *Salon de 1846.*

Diderot answers that "beauty" corresponds to an objective fact: we use the word to qualify those objects that elicit the idea of relation. A beautiful object is one that stirs the understanding to postulate relations: "J'appelle donc *beau* hors de moi, tout ce qui contient en soi de quoi réveiller dans mon entendement l'idée de rapports; et *beau* par rapport à moi, tout ce qui réveille cette idée."[8] It is the quantity and the quality of these relations that determine the beauty of the object, but if so, what accounts for the manifest

---

[4] Vernière, pp. 387-9.
[5] Diderot, p. 417.
[6] Diderot, p. 428.
[7] Diderot, p. 393.
[8] Diderot, p. 418.

variations in assessments of beauty? Diderot categorizes twelve sources of such diversity of judgment; however, his enumeration of sources of variation only serves to confirm his assertion that beauty consists in a single principle:

> Quoi qu'il en soit de toutes ces causes de diversité dans nos jugements, ce n'est point une raison de penser que le *beau* réel, celui qui consiste dans la perception des rapports, soit une chimère; l'application de ce principe peut varier à l'infini, et ses modifications accidentelles occasionner des dissertations et des guerres littéraires: mais le principe n'en est pas moins constant.[9]

Beauty exists as a concept.

Thus when in May of 1845, Baudelaire asked Champfleury to relate his *Salon de 1845* to the works of Diderot, he invited comparison with a very precise theory, one which attributes beauty to the number and kind of relations a work evokes.[10] As Claude Pichois has noted, he must have been gratified several days later, when he read in *Le Corsaire-Satan* Champfleury's account of his essay: "M. Baudelaire-Dufaÿs est hardi comme Diderot, moins le paradoxe."[11] Certainly boldness is a quality Baudelaire prized, but paradoxicalness was too, and in that case, Champfleury's compliment withholds as much as it gives. Such a compliment might in fact be one of the reasons for Baudelaire's discontent with his first *Salon,* and one of the reasons for the important departure – formal and philosophical – that his subsequent venture, the *Salon de 1846,* represents with respect to the genre. In 1846, Baudelaire was to write a work which would allow one to qualify him as "hardi *et* paradoxal, comme Diderot."

The most evident of the paradoxes with which the *Salon de 1846* abounds is Baudelaire's repudiation of any concept of beauty, and with such a concept, his repudiation of Diderot's argument:

> Toutes les beautés contiennent, comme tous les phénomènes possibles, quelque chose d'éternel et quelque chose de

---

[9] Diderot, p. 435.

[10] Baudelaire, *Correspondance,* I, 123.

[11] Claude Pichois, ed., *Œuvres,* II, 1265.

> transitoire, – d'absolu et de particulier. La beauté absolue et éternelle n'existe pas, ou plutôt elle n'est qu'une abstraction écrémée à la surface des beautés diverses. (I, 493)

That this definition of beauty recurs virtually unchanged at the end of Baudelaire's career, in *Le Peintre de la vie moderne,* serves only to prove its centrality to his thought. This assertion makes a significant advance upon Diderot's argument: if Diderot argued that beauty is constant, while perceptions of it vary, Baudelaire replies that while beauty is not constant, perceptions of it nevertheless must not vary. Beauty passes from a perception to a play of power, and aesthetic judgments pass from constatives to performatives. With this insight, Baudelaire's beauty meets Kant's, and together they open the field of modern aesthetics.

The immediate effect of this formulation is to change the tone of the work of criticism: unable to prove aesthetic judgments, the critic must elicit assent in other ways; he will use persuasion, in the form of illustration, but he will also use intimidation. Baudelaire's paradox accounts for his rude address to the bourgeois, his dismissal of Victor Hugo, and his ridiculing of individual artists.[12]

Conflict is thus built into the aesthetic judgment: when one says "this is beautiful," one cannot help but imply "and you must agree." Unlike more personal judgments, the aesthetic judgment engages debate, for it imputes its evaluation to its audience, who may disagree, and if often, Kant writes, "must put up with a rude dismissal of its claim to universal validity."[13] This predicament is registered in Baudelaire's *Salon de 1846* in the insistent use of metaphors of political struggle, which describe, in the conflict of government and rebellion, the conflict of judge and audience. This conflict produces several effects. It results, firstly, in an argumentative tendency not shared by the *Salon de 1845.*

Baudelaire tends to demonstrate the accuracy of his judgments; the marks of logical argument – *si, or, car, donc* – are widely used; comparisons (Delacroix vs. Hugo, color vs. line, school vs. individual) are frequent, and description serves to show, when

---

[12] Pierre-Georges Castex has noted this change in the tone of the *Salon de 1846:* "Il semble cependant que la réflexion théorique ait surtout conduit Baudelaire à mieux fonder ses séverités et par là-même les durcir." Castex, *La Critique d'art en France,* p. 36.

[13] Kant, p. 52.

logic can go no further, how a work merits a particular epithet. It should be noted in passing that the very point of this argument cannot be proved, since Baudelaire denies the existence of any single Beauty: such pseudo-argument simply imposes silence on a hostile audience, the Bourgeois for whom Baudelaire expresses such contempt.

The conflict between judge and audience also explains Baudelaire's use of apodictic statement:[14] it is the essence of aesthetic judgment to claim self-evidence. In this respect, Baudelaire is one of very few aestheticians to have understood that the aesthetic judgment must be intolerant of divergence, peremptory; this understanding distinguishes his work from that of many of his predecessors who took refuge in an undemanding relativism, a position which safeguards the subjectivity of the aesthetic judgment, but which reduces it, so doing, to the status of a merely subjective trait, of interest primarily to those who seek to define the psychology of the judge. Such an argument, for example, is implicit in Horace's "ut pictura poesis . . .," which evades the question "is this poem beautiful?" by saying that each one must be read "in its own light" in order to be appreciated. This argument is also used by du Bos in his *Réflexions critiques sur la poésie et sur la peinture:* "Mais la question, si le Brun est préférable au Titien; c'est-à-dire, si la partie de la composition poétique & de l'expression est préférable à celle du coloris, & laquelle de ces parties est supérieure à l'autre: je tiens qu'il est inutile de l'agiter."[15] "La chose ne dépend pas plus de lui qu'il dépend d'un homme dont le palais est conformé, de manière que le vin de Champagne lui fait plus de plaisir que le vin d'Espagne, de changer de goût, & d'aimer mieux le vin d'Espagne que l'autre."[16] Such assimilations of aesthetic judgment and taste of the palate equate questions of aesthetics with accidents of physiology. By contrast, Kantian aesthetics is founded on the premise that there is a difference, syntactic and lexical at the very least, between the two judgments, and that the autonomy of the aesthetic judgment should be maintained.

---

[14] Walter Benjamin, *A Lyric Poet in the Age of High Capitalism* (London: New Left Books, 1973), p. 71.

[15] du Bos, I, 510.

[16] du Bos, I, 513.

Finally, and most importantly, the possibility of dismissal of aesthetic claims results in a ruse: one speaks, when judging the beauty of an object, in what Kant calls a "universal voice." The aesthetic judgment's claim to universality is actually an estimate of universal taste: ". . . we believe ourselves to be speaking with a universal voice, and lay claim to the concurrence of every one, whereas no private sensation would be decisive except for the observer alone and *his* liking."[17] The fiction of universal taste serves to preempt any disagreement to aesthetic judgments.

In 1846, Baudelaire strives to speak in the universal voice, to speak to and for the greatest number. In the preface of his *Salon,* he concludes, seriously, I believe, that "tout livre qui ne s'adresse pas à la majorité – nombre et intelligence – est un sot livre." (II, 417) And later, he asserts that he speaks for a number much larger than himself, whose voice will eventually drown the voices of others:

> . . . à chaque phrase, le *je* couvre un *nous, nous* immense, *nous* silencieux et invisible, – *nous* toute une génération nouvelle, . . . une génération pleine de santé, parce qu'elle est jeune, et qui pousse déjà à la queue, coudoie et fait ses trous, – sérieuse, railleuse et menaçante! (II, 471)

The voice in which the critic speaks implies more than his opinion, and this voice arouses conflict with its listeners. The universal voice defines Baudelaire's notion of criticism; he abandons an elitist notion in favor of a more extended one. Initially, Baudelaire proposes poetry as the model of criticism:

> Je crois sincèrement que la meilleure critique est celle qui est amusante et poétique; non pas celle-ci, froide et algébrique, qui, sous prétexte de tout expliquer, n'a ni haine ni amour, et se dépouille volontairement de toute espèce de tempérament mais, – un beau tableau étant la nature réfléchie par un artiste, – celle qui sera ce tableau réfléchi par un esprit intelligent et sensible. Ainsi le meilleur compte rendu d'un tableau pourra être un sonnet ou une élégie. (II, 418)

---

[17] Kant, p. 56.

Criticism can be limited to representing the works it appreciates, and in that case, a poetic model exemplified as a sonnet or as an elegy would be the best account. Such criticism differs from "algebraic" criticism by its insistence on agency: both criticisms are reflections of works (which in turn are reflections of nature), but the poetic model which also expresses the temperament of the critic is superior to the "colder" algebraic model.

Poetic criticism is however limited: the reflection of a reflection (of a reflection), it is passive, defined entirely by its object. Moreover, it is found in smaller forms, enclosed in collections of poetry intended for poetic readers. If the critic preaches, he does so only to the converted, and such a limited audience is unacceptable. Baudelaire thus pursues to define true criticism:

> Mais ce genre de critique et destiné aux receuils de poésie et aux lecteurs poétiques. Quant à la critique proprement dite, j'espère que les philosophes comprendront ce que je vais dire: pour être juste, c'est-à-dire pour avoir sa raison d'être, la critique doit être partiale, passionnée, politique, c'est-à-dire faite à un point de vue exclusif, mais au point de vue qui ouvre le plus d'horizons. (II, 418)

Such criticism shares the temperament of poetic criticism, but extends its appeal beyond the field of readers of poetry: addressed to "philosophers," it is active, not reflective; it is argumentative, taking a position and defending it against all others; it seeks to "open horizons" to a wider audience, and, theoretically at least, to speak to all. And yet, it is "partial": partial criticism seeks to represent its object while remaining "passionate," while remaining attached to the subjective nature of the judgments it advances, and if so, such criticism is a paradox: partial in its preferences, but universal in its judgments; political in its aspiration but exclusive in its appreciations.

Such paradoxical criticism is of course a reflection of the paradoxical nature of the aesthetic judgment: while based on a preference which can only be subjective, it demands the assent of a universal audience, and this demand is at the limit of intelligibility. Baudelaire acknowledges this aspect of criticism when he says: ". . . la critique touche à chaque instant à la métaphysique." (II, 419) Whatever his definition of beauty, he does recognize a tension within aesthetics, and it will be the burden of his own critical writing to accommodate that tension.

The dedicatory chapter, "Aux Bourgeois," exemplifies the universalizing tendency in an ironic mode. Baudelaire seeks here to prove that the bourgeois, every bit as much as some unnamed *accapareurs*, have a right to aesthetic pleasure. The incongruity of defending bourgeois pleasure against the inroads of artistic monopolists is matched only by that of demanding a public right to a private pleasure but, these premises accepted, the argument is plain: if the taste of the bourgeois cannot be imposed on all, they at least can adopt a universal taste, and learn to speak in the universal voice.

Baudelaire proposes that the bourgeois model their subjective pleasure on the objective characteristics of science: ". . . il est juste que ceux qui ne sont que propriétaires aspirent à devenir savants; car la science est une jouissance non moins grande que la propriété." (II, 415) This identification of knowledge with aesthetic pleasure is important: like knowledge, pleasure must be shared; pleasure must receive the universal assent accorded to science. In the service of this assertion, Baudelaire puts forward two arguments likening aesthetic pleasure to more objective abilities. First, he assimilates political power and aesthetic sensitivity: "Vous possédez le gouvernement de la cité, et cela est juste, car vous êtes la force. Mais il faut que vous soyez aptes à sentir la beauté, car comme aucun d'entre vous ne peut aujourd'hui se passer de puissance, nul n'a le droit de se passer de poésie." (II, 415) One could, as Bentham did, found an ethics on democratic principles, but to say that a subjective pleasure should correspond to the feeling of the majority is absurd: the universality of beauty is not empirical but imputed. When the judge asserts that he speaks in a universal voice, his assertion is a challenge, not a poll. Secondly, Baudelaire associates economic ability and aesthetic sensitivity: "Cependant il est juste, si les deux tiers de votre temps sont remplis par la science, que le troisième soit occupé par le sentiment, et c'est par le sentiment que vous devez comprendre l'art . . ." (II, 416) Whatever the deficiencies of these arguments, they suggest that the bourgeois emulate in their aesthetic judgments the more global characteristics of their political and economic decisions, and if so, their judgments must abandon the parochial tendencies of conventional bourgeois preferences to acquire the universality of genuine taste.

Baudelaire is asking the bourgeois to enter the mainstream of aesthetics, to forsake the "taste" which later will be known as kitch. The fate of a single word, *science,* happily the very object of their desires, shows how their interests expand. The word recurs several times in the course of the chapter, and with each appearance, its meaning is more objective, more universal. In its first appearance, the word is taken as a source of potential pleasure, comparable in this respect to property: ". . . la science est une jouissance non moins grande que la propriété." (II, 415) *Science* and property are the objects of desire. In its second appearance, the word has acquired a new meaning: "Jouir est une science, et l'exercice des cinq sens veut une initiation particulière . . ." (II, 415) *Science* is no longer the object of a desire, but a mode of feeling pleasure, a precondition rather than an aim. In its third appearance, *science* is the very knowledge denied to the bourgeois. "La science est le comptoir et leur boutique." (II, 416) But in its fourth occurence, it is a possession of the bourgeois, and has a new meaning: it refers here to the skills of commerce, not to the appreciation of art: "Il est juste, si les deux tiers de votre temps sont remplis par la science, que le troisième soit occupé par le sentiment . . . ." (II, 416) The word's trajectory describes a progressive hardening of its meaning: from a subjective pleasure it becomes an objective fact, and this trajectory is that of the aesthetic judgment.

When in Chapter IV, Baudelaire ceases to theorize, the artist on whom he exercises his judgment is Delacroix, and he immediately attributes his preference to the "majority": "J'ignore s'il (Delacroix) est fier de sa qualité de romantique; mais sa place est ici, parce que la majorité du public l'a depuis longtemps, et même dès sa première œuvre, constitué le chef de l'école *moderne.*" (II, 427) The selection of Delacroix as a first example is of course significant, and David Kelley has commented on this choice:

> Il est vrai que les opinions de Baudelaire correspondent souvent à l'avis de la postérité. Mais dans le contexte plus précis de l'année 1846 il paraît quelque peu optimiste. . . . Si, par exemple, comme l'a très bien démontré Lucie Horner, Delacroix était soutenu par un groupe de critiques assez nombreux, cela

> ne signifie pas qu'il jouissait d'une grande popularité, et il serait difficile de prétendre qu'il a dominé le Salon de 1846.[18]

If Kelley and Horner are correct in their assessment of Delacroix's acceptance, Baudelaire is not describing a common opinion, but imposing a personal preference, and such attempts to extend personal preferences are integral to aesthetic judgments.

In his analysis of Delacroix's works, Baudelaire seeks to create a common opinion, and to that end, he cites authorities, associates Delacroix with famous men, and establishes links between the new paintings on display at the Salon and much earlier paintings which had already been accepted. The citation with which he begins his discussion, Auguste Thiers's 1822 assessment of *Dante et Virgile* proves Delacroix's universal recognition: Baudelaire refers to it as one of the *pièces du procès* by which the painter's reputation can be established. Almost immediately thereafter, he makes an extended comparison between Hugo and Delacroix, the effect of such a procedure being to set the two on a common footing; it thus confers on Delacroix something of Hugo's reputation. In fact, however, Baudelaire goes further: not simply is Delacroix like Hugo, he replaces the poet: "A coup sûr la comparaison dut paraître pénible à Eugène Delacroix, peut-être à tous deux; car si ma définition du romantisme (intimité, spiritualité, etc.) place Delacroix à la tête du romantisme, elle en exclut naturellement M. Victor Hugo." (II, 430) If Delacroix is the head of the romantic movement, his work must be recognized. The reasons for Baudelaire's preference also imply the notion of universality: Delacroix, though a painter, is more "poetic" than Hugo.

> Le premier jouit d'une certaine tranquillité, disons mieux, d'un certain égoïsme de spectateur, qui fait planer sur toute sa poésie je ne sais quelle froideur et quelle modération – que la passion tenace et bilieuse du second, aux prises avec les patiences du métier, ne lui permet pas toujours de garder –. L'un commence par le détail, l'autre par l'intelligence intime du sujet; d'où il

---

[18] Kelley, p. 53. One must not however overestimate Baudelaire's "courage" in advancing this judgment: by 1845, Delacroix had received several important commissions, indicative of official acceptance: the "Salon du Roi" at the Palais Bourbon (1833), the library of the Palais du Luxembourg (1840), the library of the Palais Bourbon (1843).

> arrive que celui-ci n'en prend que la peau, et que l'autre en arrache les entrailles. Trop matériel, trop attentif aux superficies de la nature, M. Victor Hugo est devenu un peintre en poésie; Delacroix, toujours respectueux de son idéal, est souvent, à son insu, un poète en peinture. (II, 431-2)

Superficial, too attentive to detail, leaving nothing to the imagination, Hugo's work is "cold." Delacroix's, by contrast, is "passionate": he is a creator, his work is imaginative, it is excessive. Hugo, too attentive to detail, represents the particular; Delacroix, seizing the "entrails" of his subject, represents the universal.

Just one more indication should suffice to demonstrate how Baudelaire seeks universal assent to his assessments. Before coming to his discussion of the four paintings actually displayed at the Salon, Baudelaire analyzes Delacroix's decoration of the Bibliothèque du Luxembourg at length; the painting represents the meeting of Dante and Homer in Limbo. This description is unusual in its use of citation: Baudelaire quotes the text of the *Inferno in extenso.* To a certain extent, such a procedure is necessary, for the description will account only for what the citation does not portray: Dante's text gives the narrative of the encounter; Baudelaire's gives the descriptive backdrop. But Baudelaire includes Dante's text for another reason: it describes a moment of aesthetic recognition, and traces the ambition of such judgments. Homer recognizes Virgil as a sublime poet, and this recognition is expressed through the *voix unanime* of the surrounding poets.

> 'O toi, qui honores toute science et tout art, quels sont ces esprits auxquels on fait tant d'honneur qu'on les sépare du sort des autres?'
>
> Il me répondit: 'Leur belle renommée, qui retentit là-haut dans votre monde, trouve grâce dans le ciel, qui les distingue des autres.'
>
> Cependant une voix se fit entendre: 'Honorez le sublime poète; son ombre, qui était partie, nous revient.'
>
> La voix se tut, et je vis venir à nous quatre grandes ombres; leur aspect n'était ni triste ni joyeux.
>
> Le bon maître me dit: 'Regarde celui qui marche, une épée à la main, en avant des trois autres, comme un roi: c'est Homère, poète souverain; l'autre qui le suit est Horace le satirique; Ovide

> est le troisième, et le dernier est Lucain. Comme chacun d'eux partage avec moi le nom qu'a fait retentir la voix unanime, ils me font honneur et ils font bien!'
>
> Ainsi je vis se réunir la belle école de ce maître du chant sublime, qui plane sur les autres comme l'aigle. Dès qu'ils eurent devisé ensemble quelque peu, ils se tournèrent vers moi avec un geste de salut, ce qui fit sourire mon guide. Et ils me firent encore plus d'honneur, car ils me reçurent dans leur troupe, de sorte que je fus le sixième parmi tant de génies . . . .
> . . . . (II, 437-8)

The word *voix* defines the aim of the passage. Homer utters his judgment, the other poets repeat it, but there is no delay between utterance and echo: Homer's judgment is recited as though in chorus. Their unanimous voice suppresses the difference between master and school, between instance and repetition, and finally, between judge and audience. The unanimous voice is the universal voice. Even as Dante hears this voice, he joins the chorus, for he is incorporated into the *belle école,* becoming the sixth among the poetic geniuses. It would be easy to present this citation in terms of subjectivity: that, just as Dante attributes to himself the title of genius, Baudelaire takes for himself the role of disciple of Delacroix. Such an interpretation, however accurately it describes the personal ambition of the poet, reduces the aesthetic judgment – the sublimity of Virgil, Dante, Delacroix or Baudelaire – to a subjective conceit; it is rather, the unanimity of this evaluation that is important, and such unanimity of opinion is precisely what Baudelaire, like Dante, seeks in his *Salon de 1846*.

* * *

The innovation the *Salon de 1846* represents with respect to its predecessor lies largely in its wider ambition: to speak in the universal voice. This ambition, I am sure, is what produces the belligerent tone so often noticed in this *Salon*. However, as polemical as it is, it also insists on the contrary: the private statement of subjective preferences.

By the eleventh chapter, Baudelaire has gone to considerable lengths to assure his readers of the objective character of his judgments: they are scientific, addressed to all, buttressed by authority, and cast as arguments. It comes as a surprise therefore when, discussing Horace Vernet, Baudelaire defies universal opinion, asserting the supremacy of his own judgment *envers et contre tous,* and does so in the most subjective of terms: "Je sais bien que cet homme est un Français, et qu'un Français en France est une chose sainte et sacrée – et même à l'étranger, à ce qu'on dit; mais c'est pour cela que je le hais." (II, 469) The very popularity of Vernet (which should be taken into account if Baudelaire, faithful to his announced intention, were to seek to open political horizons) is now oppressive: ". . . cette popularité, dis-je, cette *vox populi, vox Dei,* est pour moi une oppression." (II, 469) The verb *haïr,* naming the most subjective of emotions, recurs no fewer than seven times in this three-page account, including, of course, its most celebrated passage: "Je hais cet homme parce que ses tableaux ne sont point de la peinture, mais une masturbation agile et fréquente, une irritation de l'épiderme français . . ." (II, 470) Just as Baudelaire has lapsed from the objective discussion of paintings into the subjective condemnation of a man, so also does he accuse Vernet of having fallen from the dialectic of love into the monolog of masturbation.

This example should suffice to indicate that at the very heart of Baudelaire's attempt to speak in a universal voice lies a far more irrational and subjective element: can it be mere coincidence that this moment of most partial discourse is precisely that of the most explicit claim for universality: ". . . le *je* couvre un *nous* . . . "? The same difficulty troubles his effort to define his own modernity: on one hand, Baudelaire gives an objective description of Romanticism: "Qui dit romantisme dit art moderne – c'est-à-dire intimité, spiritualité, couleur, aspiration vers l'infini, exprimées par tous les moyens que contiennent les arts." (II, 421) On the other, he defines it in subjective terms: "Le romantisme n'est précisément ni dans le choix des sujets ni dans la vérité exacte, mais dans la manière de sentir." (II, 420) Finally, Baudelaire's discussion of sculpture is affected by this vacillation: on one hand, sculpture is inferior to painting because it is "positive," not "imaginative": "Brutale et positive comme la nature, elle est en même temps vague et insaisissable . . ." (II, 487) On the other, sculpture permits subjective errors of appreciation: ". . . le spectateur, qui tourne autour de la figure, peut choisir cent points de vue différents, excepté le bon . . . (II, 487) Sculpture simultaneously gives the imagination too little and too much room for play. Clearly, Baudelaire's attempt to speak in the universal voice has not entirely satisfied his desire to express his subjective preferences.

It is in the descriptions of works of art that Baudelaire's aesthetic project goes astray: as long as he confines himself to judgment, he speaks in the universal voice; as soon, however, as he describes the work, his judgments become markedly more subjective, and he speaks essentially for himself. Lucie Horner has suggested that this *Salon* was almost complete before Baudelaire ever visited the Salon, and that the descriptions were simply inserted into an already-existing manuscript;[19] such a procedure would betray suspicion of description, and an effort to keep the more general aspects of the *Salon* distinct from the details of individual accounts.

Michael Fried has shown the importance of memory as Baudelaire's criterion for judgment in this *Salon,* and suggested that the poet detects beauty when an elusive, subliminal relation between a work and its precursors can be intuited.[20] Delacroix's *Pietà,* which recasts Rosso Fiorentino's composition at the Louvre, is one such work. By contrast, Vernet's exact, photographic reproductions do not imply memory, but memorization: a precise, measurable relation to a specific model demands to be established. Art is memory, not memorization; it is imitative, but not exact imitation: ". . . l'art est une mnémotechnie du beau: or, l'imitation exacte gâte le souvenir." (II, 455)

As Baudelaire said earlier, what is true of art is also true of criticism, and here is a case in point: the very opposition between an undefinable, yet true imitation on one hand, and exact imitation on the other is part of a venerable tradition, the contemporary exponent of which was Quatremère de Quincy, and whose most celebrated version is to be found in the ninth book of Aristotle's *Poetics.*[21] Indeed, Baudelaire's indication of "history" and "poetry" as examples of the two currents of portraiture is a dead give-away:

---

[19] This hypothesis would explain the brevity of descriptions of works actually displayed at the Salon. See her *Baudelaire critique de Delacroix* (Geneva: Droz, 1956), p. 97.

[20] Fried, p. 518.

[21] "The difference, rather, lies in the fact that the historian narrates events that have actually happened, whereas the poet writes about things as they might possibly occur. Poetry, therefore, is more philosophical and more significant than

> Il y a deux manières de comprendre le portrait – l'histoire et le roman.
>
> L'une est de rendre fidèlement, sévèrement, minutieusement, le contour et le modelé du modèle, ce qui n'exclut pas l'idéalisation, qui consistera pour les naturalistes éclairés à choisir l'attitude la plus caractéristique, celle qui exprime le mieux les habitudes de l'esprit. . . .
>
> La seconde méthode, celle particulière aux coloristes, est de faire du portrait un tableau, un poème avec ses accessoires, plein d'espace et de rêverie. Ici l'art est plus difficile, parce qu'il est plus ambitieux. Il faut savoir baigner une tête dans les molles vapeurs d'une chaude atmosphère, ou la faire sortir des profondeurs d'un crépuscule. Ici, l'imagination a une plus grande part, et cependant, comme il arrive souvent que le roman est plus vrai que l'histoire, il arrive aussi qu'un modèle est plus clairement exprimé par le pinceau abondant et facile d'un coloriste que par le crayon d'un dessinateur. (II, 464)

Linear portraiture insists on detail; colorist insists on atmosphere; the former respects fact, the latter, imagination; the model for linear art is history, that of colorist art is the novel, or, as Baudelaire also says, the poem. As long as the artist avoids exact imitation, imitation is beautiful, living, and true. But at what point does imitation fall into exactitude, memory into memorization? Correlatively, and most importantly for the critic, at what point does the critical "reflection" cease expressing a temperament, and fall into "cold," "algebraic" exactitude? Can description tread this fine line?

The very first description in the *Salon*, that of Delacroix's *Pietà*, suggests that it cannot. The painting is, and always has been, located at the church of Saint-Denis du Saint-Sacrement. It is structured by binary relations, and by consistent valorization of one of two alternatives, Delacroix actually argues a thesis. Further, these oppositions and this thesis are the very ones which are under discussion: Delacroix opposes objective and subjective registers and insists on the importance of the former. The painting depicts Mary before the tomb, with the dead Christ on her lap, and surrounded by other figures from the Passion. Although Christ is

---

history, for poetry is more concerned with the universal, and history more with the individual." Aristotle, p. 17.

dead, and Mary alive, the two figure share the same cadaverous pallor, and thus constitute a pair. But Mary's rigidity (her arms are stretched out in a crucified position) contrasts with Christ's droopiness, whose head rolls to one side, and who seems to be falling between Mary's knees. The surrounding figures repeat this formal opposition and translate it into more recognizable emotional terms. The men, whose faces are composed, if sad, stand, and their gazes converge on Mary's head. This self-possession is not shared by the holy women, who crawl or crouch on the ground, their attitudes signifying excessive grief, their gazes directed in divergent directions, and their postures picking up and amplifying the undulating movement of Christ's body. The men and Mary form a stable focus of interest, signifying composed grief, while Jesus and the holy women constitute a writhing unstable and unbalanced form, signifying a grief which has overcome the constraint imposed on it. The latter are lower in the composition, the former higher, this placement connoting their relative moral value.

This system of oppositions is repeated with respect to form and light. The group is found, as is customary, at the entry to the tomb. The ointments for embalming are contained in jugs placed on the left; the edge of the tomb is visible on the right. The tomb is located, it would seem, in a cave on the side of a hill, and from its entrance a wide landscape can be seen. If the viewer is looking out from within the tomb, most of the participants are looking back at him, away from the landscape behind them: they thus are making a choice between the restricted space ot the tomb and the expanse of the landscape. This opposition is brought out by the articulation of another: at the crest of the hills in the distance, behind the figures, the last light of the setting sun is visible. It is not though this light that illuminates the figures, but a light in front of them, to Mary's right, a light which leaves half of their features in darkness. This light must come from within the tomb. The two lights imply two distinct spaces: a natural landscape to which which the figures turn their backs, and an artificial construction which is the end of their lives and the aim of their thoughts. At each point in these oppositions of nature and artifice, Delacroix indicates the superiority of the latter. If a *Pietà* represents the moment in which a mother's private grief is opposed to the hope of the world, then what Delacroix argues is that the universal signification of the image is of greater importance than its private pathos. While it is difficult in most cases to assign a propositional meaning to a painting, Delacroix's use of binary oppositions and consistent valorizations imposes a meaning on this painting: the universal is of greater importance than the individual, the objective of greater importance than the subjective. Baudelaire seems to understand this thrust, for he offers his description of the work (which was not displayed at the Salon) to prove the contention that the painter, alone among those two displayed works at the salon, is "universal":

> Cela se comprend facilement, si l'on veut considérer que Delacroix est, comme tous les grands maîtres, un mélange admirable de science – c'est-à-dire un peintre complet – et de naïveté, c'est-à-dire un homme complet. Allez voir à Saint-Louis au Marais cette *Pietà*, où la majestueuse reine des douleurs tient sur ses genoux le corps de son enfant mort, les deux bras étendus horizontalement dans un accès de désespoir, une attaque de nerfs maternelle. L'un des deux personnages qui soutient et modère sa douleur est éploré comme les figures les plus lamentables de l'*Hamlet*, avec laquelle œuvre celle-ci a plus d'un rapport. – Des deux saintes femmes, la première rampe convulsivement à terre, encore revêtue des bijoux et des insignes du luxe; l'autre, blonde et dorée, s'affaisse plus mollement sous le poids énorme de son désespoir.
>
> Le groupe est échelonné et disposé tout entier sur un fond d'un vert sombre et uniforme, qui ressemble autant à des amas de rochers qu'à une mer bouleversée par l'orage. Ce fond est d'une simplicité fantastique, et E. Delacroix a sans doute, comme Michel-Ange, supprimé l'accessoire pour ne pas nuire à la clarté de son idée. Ce chef-d'œuvre laisse dans l'esprit un sillon profond de mélancolie. (II, 435-6)

The tone of Baudelaire's description is what alerts the reader to the difference between his interpretation and Delacroix's: his vocabulary is incongruous, not sufficiently elevated to transmit a hope of salvation, and indicates a highy idiosyncratic reading. If Mary is "la majestueuse reine des douleurs," Christ is an "enfant mort"; if Mary's gesture implies "un accès de douleur," that pain also is an "attaque de nerfs maternelle"; if in their dignity the men resemble the figures of Delacroix's illustrations to *Hamlet,*[22] one of the holy women "rampe convulsivement à terre." Baudelaire respects the binary structure of the painting, but gives greater importance – the more striking formulations, the significant last place – to the subjective register. As he concludes his description, he analogizes the background to "une mer bouleversée par l'orage": such an analogy is hardly evident; at the very least, Baudelaire should be spelling *mer* as *mère.* The painting does not signify salvation, but *mélancolie.* While such an interpretation is by no means extraordinary, this conclusion does indicate that Baudelaire considers the subjective and the particular to be the primary aims of critical description.

A second example should suffice to show how Baudelaire's assessments of works tend to stray from their initial focus of interest. He refers in Chapter VI to two portraits by the frontier artist George Catlin of American Indians, Shon-ta-y-e-ga and Stumich-a-Sucks, in order to prove how unfounded earlier dismissals of Catlin's abilities were: "Il est aujourd'hui avéré que M. Catlin sait fort bien peindre et fort bien dessiner. Ces deux portraits suffiraient pour me le prouver, si ma mémoire ne me rappelait beaucoup d'autres morceaux également beaux." (II, 446) The following discussion of the portraits is thus resolutely argumentative, and the aim of the argument is to prove the beauty of Catlin's works, not simply those displayed at the Salon, but those which were included in Catlin's earlier travelling museum.[23] The thrust of the argument is familiar: Baudelaire seeks to impose and to extend an aesthetic judgment.

His first analysis serves this argument: qualifications of character, expression and bone structure are, in 1846, supported by the sciences of physiognomy and physiology, and constitute objective

---

[22] Delacroix published a series of thirteen engravings illustrating scenes from *Hamlet: Hamlet; treize sujets dessinés par Eug. Delacroix* (Paris: Gihaut frères, 1843). The last of these engravings, "Mort d'Hamlet," depicting Laertes supporting the dying Hamlet, bears comparison with the "Pietà."

[23] Catlin showed his "Indian Gallery" in Europe and in England between 1839 and 1870. See M. Halpin, ed., *North American Indians,* by George Catlin (New York: Dover Publications, 1973), I, xii. It would seem than Catlin was generally better appreciated in Europe than in the United States: see Ruskin, III, 145.

references.[24] However, midway through the paragraph, a shift occurs in the argument: Baudelaire no longer speaks from vision, but from memory; he no longer describes the Salon, but the travelling exposition:[25]

> Quant à la couleur, elle a quelque chose de mystérieux qui me plaît plus que je ne saurais dire. Le rouge, la couleur du sang, la couleur de la vie, abondait tellement dans ce sombre musée, que c'était une ivresse; quant aux paysages – montagnes boisées, savanes immenses, rivières désertes – ils étaient monotonement, éternellement verts; le rouge, cette couleur si obscure, si épaisse, plus difficile à pénétrer que les yeux d'un serpent – le vert, cette couleur calme et gaie et souriante de la nature, je les retrouve chantant leur antithèse mélodique jusque sur le visage de ces deux héros –. Ce qu'il y a de certain, c'est que tous leurs tatouages et coloriages étaient faits selon des gammes naturelles et harmoniques. (II, 446)

The vocabulary is no longer one of knowledge, but one of pleasure: Baudelaire speaks of color, not line (which, in Chapter IX, "Du Portrait," he associates with exact knowledge). Words such as *plaît, ivresse, gaie* serve to advance the description; musical metaphors – *chante, mélodique* – express the meaning found in these works. And yet, Baudelaire discovers certain knowledge in these paintings, natural knowledge, which we would name "intuition." In other words, the pleasure that Baudelaire experiences is mnemonic, not perceptual, musical, not propositional, natural, not conventional, but this obviously subjective pleasure is the necessary point of departure for aesthetic judgments.

These problems come together in a particularly rich fashion in a poem first published in 1860, "Hymne à la Beauté." A debate circles around the date of the poem: Antoine Adam dates the poem from the moment of its first publication;[26] Claude Pichois, likening the poem to "La Beauté," suggests that an unfound earlier

---

[24] Walter Benjamin has commented on the fashion of "physiologies" in France at the time of Baudelaire's first entry into the literary market-place. See Benjamin, *Charles Baudelaire,* pp. 35-40.

[25] Only the two portraits were displayed at the Salon. See City of Paris, *Salon de 1846* (Paris: Vinchon, 1846), p. 41.

[26] Antoine Adam, ed., *Les Fleurs du mal,* by Charles Baudelaire (Paris: Garnier, 1961), p. 300.

version might date from the forties.[27] While it might be impossible to determine once and for all the answer to this question, I would suggest that this difficulty is itself indicative of a quality of the poem: it is about beauty, and the fact that it is at home at any point in Baudelaire's career implies the centrality of beauty to his poetic reflection. The poem, Pichois points out further, takes up a theme which would seem to be perennial: Crépet and Blin put forward very similar formulations of beauty taken from Voltaire and Xavier de Montépin.[28] This poem about beauty formulates a conception of beauty found in many other places, both in Baudelaire's own works and outside of them, and consequently suggests that he is dealing with a cliché.

The beauty Baudelaire invokes is antithetical: it comes either from the heavens or the abyss; its gaze is infernal or divine; it produces good deeds and crimes, etc. In all, Baudelaire employs eleven alternatives for formulating beauty; the poem could be considered a near-perfect illustration of a tendency in Baudelaire to which Leo Bersani objects: "Baudelaire's works can indeed be read as a dramatic confirmation of this traditional dualism between spirit and flesh, between aspirations toward purity and an equally intense appetite for self-degradation or 'evil.' "[29] Michael Riffaterre uses the poem to show how even paradoxes can be clichés. For him, its most famous line – "O Beauté, monstre énorme, effrayant, ingénu" – repeats over and over an entirely conventional notion of beauty: "From the stand-point of meaning, the whole line merely develops simultaneously two opposite semantic potentialities of its nuclear word; the line is simply the transformation of that word into a sentence that is *about* the word, and is made entirely out of the *stuff* of the word."[30]

The view Baudelaire puts forward here is indeed antithetical; however, his poem does advance upon these dualisms in two important respects, and it does so because the writer insists on the subjective aspects of beauty. Here is the poem:

---

[27] Claude Pichois, ed., *Œuvres,* I, 877: ". . . avant 1852, la pièce pouvait ne pas le satisfaire, dans une première version."

[28] Jacques Crépet and Georges Blin, eds., *Les Fleurs du mal,* by Charles Baudelaire (Paris: Corti, 1942), p. 334.

[29] Bersani, pp. 1-2.

[30] Riffaterre, *Semiotics,* p. 25.

Viens-tu du ciel profond ou sors-tu de l'abîme,
O Beauté? ton regard, infernal et divin,
Verse confusément le bienfait et le crime,
Et l'on peut pour cela te comparer au vin.

Tu contiens dans ton œil le couchant et l'aurore;
Tu répands des parfums comme un soir orageux;
Tes baisers sont un philtre et ta bouche une amphore
Qui font le héros lâche et l'enfant courageux.

Sors-tu du gouffre noir ou descends-tu des astres?
Le Destin charmé suit tes jupons comme un chien;
Tu sèmes au hasard la joie et les désastres,
Et tu gouvernes tout et ne réponds de rien.

Tu marches sur des morts, Beauté, dont tu te moques;
De tes bijoux, l'Horreur n'est pas le moins charmant,
Et le Meurtre, parmi tes plus chères breloques,
Sur ton ventre orgueilleux danse amoureusement.

L'éphémère ébloui vole vers toi, chandelle,
Crépite, flambe et dit: Bénissons ce flambeau!
L'amoureux pantelant incliné sur sa belle
A l'air d'un moribond caressant son tombeau.

Que tu viennes du ciel ou de l'enfer, qu'importe,
O Beauté! monstre énorme, effrayant, ingénu!
Si ton œil, ton souris, ton pied, m'ouvrent la porte
D'un Infini que j'aime et n'ai jamais connu?

De Satan ou de Dieu, qu'importe? Ange ou Sirène,
Qu'importe, si tu rends – fée aux yeux de velours,
Rythme, parfum, lueur, ô mon unique reine! –
L'univers moins hideux et les instants moins lourds? (I, 24-5)

Too simply put, the poem argues that beauty is antithetical (stanzas 1-3); because beauty is antithetical, it must contain some element of evil (4, 5); despite its necessary evil, the poet loves beauty (6, 7). The poem thus illustrates an about-face on the part of the poet: initially, he entertains a vision of beauty as antithesis, only to disregard the implications of that vision. This about-face is audible in a change in the poem's tone: initially, as any "hymn" should be, its tone is religious: the vocative "ô Beauté," which occurs three times, the insistent interrogatives ("viens-tu," "descends-tu," etc.), the use of sensual metaphors ("vin," "amphore") recall the structure of the Psalms.[31] These devices are visible especially in the first three stanzas. However, in the last two stanzas, the exclamation replaces the question; the rhetorical "qu'importe" is repeated three times; the first person pronoun "je" appears in opposition to the "tu" accorded to beauty: the poet finally insists on his own opinion, and the tone is one of exasperation.

The change in direction is also visible in the change in the nature of questions addressed to beauty: initially, as in verses 1 and 2, the questions are real: the poet asks which element of the alternative he puts forward truly describes beauty: infernal/divine, beneficial/criminal, cowardly/heroic, powerful/responsible. At the end of the poem, however, the questions are not real but rhetorical. In verse 25, for example, the poet does not care to know whether beauty comes from God or from Satan; even less does he care to know what the significance of such a choice is: the "qu'importe" so insistently used indicates that the poet has already concluded that the issue is trivial, and does not seek any answer to these questions. In sum, the poem illustrates a change in attitude respecting beauty.

However, the poem also indicates why this change comes about. When the poet asks who beauty is, what she does, and what her origins are, he presupposes that she has a claim on each of the alternatives he puts forward. That he should ask whether beauty comes from the heavens or the abyss implies that both are possible, that he should ask which of her effects is more properly hers, good deeds or crimes, implies that she contributes to both. Every antithetical question the poet asks serves to extend the definition of beauty, and if so, the field of those who recognize beauty is also extended. Thus the poet can conclude: "Tu contiens dans ton œil le couchant, l'aurore." As in the *Salon de 1846,* beauty must be recognized by all. However, Baudelaire refuses here, as there, to define beauty: just as Kant's judge is technically irresponsible (because he cannot defend his judgment), so is Baudelaire's

---

[31] See especially Psalm 13.

beauty irresponsible: "Tu gouvernes tout et ne réponds de rien." The poem perfectly illustrates the paradox of beauty: it must be universally recognized, but cannot be defined.

The poem also illustrates the consequences of this antithetical formulation: if beauty contains traces of divine and infernal origins, it must contain evil, and thus horror, murder, self-destruction and death can be put to its account. The two stanzas which show these consequences differ from the rest of the poem in that they contain none of the antithetical formulations found everywhere else: they are pure description, pure elaboration of one aspect of beauty, its necessary evil. Rhetorically, they constitute a hypotyposis: they show something already stated, and advance upon that prior statement only in the vividness of their description. These eight verses are appropriately characterized by a redundancy stronger here than in other parts of the poem: "marcher sur des morts" implies "se moquer," "chandelle" implies "crépiter" and "flamber," "moribond" implies "tombeau." As such, this description does not advance the argument.

Nevertheless, it does have an effect, for it is immediately upon painting this scene that the poet's about-face poem occurs: the description has endowed the paradox with an immediacy that requires a response from him, one that concerns his own ethical outlook. The poet sticks to his guns, as it were, responding "qu'importe": thus the exasperation, and thus, most significantly, the "j'aime." The depiction of evil has caused the poet to shift from an indefensible aesthetic position to a defensible subjective preference. Despite the poet's awareness of beauty's claim to universality, description has caused him to redefine beauty as subjective.

6

THE ENDS OF BEAUTY: *EXPOSITION UNIVERSELLE*

> Sans analyser ici le but qu'ils poursuivirent, sans en vérifier la légitimité, sans examiner s'ils ne l'ont pas outrepassé, constatons simplement qu'ils avaient un but . . . (II, 583)

For centuries, criticism has been considered the parasite of literature, writing that lives off the body of works more vigorous than it is. If the artist seeks to create, the critic seeks only to relay the artist's message, and the work of the critic is correspondingly secondary. The longevity of this opinion is easily matched by its geographic extension, and the inferiority of criticism is a fact of which we are so sure that it can only be a preconception. Such universality suggests that ideological factors are at work, and there is every reason to believe that this opinion is another instance of what Roland Barthes has called "la grande opposition mythique du vécu (du vivant) et de l'intelligible."[1] The artist, a creator, is involved in real, deeply felt work; the critic, a messenger, seeks only to elaborate a meaning he did not generate. The former experiences, the latter only knows. It is difficult to overcome this preconception; even so convinced a proponent of criticism as Geoffrey Hartman has sought to improve its standing by comparing it to literature. In his article "Literary Commentary as Literature," Hartman writes ". . . that literary commentary may cross the line and become as demanding as literature: it is an unpredictable or unstable genre that cannot be subordinated, a priori, to its

---

[1] Roland Barthes, "Effet," 172.

referential or commentating function."[2] Criticism can be as artistic as art.

An assumption dominates this comparison, and tends to cast it in terms of a single question: "How good is the critic as artist?" Does the ability to understand imply the ability to create? Can the critic play the role of the writer? Such questions imply an entirely accidental relation between criticism and literature. When one considers, for example, the criticism of such authors as Baudelaire, Mallarmé or Valéry, it is because of their interest as poets. But conversely, when one studies Ruskin or Sainte-Beuve, it is to study their criticism. Isolating the two fields serves only to emphasize the prerogatives of art.

Perhaps then it would be better not to consider individual cases, with their implicitly contingent aspect; perhaps it would be better to discuss the more general relation of literary creation to literary criticism. Here I turn to the work of Paul de Man, who in a 1969 essay on Georges Poulet describes the "demanding" criticism of Baudelaire, Mallarmé, Valéry and Blanchot: ". . . the reasons that prompted these writers to take up criticism have only a limited interest. What matters a great deal is that Baudelaire's *Essay on Laughter,* Mallarmé's *La Musique et les lettres,* or Blanchot's *Chant des sirènes* are more than equal in verbal and thematic complexity to a prose poem from the *Spleen de Paris,* a page from *Un Coup de dés* or a chapter of *Thomas l'obscur.*"[3] It is of course safe to make this assertion for Baudelaire, Mallarmé or Valéry; it is less so to make it with regard to Poulet's work; but at any event, it is quite plausible, for this judgment still reflects an opinion with which we are at home: that artistic "creation" is essentially different from criticism. And this assumption implies, whenever one compares criticism and poetry, that one consider the critic *as* poet.

I would like instead to consider the poet as critic, and not simply in order to ask how well the poet scores in his prediction of future taste. In 1798, Friedrich Schlegel defined modern liter-

---

[2] Geoffrey Hartman, "Literary Commentary as Literature," in *Criticism in the Wilderness* (New Haven: Yale University Press, 1980), 201.

[3] Paul de Man, "The Literary Self as Origin: The Work of Georges Poulet," in *Blindness and Insight* (New York: Oxford University Press, 1971), 79-80.

ature as one which should contain a critical dimension, and thus implied that the poet should be a critic:

> . . . that poetry which is not infrequently encountered in modern poets should combine those transcendental materials and preliminary exercises for a poetic theory of the creative power with the artistic theory and beautiful self-mirroring . . . poetry should portray itself with each of its portrayals; everywhere and the same time, it should be poetry and the poetry of poetry.[4]

Such an assertion is of course vast; however, it does suggest a novel twist to the comparison: if one considers the poet as critic, should one not consider the two fields as potentially related, and thus ask whether a writer's critical ambition helps or hinders his literary achievement?

No writer is better placed to furnish answers to these questions than Baudelaire: his critical career runs parallel to his poetic career, and frequently, his criticism is used to mirror his poetry. More importantly, his poetry was also criticism: poems such as his accounts of Delacroix's "Ovide en exil chez les Scythes," and of Christophe's statues all indicate that he conceived of criticism as potentially poetic, and certainly, of critical writing as essentially literary. He wrote in his *Salon de 1846* that the best criticism could be poetic: ". . . le meilleur compte rendu d'un tableau pourra être un sonnet ou une élégie." One could also infer from the examples of the poems "Horreur sympathique," "Danse macabre," "Le Masque," and, of course, "Les Phares" that the best poetry would conversely be critical.

Of Baudelaire's works the one that both discusses and exemplifies most fully the relation of creative writing to criticism is his *Exposition universelle de 1855.* Here Baudelaire puts forward a theory of criticism which calls into question the abilities and interest of professional criticism, and thus clears the field for the work of poets and novelists. In the place of Alphonse Karr, "l'homme au bon sens de travers," (II, 592) Baudelaire proposes Théophile Gautier, Honoré de Balzac, and yes, Charles Baudelaire.

---

[4] Friedrich Schlegel, *Dialogue on Poetry* and *Literary Aphorisms,* E. Behler and R. Struc, trans. (University Park, Pennsylvania: The Pennsylvania State University Press, 1968), 145.

These examples, "excellente(s) leçon(s) de critique," (II, 579) are so many promises that literature can fulfill the obligations of criticism better than criticism itself can, and for my part, I would like to ask why.

The show opened on May 15, 1855; a "universal" exposition in the mode of the London exposition in the Crystal Palace four years earlier, its aim was to display the technology and the arts of the nations of the world.[5] Even if it was dominated by France and England, Baudelaire's choice of discussing only the works Delacroix and Ingres – the poles of painting perhaps, but of French painting for sure – is a conspicuous gesture of critical selectivity, and the notion of judgment is correspondingly at the fore.

Claude Pichois has argued that Baudelaire's article is incomplete: its three chapters – "Méthode de critique," "Ingres," and "Delacroix" – would have been complemented by a fourth, perhaps on English artists, perhaps on other French painters, but Baudelaire, discouraged by the refusal of *Le Pays* to publish the chapter on Ingres, abandoned this project.[6] The choice of two painters is very restricted, and, surprisingly for an account of a "Universal exposition," the two painters are very familiar. Nevertheless, in his introductory chapter, Baudelaire pleads for greater openness to the art of other cultures, and as he does so argues that beauty is not the attribute of western art alone. Since criticism is ordinarily capable only of reflecting the values of the culture that produces it, Baudelaire proposes to abandon academic criticism, and in its place, suggests an artistic criticism which, because it is unsystem-

---

[5] Frank Anderson Trapp writes:

> In one important respect, however, the Paris exhibition differed from all previous ventures of its kind: in the effort to be more truly "universal," its organizers included with its industrial display a vast retrospective exhibition of paintings, sculpture, prints and architecture to recall man's accomplishments in the arts, as well as science, technology, and business. In this way the international prestige of French culture could be reaffirmed. Under the direction of a special commission headed by the Emperor's cousin and including Delacroix and Ingres among its members, over 5,000 works of art (more than half of them French) were selected for exhibition.

See "The Universal Exposition of 1855," *The Burlington Magazine,* June, 1965, 300-305.

[6] Claude Pichois, ed., *Œuvres,* II, 1366.

atic, can apprehend elusive beauty. In response to the blindness of academic criticism, Baudelaire proposes the poet as critic.

Doing so, he challenges some of the fundamental presuppositions of art criticism. Academic criticism is characterized by measurement, verification, identification; in order to judge, the academic compares the work to rules (of beauty, of anatomy, of decorum) and measures the play between the two. As he does so, the academic critic tells his public how the artist has succeeded, or, more frequently, why he has failed. He has an aim: to instruct his readers in the rules of taste, rules which, according to Baudelaire, blind him to beauties lying outside of the field they limit for him. Baudelaire is here suggesting a new critical gesture: the critic senses, he does not compare; he employs taste, not memory. On one side, there is the professional critic, whose very knowledge inhibits his ability to detect beauty:

> . . . science barbouillée d'encre, goût bâtard, plus barbares que les barbares, qui a oublié la couleur du ciel, la forme du végétal, le mouvement et l'odeur de l'animalité, et dont les doigts crispés, paralysés par la plume, ne peuvent plus courir avec agilité sur l'immense clavier des *correspondances!* (II, 577)

On the other, there is the "man of the world," whose abilities in criticism are like those of an explorer in the wilderness:

> Les mieux doués à cet égard sont ces voyageurs solitaires qui ont vécu pendant des années au fond des bois, au milieu des vertigineuses prairies, sans autre compagnon que leur fusil, contemplant, disséquant, écrivant. Aucun voile scolaire, aucun paradoxe universitaire, aucune utopie pédagogique, ne se sont interposés entre eux et la complexe vérité. (II, 576)

Not obscured by any veil or paradox, his evaluations are accurate; unmediated by any knowledge, this judgment is purely sensory.

Of the academic critics invoked by Baudelaire, none could be more systematic than the Abbé Charles Batteux, the title of whose treatise on beauty is *Les Beaux-Arts réduits à un même principe,* and of those critics, only one could incarnate better the *professeur-juré* than Quatremère de Quincy, *Secrétaire Perpétuelle de l'Académie des Beaux-Arts.* The views of Batteux and Quatremère are precisely those Baudelaire rejects. Batteux, for example, asserts that beauty serves a purpose. At first, as Baudelaire will, he claims that the object of the fine arts is pleasure:

> Les autres (arts) ont pour objet le plaisir. Ceux-ci n'ont pu naître que dans le sein de la joie & des sentimens que produisent l'abondance & et la tranquillité: on les appelle les beaux Arts par excellence.[7]

As he pursues his argument, however, Batteux writes that the faculty that senses this pleasure is "taste":

> Je puis donc définir l'Intelligence: la facilité de connoître le vrai & le faux, & et de les distinguer l'un de l'autre: & et le Goût, la facilité de sentir le bon, le mauvais, le médiocre & de les distinguer avec certitude.[8]

At this point in his reasoning, it is still plausible that Batteux will assert the autonomy of the aesthetic judgment: that the pleasure produced by beauty will be distinct, and that the faculty that detects it will be autonomous. However, he writes:

> . . . en nous donnant la faculté de connoître, elle (Nature) ne pouvoit nous refuser celle de sentir le rapport de l'objet connu avec notre utilité, & d'y être attiré par ce sentiment. C'est ce sentiment qu'on appelle le Goût naturel, parce que c'est la Nature qui nous l'a donné. Mais pourquoi nous l'a-t'elle donné? Etoit-ce pour juger des Arts qu'elle n'a point faits? Non: c'étoit pour juger des choses naturelles par rapport à nos plaisirs ou à nos besoins.[9]

In other words, beauty signifies that an object corresponds to a need; by indicating what is useful, beauty serves a purpose, and one can thus infer what will be beautiful by considering what is useful.

Closer to Baudelaire's own time, Quatremère de Quincy advanced a similar argument; like Batteux, he paid initial lip-service

---

[7] Batteux, p. 27.
[8] Batteux, p. 80.
[9] Batteux, pp. 84-5.

to the notion of beauty's independence. Early in his description of the imitative arts he asserts that the aim of art *(imitation)* is beauty *(plaisir moral)*: "Le plaisir que nous donnons pour but à l'imitation, le place donc fort au-dessus de celui qu'on appelle *physique*, c'est-à-dire que c'est un plaisir *moral*."[10] As he pursues his argument, however, Quatremère asserts that this pleasure is itself subordinated to a further consideration: utility. The pleasure of imitation provokes one to enrich one's stock of sensations, of ideas, of images:

> L'effet utile du plaisir de l'imitation, doit consister dans ce que nous acquérons par elle, en connoissances, en sensations, en idées, en images, autrement dit, dans ce qui augmente le domaine de notre intelligence, enrichit notre esprit de conceptions nouvelles, ouvre à notre imagination des routes sans nombre vers des points de vue sans terme.[11]

Thought of this kind tempted Baudelaire, but he also realized that judging according to rules confines the critic as much as it limits his objects:

> J'ai essayé plus d'une fois, comme tous mes amis, de m'enfermer dans un système pour y prêcher à mon aise. Mais un système est une espèce de damnation qui nous pousse à une abjuration perpétuelle; il en faut toujours inventer un autre . . . (II, 577)

Thus, advancing a proposition taken from Poe, Baudelaire rejects any external purpose for poetry: "La poésie ne peut pas, sous peine de mort ou de défaillance, s'assimiler à la science ou à la morale; elle n'a pas la Vérité pour objet, elle n'a qu'Elle-même." (II, 333)

As a result, beauty fails to correspond to any expectations; it might consist, as it did for Diderot, in "relation"[12] or in "correspondences," but only accidentally will it correspond to "rules" of

---

[10] Quatremère de Quincy, *De l'imitation,* pp. 161-2.

[11] Quatremère de Quincy, *De l'imitation,* pp. 168-9.

[12] Diderot, pp. 418: "J'appelle donc *beau* hors de moi, tout ce qui contient en soi de quoi réveiller dans mon entendement l'idée de rapports; et *beau* par rapport à moi, tout ce qui réveille cette idée."

beauty. It springs more from a principle of difference than from one of identity:[13]

> *Le beau est toujours bizarre.* Je ne veux pas dire qu'il soit volontairement, froidement bizarre, car dans ce cas il serait un monstre sorti des rails de la vie. Je dis qu'il contient toujours un peu de bizarrerie, de bizarrerie naïve, non voulue, inconsciente, et que c'est cette bizarrerie qui le fait être particulièrement le Beau. (II, 578)

Beauty's freedom is thus radical: it obeys no rules, reflects no interest, serves no purpose. The critic senses beauty, he does not perceive it, in an argument which one finds earlier in Rousseau's first discourse: learning prevents the recognition of the truth. If the paradox is familiar, its ramifications are not: what alternative is there to learning when it comes to recognizing beauty? What faculty performs the discriminations of aesthetic judgment? What does the writer have that the critic has not?

Baudelaire delays responding to these questions by invoking the notion of "taste," but taste conceived of as a sense, not as a set of principles: ". . . je me suis contenté de sentir; je suis revenu chercher un asile dans l'impeccable naïveté." (II, 578) Baudelaire thus sets "naïveté" against "knowledge," "sensation" against "understanding" in oppositions that require no commentary. But to say that the writer judges by taste where the critic judges by system is hardly to explain matters: what is this faculty, that allows judgment but refuses to refer to a concept, that demands universal assent while remaining entirely subjective?[14] And why is it the prerogative of the poet, not the professor?

Baudelaire explains his conception of taste in a bizarre paragraph, as elusive as it is suggestive, where he describes the adjustment of *un homme du monde* to a new culture:

---

[13] For a persuasive presentation of the idea of difference in Baudelaire's *Exposition universelle,* see Christopher Miller, *Blank Darkness,* pp. 87-91 and 125-136. It will be noted that I do not accept Miller's contention that Baudelaire seeks in 1855 to impose a French concept of beauty. Precisely the contrary is true: for Baudelaire, exotic beauty modifies the judge.

[14] Kant, pp. 50-60.

> Ces formes de bâtiments, qui contrariaient d'abord son œil académique . . . , ces végétaux inquiétants pour sa mémoire chargée de souvenirs natals, ces femmes et ces hommes dont les muscles ne vibrent pas suivant l'allure classique de son pays, dont la démarche n'est pas cadencée selon le rythme accoutumé, dont le regard n'est pas projeté avec le même magnétisme, ces odeurs qui ne sont plus celles du boudoir maternel, ces fleurs mystérieuses dont la couleur profonde entre dans le regard, ces fruits dont le goût trompe et déplace les sens et révèle au palais des idées qui appartiennent à l'odorat, tout ce monde d'harmonies nouvelles entrera lentement en lui, le pénétrera patiemment, comme la vapeur d'une étuve aromatisée; toute cette vitalité inconnue sera ajoutée à sa vitalité propre; quelques milliers d'idées et de sensations enrichiront son dictionnaire de mortel, et même, il est possible que, dépassant la mesure et transformant la justice en révolte, . . . il brûle ce qu'il avait adoré, et qu'il adore ce qu'il avait brûlé. (II, 567-7)

The "man of the world" is contradicted, disturbed, overpowered, and duped, as though the plaything of some *malin génie*. He is passive, an object; if this paragraph describes the acquisition of taste, Baudelaire conceives of taste as flavor, not as a faculty. The traveller acquires his taste through osmosis, not training: one could almost say that the man of good taste is a man who tastes good. This confusion results in aberrant behavior: instead of extending the application of his judgments, he reverses his values, destroying what he once loved. It is plain though that the man of the world appreciates the new culture; it is plain also that Baudelaire advocates this appreciation, but what is not plain is why.

The passage reverses the relations of conventional conceptions of judgment: that the judge is subject, work object; that discrete faculties apply to distinct objects; that judgment establishes correspondences between object and rules; that judgment calculates the difference between an objet and its corresponding rules; finally, that taste is an education, not a sense. Here, objects act; the judge is passive: he is the direct object of transitive verbs whose subjects are the objects he nominally judges. His faculties of judgment are "displaced" with regard to their objects. The culture does not affirm, but negates his expectations *(contrariaient, ne vibrent pas, n'est pas cadencée, n'est pas projeté)*. The judge does not subtract this experience from his expectations but adds it to his knowledge. In a word, *il ne cherche pas; il trouve:* purpose, and all its implications are excluded from the aesthetic experience. It is thus with relation to such a non-concept of beauty that Baudelaire proposes to evaluate the works of Ingres and Delacroix.

* * *

Baudelaire qualifies the works of both Ingres and Delacroix as *bizarre,* but only Delacroix merits the epithet *beau:* "Parce que le Beau est *toujours* étonnant, il serait absurde de supposer que ce qui est étonnant est *toujours* beau." (II, 616) At the very best, parts of Ingres's works are *charmant;* more often, however, the figure Baudelaire uses to qualify Ingres's works is that of force: Ingres dominates his model, imposes his will on it, does not grant it independence:

> On avait dit jusqu'ici que la nature devait être interprétée, traduite dans son ensemble et avec toute sa logique; mais dans les œuvres du maître en question il y a souvent dol, ruse, violence, quelquefois tricherie et croc-en-jambe. (II, 587)

> . . . la faculté qui a fait de M. Ingres ce qu'il est, le puissant, l'indiscutable, l'incontrôlable dominateur, c'est la volonté, ou plutôt un immense abus de la volonté. (II, 589)

These characteristics hide some major failings: Ingres has no imagination: ". . . l'imagination, cette reine des facultés, a disparu." (II, 585) Ingres has no genius, nor does he possess the "energy" that Baudelaire considers its source: ". . . M. Ingres peut être considéré . . . comme dénué de ce tempérament énergique qui fait la fatalité du génie. . . ." (II, 588) These lacks result from a deliberate sacrifice: ". . . c'est de sa part une immolation héroïque, un sacrifice sur l'autel des facultés qu'il considère sincèrement comme plus grandioses et plus importantes." (II, 585) Ingres builds then, but only where he has destroyed; he is like a conquering army which erects monuments to its own glory on the ruins of the cities it has razed.

Ingres is destructive because he has imposed a model of classical beauty taken from Raphael on contemporary subjects; out of a sense of moral obligation, he has "corrected" nature: "Il croit que la nature doit être corrigée, amendée; que la tricherie heureuse, agréable, faite en vue du plaisir des yeux, est non seulement un droit, mais un devoir." (II, 587) Instead of producing pleasure, however, these corrections have betrayed their subjects: "Voici une armée de doigts trop uniformément allongés en fuseaux et dont les extrémités étroites oppriment les ongles. . . ." (II, 587) Formal perfection has its limits.

Ingres's corrections are the very type of purposeful activity; when one corrects, one has a purpose, an aim beyond the present work which one would realize. Whether one refers to a notion of utility, as Batteux and Quatremère do, or to one of formal perfection, as does Ingres, one is assigning some exterior aim to art.[15] This, Baudelaire argues, is an error, for it is only when Ingres "adulterates" his classical ideal that he produces works of "charm."

> Je croirais volontiers que son idéal est une espèce d'idéal fait moitié de santé, moitié de calme, presque d'indifférence, quelque chose d'analogue à l'idéal antique, auquel il a ajouté les curiosités et les minuties de l'art moderne. C'est cet accouplement qui donne souvent à ses œuvres leur charme bizarre. (II, 586)

In other words, as long as Ingres assigns to his art the task of resurrecting classical form, of imitating Raphael in the 19th century, he fails to produce beauty; as soon, however, as he strays from this purpose, he creates works of charm. Purpose obscures the beauty of a work of art, and conversely, when its purpose is obscure, its beauty can be perceived.[16]

---

[15] "Objective finality is either external, i.e. the *utility,* or internal, i.e. the *perfection,* of the object. That the delight in an object on account of which we call it beautiful is incapable of resting on the representation of its utility, is abundantly evident from the two preceding articles. . . . Beauty . . . involves no thought whatsoever of a perfection of the object . . ." Kant, pp. 69-70.

[16] Kant exemplifies the destructive effect of the perception of purpose in aesthetic judgment thus: "What do poets set more store on than the nightingale's bewitching and beautiful note, in a lonely thicket on a still summer evening by the soft light of the moon? And yet we have instances of how, where no such songster was to be found, a jovial host has played a trick on the guests with him on a visit to enjoy the country air, and has done so their huge satisfaction, by hiding in a thicket a rogue of a youth who (with a reed or rush in his mouth)

If Ingres abusively imposes a classical notion of perfection on painting, Delacroix does something else. He too uses consecrated forms, but unlike Ingres, he does not overpower his models with them: a play exists between his vocabulary and his subjects, allowing one to call his works beautiful. Both ideal and model are present here. If the paintings both of Ingres and of Delacroix receive the epithet *bizarre* only those of Delacroix receive that of *beau,* for he alone renounced the use of force. While Baudelaire characterized Ingres's painting with figures of constraint, he employs figures of freedom to describe Delacroix's; if Ingres excluded elements which do not correspond to his preconceived model, Delacroix incorporates specifically modern elements, and thus releases beauty from classical domination. For example, Delacroix's figures of women are physically *abondantes,* and their physical "abundance" allegorizes their abundance of meaning: "On dirait qu'elles portent dans les yeux un secret douleureux, impossible à enfouir dans les profondeurs de la dissimulation. Leur pâleur est comme une révélation de batailles intérieures." (II, 594) Unlike Ingres's, Delacroix's figures make simultaneous references to modern and to classical models, combining physical strength and moral fever.

Baudelaire's effort to free beauty from exterior references appears in his strange reference to Alphonse Karr's article on *La Justice de Trajan.* There, Karr criticized Delacroix's use of color;[17] fifteen years later, Baudelaire resurrects this quarrel:

> Ce tableau est celui qui fut *illustré* jadis par les petites plaisanteries de M. Karr, l'homme au bon sens de travers, sur le cheval rose; comme s'il n'existait pas de chevaux légèrement rosés, et comme si, en tout cas, le peintre n'avait pas le droit d'en faire. (II, 592)

The painter is not held to perfect accuracy, even if some pages earlier, Baudelaire did criticize Ingres's comparable deformation of human anatomy. When Ingres proposes stylization *à la mode de*

---

knew how to reproduce this note so as to hit off nature to perfection. But the instant one realizes that it all is a fraud no one will long endure listening to this song that was regarded as so attractive" (Kant, p. 162).

[17] In *Les Guêpes,* April, 1840. See Pichois, *Œuvres,* ed., II, 1367.

Raphael, Baudelaire advocates accurate representation; when Karr requires accurate color, Baudelaire calls for artistic freedom. To maintain his independence of judgment, he invokes different authorities and one can only conclude before this contradiction that while accepting the notion of representation generally in painting, he refutes any specific representation.

The passage of the chapter that questions purpose most insistently is the discussion of Delacroix's formal achievements, and understandably, for form is the object *par excellence* of aesthetic response, which in turn claims always to be free: it would follow that a "free" judgment could only detect freedom in its object. Baudelaire argues here that form is not the servant of content, but is autonomous; such autonomy is proved by form's lack of purpose, its ability to transmit a content different from that of the subject of the painting.

> D'abord, il faut remarquer, et c'est très important, que, vu à une distance trop grande pour analyser ou même comprendre le sujet, un tableau de Delacroix a déjà produit sur l'âme une impression riche, heureuse ou mélancolique. On dirait que cette peinture, comme les sorciers ou les magnétiseurs, projette sa pensée à distance. Ce singulier phénomène tient à la puissance du coloriste, à l'accord parfait des tons, et à l'harmonie (préétablie dans le cerveau du peintre) entre la couleur et le sujet. Il semble que cette couleur, qu'on me pardonne ces subterfuges de langage pour exprimer des idées fort délicates, pense par elle-même, indépendamment des objets qu'elle habille. (II, 594-5)

In other words, form can possess a beauty and produce an effect without reference to the subject it vehicles; it is not necessary to establish any relation (analogy, instrumentality, antithesis) between form and content in order to appreciate form. Form, like poetry, can be its own object.

This is true even of Delacroix's line. In the case of Ingres, line indicated his obedience to an authoritative model (Raphael), while at the same time, line, "constraining" the forms that it enclosed, symbolized the lack of freedom implied by such obedience. By contrast, Delacroix's line is essentially free:

> . . . un bon dessin n'est pas une ligne dure, cruelle, despotique, immobile, enfermant une figure comme une camisole de force; . . . le dessin doit être comme la nature, vivant et agité; . . . la simplification dans le dessin est une monstruosité, comme la tragédie dans le monde dramatique; . . . la nature nous présente une série infinie de lignes courbes, fuyantes, brisées, suivant une loi de génération impeccable, où le parallélisme est toujours indécis et sinueux, où les concavités et les convexités se correspondent et se poursuivent . . . (II, 595)

Closure, force, and inevitability ordinarily characterize line; in these respects, it resembles the cliché descriptive of racinian tragedy: an infernal machine. By contrast, Delacroix's line is "living," "moving," and "undecided": not bound to a purpose, its only aims are to "correspond" to itself and to "follow" its own direction.

Baudelaire illustrates how the beautiful is self-contained in his gloss of a citation from "Les Phares;" the stanza concerns Delacroix, of course, and in his gloss, the poet hopes to show how the painter's color harmonies evoke quasi-musical *rêveries:*

> Un poète a essayé d'exprimer ces sensations subtiles dans des vers dont la sincérité peut faire passer la bizarrerie:
>
> Delacroix, lac de sang, hanté des mauvais anges,
> Ombragé par un bois de sapins toujours vert,
> Où, sous un ciel chagrin, des fanfares étranges
> Passent comme un soupir étouffé de Weber.
>
> *Lac de sang:* le rouge; — *hanté des mauvais anges:* surnaturalisme; — *un bois toujours vert:* le vert, complémentaire du rouge; — *un ciel chagrin:* les fonds tumultueux et orageux de ses tableaux; — *les fanfares et Weber:* idées de musique romantique que réveillent les harmonies de sa couleur. (II, 594-5)

One would expect such a word-by-word commentary to explain the stanza, to spell out pictorial signifieds to illustrate the poet's figures. Instead, Baudelaire indicates painterly signifiers *(rouge, vert)* and connotations *(surnaturalisme* and *idées de musique romantique).* In other words, he does not conceive of Delacroix's paintings (or his own poetry, for that matter) as windows that serve only to look out onto a field of meanings more important than they are; rather, the duty of these signifieds (works or pigments) is to themselves: "red" refers only to "green;" "music" refers only to "harmony." The work of art is self-contained, repudiating even the function of representation.

It is not sufficient however to assert that Baudelaire denies any exterior purpose to beauty; to be sure, he refutes utility and perfection (to the extent that such perfection comes from outside), but does recognize in beautiful objects a movement away from themselves that might be called their appeal. This movement, to return to Kantian terminology, is "purposiveness," and the paradox of beauty is that in aesthetic judgment, purpose is denied even while purposiveness is asserted: "*Beauty* is the form of *purposiveness* of an object, so far as this is perceived in it *without any representation of a purpose.*"[18] Baudelaire's notion of beauty betrays this paradoxical aspect when, for instance, he indicates that color "projects its thought into the distance" even as he asserts the independence of formal beauty.

The paradox is worked out most fully in "Les Phares," from which the quatrain was taken. The poem argues that the communication subtended by the work of art is unlike that of ordinary language: the aim of the artistic statement differs from that of ordinary speech. The poem lists eight medallions, each naming an artist and associating his name with a group of figures. Three stanzas summarizing these medallions follow them, and interpret their movement as an appeal to God.

Rubens, fleuve d'oubli, jardin de la paresse,
Oreiller de chair fraîche où l'on ne peut aimer,
Mais où la vie afflue et s'agite sans cesse,
Comme l'air dans le ciel et la mer dans la mer;

Léonard de Vinci, miroir profond et sombre,
Où des anges charmants, avec un doux souris

[18] Immanuel Kant, *Kant's Critique of Judgement,* J. H. Bernard, trans. (London: Macmillan and Co., 1931), p. 90. I have used the Bernard translation here, because this translation comes closer than does Meredith's to the standard formulation, "purposiveness without purpose." In his *Aesthetics,* Hegel explains this statement thus: ". . . the beautiful is to have the form of *purposiveness* in so far as the purposiveness is perceived in the object without any presentation of a purpose." Hegel, p. 59.

Tout chargé de mystère, apparaissent à l'ombre
Des glaciers et des pins qui ferment leur pays;

Rembrandt, triste hôpital tout rempli de murmures,
Et d'un grand crucifix décoré seulement,
Où la prière en pleurs s'exhale des ordures,
Et d'un rayon d'hiver traversé brusquement;

Michel-Ange, lieu vague où l'on voit des Hercules
Se mêler à des Christs, et se lever tout droits
Des fantômes puissants qui dans les crépuscules
Déchirent leur suaire en étirant leurs doigts;

Colères de boxeur, impudences de faune,
Toi qui sus ramasser la beauté des goujats,
Grand cœur gonflé d'orgueil, homme débile et jaune,
Puget, mélancolique empereur des forçats;

Watteau, ce carnaval où bien des cœurs illustres,
Comme des papillons, errent en flamboyant,
Décors frais et légers éclairés par des lustres
Qui versent la folie à ce bal tournoyant;

Goya, cauchemar plein de choses inconnues,
Des fœtus qu'on fait cuire au milieu des sabbats,
De vieilles au miroir et d'enfants toutes nues,
Pour tenter les démons ajustant bien leurs bas;

Delacroix, lac de sang hanté des mauvais anges,
Ombragé par un bois de sapins toujours vert,
Où, sous un ciel chagrin, des fanfares étranges
Passent, comme un soupir étouffé de Wéber;

Ces malédictions, ces blasphèmes, ces plaintes,
Ces extases, ces cris, ces pleurs, ces *Te Deum,*
Sont un écho redit par mille labyrinthes,
C'est pour les cœurs mortels un divin opium!

C'est un cri répéte par mille sentinelles,
Un ordre renvoyé par mille porte-voix;
C'est un phare allumé sur mille citadelles,
Un appel de chasseurs perdus dans le grand bois!

Car c'est vraiment, Seigneur, le meilleur témoignage
Que nous puissions donner de notre dignité
Que cet ardent sanglot qui roule d'âge en âge
44 Et vient mourir au bord de votre éternité! (I, 13)

Each medallion identifies an artist with a brief description of his works; the name is associated with the works that ensure its continued meaning. This device, used simply in the medallions, is explained in the last three stanzas, where its mechanism and its aspiration become explicit. There, through condensation and reduction, one term takes on the meaning of several, acquiring thereby force sufficient to project its meaning into the future. The structures of the medallions individually, and that of the last three stanzas together are analogous: each medallion associates a message with a source, while the last stanzas associate those messages with a receiver.

I focus on this aspect of the medallions because, investing so heavily in this transformation, Baudelaire singles it out as important. One medallion alone has a grammatical structure different from that of the others, and its difference has to do precisely with the relation of its proper noun to its description of works of art. In each of the seven stanzas devoted to painters, the artist's name, apposed to a figure, is the first word: thus, Rubens is a *fleuve d'oubli,* Leonardo, a *miroir profond et sombre.* The figure is then qualified with a subordinate clause introduced by the conjunction *où,* or, perhaps, a spatial adjective. Thus "life" fills Rubens' river; "angels" and "glaciers," are contained in Leonardo's mirror; "prayers" rise from Rembrandt's hospital.

The stanza devoted to Puget employs a different order and syntax, reflecting through its use of reversal perhaps the Baroque aesthetic the 17th-century sculptor tried in vain to import into France, perhaps the reversals the artist endured at the end of his career. Here, the proper noun comes in the last verse, and here, there is no clear-cut subordination which would allow one to say that one figure "contains" others. Further, the order of the verses is not critical: they may be read in reverse order without loss of grammar or sense. The anomalous syntax indicates a lesser beauty and more restricted meaning assigned to the name of the artist.

The low opinion expressed here has a precedent. In 1846, Baudelaire distinguished painting and sculpture through the notion of point of view: painting imposed a single point of view while sculpture admitted multiple viewpoints.

> C'est en vain que le sculpteur s'efforce de se mettre à un point de vue unique; le spectateur, qui tourne autour de la figure, peut choisir cent points de vue différents, excepté le bon, et il arrive souvent, ce qui est humiliant pour l'artiste, qu'un hasard de lumière, un effet de lampe, découvrent une beauté qui n'est pas celle à laquelle il avait songé. Un tableau n'est que ce qu'il veut; il n'y a pas moyen de le regarder autrement que dans son jour. La peinture n'a qu'un point de vue; elle est exclusive et despotique: aussi l'expression du peintre est-elle bien plus forte. (II, 487)

In "Les Phares," painters are distinguished from sculptor according to syntax: the syntax of the painters' medallions imposes a subject despotically, and subordinates qualifications to it; the syntax of the sculptor's stanza allows one to attribute *colère* and *impudences* to Puget or to his work. This stanza also addresses the artist directly with a vocative: "Toi, qui sus ramasser la beauté des goujats." "Puget" refers then to an artist: the proper noun has not achieved the extension of meaning of "Rubens" or "Michel-Ange": While "Rembrandt" can mean a painting, "Puget" does not mean a statue; "Puget" is only a person, while "Rembrandt" is also a place; a "Rembrandt" is universally acknowledged as beautiful, while a "Puget" is not.

In the last stanzas of the poem, Baudelaire reproduces in moral language what the medallions illustrated. Instead of scenes from the artists' works we find curses, blasphemies, complaints, extasies, cries, tears and *Te Deum.* While it is clear that these messages come from the artists, it is no longer clear who says what: the messages are so brief that the artists they express cannot be named. Also, only seven messages are derived from the medallions, as though one artist had been unable to project his fame into the future: perhaps Puget, unable to give his name to his works, is also unable to transmit his thought to posterity. Certainly there is a lesson to be drawn from this comparison, but given the difficulty of deriving it, I would like to call "Les Phares" parabolic.

I like the term "parabolic" because it is applicable to a geometric figure as well as to a rhetorical one, and because the properties of the former are analogous to the intentions of the latter. I like it all the more because the parabolic reflector, i.e., a mirror in the form of a parabola, was the device that permitted the development of the lighthouse. Further, the heroic moment of light-house building coincided with Baudelaire's lifetime, the lighthouse being a common symbol of the progress referred to in the *Exposition universelle.*[19] The principle of the invention is significant. When a source of light is placed at the focus of a parabolic reflector, the light ordinarily dispersed by the course will be projected in a single beam of parallel rays: this collection amplifies the light, and is necessary in devices such as lighthouses. Conversely, waves travelling parallel to the axis of the reflector will be returned to the focus, where they are collected: thus the parabolic microphone.

The notions of amplification and condensation are also part of conventional interpretation of the parable: this figure appends a brief, perhaps ambiguous reflection to the illustration of a moral problem; the comparison of the two elements results in the proverbial obscurity of the figure, and also intensifies its message, if it can be understood. In several of Jesus' parables, for instance, the difficulty of determining the relation of moral to illustration produces an effect of profundity.[20]

---

[19] In an article entitled "De la lumière artificielle," from *La Revue des Deux Mondes* (25ème année, seconde série, nouvelle période, vol. 1212 (1855)), p. 673, M. Babinet indicates that one of the popular attractions of the "Exposition universelle" was a life-size lighthouse. He also interprets the lighthouse as a moral allegory, and attributes to it a mediating function in terms which echo some of Baudelaire's antithetical constructions: "Les rayons qui allaient se perdre vers le ciel furent ramenés par des bandes de terre assemblées circulairement qui réfléchissaient tous ces rayons vers l'horizon. D'autres bandes, placées plus bas que la flamme, ramenèrent de même vers l'horizon les rayons qui s'égaraient vers la terre. . . ."

[20] The parable of the marriage of the king's son (Matthew 22: 1-14) is typically obscure: after compelling unknown travellers to come to his son's marriage, the king throws out those who are not dressed for the occasion, saying: "Many are called, but few are chosen." One is not sure whether to side with the traveller for the king's apparent injustice, or with the king, for the traveller's unpreparedness. For an extended analysis of the function of obscurity in narrative, and in the parable in particular, see Frank Kermode, *The Genesis of Secrecy* (Cambridge: Harvard University Press: 1979), pp. 23-47.

"Les Phares," initiating a certain kind of art criticism,[21] argues that great art seeks to communicate with God, with posterity. Its aim is recognizable across the universe and throughout eternity. Great art transmits a message which has been amplified much the way the light of a flame is intensified by a parabolic reflector. The message it finally transmits is magified a thousandfold: it is repeated by *mille sentinelles,* relayed by *mille porte-voix,* displayed on *mille citadelles.* This amplification allows it to reach to the limits of human existence, an "ardent sanglot qui roule d'âge en âge / Et vient mourir au bord de votre éternité." Art has an aim, and that aim is God.

But a price must be paid by any artist whose voice is to be heard at an infinite distance: the price is reduction, or condensation. The light projected by a lighthouse is the image of a flame, but the reflector has so distorted it that it is no longer recognized, visible only as a flash. In like manner, Baudelaire writes that the message of the artist is garbled, losing all nuances in order simply to be heard. The messages, which become *un cri, un ordre, un appel* were originally more complicated: *malédictions, blasphèmes, Te Deum,* etc. Plurals have become singulars; possible inflections of meaning have disappeared. The artist's message acquires force at the price of such enormous simplification that one wonders whether it still can be called the artist's.

Baudelaire thus argues that the work of art is self-contradictory: on one hand, it postulates an aim, invokes a receiver, just as one does in ordinary communication. On the other, it suppresses its message by reducing it to a mere signal: the work does not communicate a thought so much as it asserts its existence. The work aims, but has nothing to send; it has direction, but no purpose. Losing message, purpose, function, the work however acquires an elusive posterity. If one understands, as Sartre does,

---

[21] The kind of criticism Baudelaire sketches in "Les Phares" is implemented by André Malraux in *Les Voix du silence* (Paris: Gallimard, 1951). Like Baudelaire whom he invokes on many occasions, Malraux conceives of art as an "appeal," and of the history of art as the relaying of a message from great artist to great artist through masterworks. This silent communication produces the always-evolving concept of "style": "Et à 'Qu'est-ce que l'art?' nous sommes portés à répondre: 'Ce par quoi les formes deviennent style.' " (p. 270)

the quality that guarantees longevity to be beauty,[22] the restrictions Baudelaire suggests ensure such beauty. When purpose, content, and function recede, criticism becomes poetry.

---

[22] For Sartre, the link between beauty and posterity is so strong that beauty will alleviate intimations of mortality: ". . . j'ai pris l'avion deux cents fois, sans m'y habituer. . . .; de temps en temps la peur se réveille – tout particulièrement lorsque mes compagnons sont aussi laids que moi; mais il suffit qu'une belle jeune femme soit du voyage ou un beau garçon ou un couple charmant et qui s'aime: la peur s'évanouit; la laideur est une prophétie: il y a en elle je ne sais quel extrémisme qui veut porter la négation jusqu'à l'horreur. Le Beau paraît indestructible; son image sacrée nous protège . ." Jean-Paul Sartre, "Le Séquestré de Venise," in *Situations, IV* (Paris: Gallimard, 1964), p. 341.

7

INTEREST AND IMAGINATION: *LE SALON DE 1859*

> Le goût exclusif du Vrai (si noble quand il est limité à ses véritables applications) opprime ici et étouffe le goût du Beau. (II, 616)

In the first paragraphs of his *Salon de 1859* Baudelaire excuses the banality of the essay that will follow, saying that his commonplaces are the necessary comcomitant of an uninspired exposition: "Ne vous étonnez donc pas que la banalité dans le peintre ait engendré le *lieu commun* dans l'écrivain." (II, 608-9) Such an assertion disarms criticism (of course), but more importantly, it transforms the *Salon* from a presentation of what is visible at the Salon to an answer to the question: "What is wrong with the paintings at the Salon"?

Its painting is banal because its painters are "spoiled"; they have never had to exercise their "imagination." "L'artist, aujourd'hui et depuis de nombreuses années, est, malgré son absence de mérite, un simple *enfant gâté.* Que d'honneurs, que d'argent prodigués à des hommes sans âme et sans instruction!" (II, 611) Prizes, privileges, and honors have satisfied the artist's desires, who has thus never had to justify his own self-esteem or argue the principles of his works. Rather, the modern artist directs his efforts toward conventional marks of success, the validity of which he never questions. "Il peint, il peint; et il bouche son âme, et il peint encore, jusqu'à ce qui ressemble enfin à l'artiste à la mode, et que par sa bêtise et son habileté il mérite le suffrage et l'argent du public." (II, 613) The notion of compensation permeates this discussion; the Salon's artists are guided not by intellectual ambitions but by material interests.

Interest is thus the problem that the theory of "imagination," for which the *Salon* is famous, seeks to answer: because the former dominates contemporary art, the latter must be encouraged. This opposition entails a much larger opposition: that of reality and fiction. One is *interested* in *real* things, while one takes *aesthetic pleasure* in things both real and unreal. To explain further: if one's appreciation of an object is affected by the reality of the object appreciated, that appreciation is interested. If, on the contrary, one's appreciation is unaffected, that appreciation is aesthetic.[1] To illustrate: I can contemplate a picture representing food, a Chardin still-life, for example. If it pleases me even when I am not hungry (as in Proust's example), my judgment is *disinterested,* but if I reject it because it does not satisfy my hunger, my judgment is *interested.*

What Baudelaire detects in the art of 1859 is *interest:* its emphasis on reality, its effort to acquire the visible world indicates desire, not aesthetic pleasure. The Salon artists produce realistic images of those things their buyers desire,[2] and such pandering has nothing to do with beauty. "De jour en jour l'art diminue le respect de lui-même, se prosterne devant la réalité extérieure, et le peintre devient de plus en plus enclin à peindre, non pas ce qu'il rêve, mais ce qu'il voit." (II, 619) Baudelaire finds an indication of the extent of this obsession in the popular success of photography, which, if

---

[1] "Now, where the question is whether something is beautiful, we do not want to know, whether we, or any one else are, or even could be, concerned with the real existence of the thing, but rather what estimate we form of it on mere contemplation (intuition or reflection). . . . Everyone must allow that a judgement on the beautiful which is tinged with the slightest interest, is very partial and not a pure judgement of taste. One must not be in the least prepossessed in favor of the real existence of the thing, but must preserve complete indifference in this respect, in order to play the part of the judge in matters of taste." (Kant, pp. 42-3)

[2] The historical moment of the *Salon de 1859* should not be forgotten: written only a few months before "Le Cygne," it too reflects the effects of the "Haussmanization" of Paris, largely in the presuppositions it makes about the buying public. Timothy Clark has characterized this public thus: "This was the city of courtesans and bull markets. Here was ostentation, not luxury; frippery, not fashion; consumption, not trade." (pp. 46-7) Clark argues that the transformations of Paris during the Empire prepared the ground for "consumer society" (p. 69); he also insists on the sexual nature of such consumption: "The bourgeoisie believed in Desire. The papers and streets were supposed to be full of it, and its force was imagined as working and changing the whole social body – breaking down the old distinctions between urbanity, sexual tolerance, *galanterie,* adultery, debauchery, and prostitution proper." (p. 107)

nothing else, implies the reality of its subject, and he thus denounces photography's realism as "unimaginative." His denunciation – which might strike us as unfair – comes in the very infancy of photography and indicates how quickly Baudelaire understood the rhetoric of photography.[3] This rhetoric has been explained recently by Susan Sontag and Roland Barthes, but Baudelaire's example proves that one tenet was already in place: the assumption of the perfect transparency of the photograph: that, unlike painting, photography "tells it like it is." Barthes writes: ". . . percevoir le signifiant photographique n'est pas impossible . . . , mais cela demande un acte de savoir ou de réflexion. . . . On dirait que la Photographie emporte toujours son référent avec elle . . ."[4]

Because photography enjoys this unearned reputation for veracity, its status as sign is equivocal: the photograph does not *represent* its subject, it *is* its subject:

> Dans la photographie, en effet – du moins au niveau du message littéral –, le rapport des signifiés et des signifiants n'est pas de 'transformation' mais d''enregistrement,' et l'absence de code renforce évidemment le mythe du 'naturel' photographique: la scène *est là,* captée mécaniquement, mais non humainement (le mécanique est ici gage d'objectivité) . . .[5]

---

[3] For instance, human figure photography was only about 15 years old at the time Baudelaire was writing; nevertheless, erotic subject matter was already common: "The first attempts to portray the human body by daguerreotype as an aid in the fine arts or for attractive subjects for sale were made in the forties of the last century in Paris. The earliest daguerreotypes of this class which I have seen date from 1844-1849 and represent the most technically perfect daguerreotypes which have been preserved from that time. They bear only the name and age of the model and were undoubtedly made for erotic purposes." See Joseph Maria Eder, *History of Photography,* Edward Epstean, trans. (New York: Columbia University Press, 1945), pp. 314-5.

[4] Roland Barthes, *La Chambre claire* (Paris: Edition du Seuil, 1980), pp. 16-7. Walter Benjamin agrees: "In photography, however, one encounters something strange and new: in that fishwife from Newhaven who looks at the ground with such relaxed and seductive shame something remains that does not testify merely to the art of the photographer Hill, something that is not to be silenced, something demanding the name of the person who had lived then, who even now is still real and will never entirely perish into *art.*" "A Short History of Photography," P. Patton, trans., in *Classic Essays on Photography,* Alan Trachtenberg, ed. (New Haven: Leete's Island Books, Inc., 1980), p. 200.

[5] Barthes, "Rhétorique," p. 35.

Before a photograph, naiveté returns, and one regains trust in a "natural" meaning: one forgets the difference between signifier and signified, and this allows one to seek in the photograph the satisfactions of the real world. Sontag calls this forgetfulness "magic": photographs, she writes, "trade simultaneously on the prestige of art and the magic of the real."[6] When Baudelaire detects this naiveté, he correctly labels it "idolatry":

> Dans ces jours déplorables, une industrie nouvelle se produisit, qui ne contribua pas peu à confirmer la sottise dans sa foi et à ruiner ce qui pouvait rester de divin dans l'esprit français. Cette foule idolâtre postulait un idéal digne d'elle et approprié à sa nature, cela est bien entendu. (II, 610)

Photography is idolatrous because it conflates signifier and signified, refusing to admit the autonomous existence of the latter. Further, photography takes the place not simply of its objects, but also of those forms of art it most resembles, painting and drawing: "S'il est permis à la photographie de suppléer l'art dans quelques-unes de ses fonctions, elle l'aura bientôt supplanté ou corrompu tout à fait . . ." (II, 618) The photograph is thus both a sign and a non-sign; it both signifies and is; because of this ambiguity, photography is loved by the nineteenth century, which, seeking its interest in the artistic market-place, uses photography as a stand-in for the real objects it desires.[7]

Photography responds thus to desires which require real objects: sexual attraction is the very type of such desires, for appreciation of the attractiveness of another person is predicated on the real existence of that person, and on the possibility of satisfaction that person offers. Photography, which implies the reality of its objects, awakens these desires:

> . . . des milliers d'yeux avides se penchaient sur les trous du stéréoscope comme sur les lucarnes de l'infini. L'amour de l'obscénité, qui est aussi vivace dans le cœur naturel de l'homme

[6] Susan Sontag, *On Photography* (New York: Farrar, Straus and Giroux, 1977), p. 69.

[7] Sontag writes "Photographs are a way of imprisoning reality, understood as recalcitrant, inaccessible; of making it stand still. . . . One can't possess reality, one can possess (and be possessed by) images . . ." (p. 163)

> que l'amour de soi-même, ne laissa pas échapper une si belle occasion de se satisfaire. (II, 617)

Because photography is interested, it is not beautiful, but in 1859, beauty is not sought by the buying public. Consequently, the popular success of photography is matched only by the commercial failure of imaginative art, for if photography succeeds because of its capacity to awaken desire, imaginative art fails because of its refusal to do likewise. The failure of imaginative art results from its inherent disinterestedness.

Why then produce imaginative art? Because imagination adds where realism only repeats. Baudelaire explains the advantage of imagination by way of contrasting examples, one of an unimaginative artist, the other of an imaginative peasant:

> Une fille de concierge se dit: 'J'irai au Conservatoire, je débuterai à la Comédie-Française, et je réciterai les vers de Corneille jusqu'à ce que j'obtienne les droits de ceux qui les ont récités très longtemps.' Et elle le fait comme elle l'a dit. Elle est très classiquement monotone et très classiquement ennuyeuse et ignorante; mais elle a réussi à ce qui était très facile, c'est-à-dire à obtenir par sa patience les privilèges de sociétaire. (II, 612)

She recites a text consecrated by years of repetition, imitating the gestures of generations of actors, until she obtains privileges foreign to acting. She contributes nothing to art but the obstinacy of her effort. By contrast, a peasant's notion of art, misguided as it is, implies something more: he requires that the painter add to the portrait he has ordered, and Baudelaire labels these recommendations "imaginative."

> 'Monsieur le peintre, je veux que vous fassiez *mon portrait.* Vous me représenterez assis à l'entrée principale de ma ferme, dans le grand fauteuil qui me vient de mon père. A côté de moi, vous peindrez ma femme avec sa quenouille; derrière nous, allant et venant, mes filles qui préparent notre souper de famille. Par la grande avenue à gauche débouchent ceux de mes fils qui reviennent des champs, après avoir ramené les bœufs à l'étable; d'autres, avec mes petits fils, font rentrer les charrettes remplies de foin. Pendant que je contemple ce spectacle, n'oubliez pas, je vous prie, les bouffées de ma pipe qui sont nuancées par le

> soleil couchant. Je veux aussi *qu'on entende* les sons de l'Angélus qui sonne au clocher voisin. C'est là que nous nous sommes tous mariés, les pères et les fils. Il est important que vous peigniez *l'air de satisfaction* dont je jouis à cet instant de la journée, en contemplant à la fois *ma famille et ma richesse augmentée du labeur d'une journée!*'
>
> Vive ce paysan! Sans s'en douter, il comprenait la peinture. L'amour de sa profession avait élevé son *imagination.* (II, 613)

The peasant asks the painter to represent the unrepresentable: time, sound, family relations, and a particular, undefinable expression which does not yet exist. He proposes additions rather than duplications; just as labor augments the wealth of the peasant, so does imagination make his portrait more expressive.

Criticism too can be an art, but if it is to be one, like painting, it must add to the work it discusses. Explaining how Alexandre Dumas can write good criticism, Baudelaire concludes:

> Si Alexandre Dumas, qui n'est pas un savant, ne possédait pas heureusement une riche imagination, il n'aurait dit que des sottises; il a dit des choses sensées et les a bien dites, parce que . . . (il faut bien achever) parce que l'imagination, grâce à sa nature suppléante, contient l'esprit critique. (II, 623)

What is in question is the supplement; a work (criticism, painting, poetry) is imaginative to the extent it is supplementary.[8] But how, in such a concise formulation, does one attribute a definite meaning to the word *suppléante?* In these examples, *suppléer* seems to mean "to supplement," although it is impossible to decide on the basis of grammar alone whether it does not mean "to replace." Does imagination supplement its object or replace it? In other contexts, its meaning is "to replace." Comparing imagination to the other faculties, Baudelaire writes: "Aucune ne peut se passer d'elle, et elle peut suppléer quelques-unes." (II, 621) Imagination aids all faculties and replaces some of them. Baudelaire's notion of imagination lies somewhere between addition and replacement, between creation and building on what already exists.

---

[8] The verb is perhaps taken from Diderot, who, in 1763, writes in his article on Boucher's *La Bergerie:* "De grâce, laissez quelque chose à suppléer par mon imagination . . ." See Diderot, p. 552.

Further, not all additions are imaginative: Ingres, for example, arbitrarily adds "style" (qualified as *une poésie étrangère*) to his subject; Baudelaire condemns this stylization:

> M. Ingres trouve un modèle grand, pittoresque, séduisant. 'Voilà sans doute, se dit-il, un curieux caractère; beauté ou grandeur, j'exprimerai cela soigneusement; je n'en omettrai rien, mais j'y *ajouterai quelque chose qui est indispensable:* le style.' Et nous savons ce qu'il entend par le style; ce n'est pas la qualité naturellement poétique du sujet qu'il en faut extraire pour la rendre plus visible. C'est une poésie étrangère, empruntée généralement au passé. . . . De quel droit ajouter? (II, 657)

Such stylization does not spring from the subject, but pre-exists to it: it is preconceived.

> Ces bras sont d'un galbe très pur et d'un contour bien séduisant, sans aucun doute; mais un peu graciles, il leur manque, pour arriver au style *préconçu* une certaine dose d'embonpoint et de suc matronal. (II, 657)

In other cases, however, addition is acceptable; both Reynolds and Gérard supplement the straightforward representation of their subjects, and Baudelaire praises their additions, discovering a "natural," not a "preconceived" relation between addition and subject:

> Reynolds et Gérard ont ajouté l'élément romanesque, toujours en accord avec le naturel du personnage; ainsi, un ciel orageux et tourmenté, des fonds légers et aériens, un mobilier poétique, . . . un bon portrait m'apparaît toujours comme une biographie dramatisée, ou plutôt comme le drame naturel inhérent à tout homme. (II, 655)

The difference between Ingres's additions and those of Reynolds and Gérard is crucial: what Ingres adds is pictorial, *le style,* a form taken from another painter; what Reynolds and Gérard add is narrative – *romanesque,* biographical, dramatic – just as the peasant added time to his account. This context should help to interpret Baudelaire's much-commented definition of the imagination:

> Elle est l'analyse, elle est la synthèse; et cependant des hommes habiles dans l'analyse et suffisamment aptes à faire un résumé peuvent être privés d'imagination. Elle est cela, et elle n'est pas tout à fait cela. . . . Que dit-on d'un guerrier sans imagination? Qu'il peut faire un excellent soldat, mais que, s'il commande des armées, il ne fera pas de conquêtes. . . . Que dit-on d'un diplomate sans imagination? Qu'il peut très bien connaître l'histoire des traités et des alliances dans le passé, mais qu'il ne devinera pas les traités et les alliances contenus dans l'avenir. D'un savant sans imagination? Qu'il a appris tout ce qui, ayant été enseigné, pouvait être appris, mais qu'il ne trouvera pas les lois non encore devinées. (II, 621)

The lack of imagination closes the door to the future, for imagination derives laws from study of the past and employs them in future action. Doing so, it generates narratives, hypothetical sequences of actions that create significance. I would argue then that for Baudelaire, the imagination is not the ability to produce images (possessed by Ingres and by photographers), but the faculty of producing fictions, in the restricted sense of narratives.[9] If the artists and public of 1859 are unimaginative, it is because they reject fictions, and if they reject fictions, it is because fictions cannot satisfy their desires. The only "interest" a fiction can awaken is disinterested, i.e., aesthetic.

Baudelaire presents his *Salon de 1859* as a search for "imagination" at the Salon. Since, however, he has assimilated criticism and painting, I would ask whether his criticism meets the requirements he makes of the works of the Salon, and if so, whether such criticism might not subvert the very notion of judgment, by producing imagination and beauty there where it found none. The

---

[9] Sartre's technical definition of the imagination bears a strong resemblance to this theory: defining the image as an act, not a thing, he comes close to Baudelaire's definition of the imagination as a fiction-producing, not a picture-producing faculty. "Il n'y a pas, il ne saurait y avoir d'images *dans* la conscience. Mais l'image *est un certaine type de conscience.* L'image est un acte et non une chose. L'image est conscience *de* quelque chose." Jean-Paul Sartre, *L'Imagination* (Paris: Presses Universitaires de France, 1936), p. 162. When Baudelaire writes that the imagination exists only as consciousness of time, he is refuting the reified notion of imagination proposed by Ingres or the *fille de concièrge,* for whom beauty is a commodity to be acquired.

model of criticism Baudelaire proposes is quite plain: he formulated this model four years earlier in his *Exposition universelle:*

> On raconte que Balzac (qui n'écouterait avec respect toutes les anecdotes, si petites qu'elles soient, qui se rapportent à ce grand génie?), se trouvant un jour en face d'un beau tableau, un tableau d'hiver, tout mélancolique et chargé de frimas, clairsemé de cabanes et de paysans chétifs, – après avoir contemplé une maisonette d'où montait une maigre fumée, s'écria: 'Que c'est beau! Mais que font-ils dans cette cabane? à quoi pensent-ils, quels sont leurs chagrins? les récoltes ont-elles été bonnes? *ils ont sans doute des échéances à payer?*'
>
> Rira qui voudra de M. de Balzac. J'ignore quel est le peintre qui a eu l'honneur de faire vibrer, conjecturer et s'inquiéter l'âme du grand romancier, mais je pense qu'il nous a donné ainsi, avec son admirable naïveté, une excellente leçon de critique. (II, 579)

The critic invents a fiction surrounding the picture: the activities, thoughts, and emotions of its figures, their past and their future. He dramatizes the pictorial, suggesting a plot where there had not even been time.[10] If this is in fact an "excellent lesson in criticism," one would expect Baudelaire's own commentaries to employ fictions, construct plots, suggest psychological causality, and produce pathos.

I will read several descriptive passages from the *Salon de 1859* in order to determine how this model functions in practice. The entire *Salon* is written under the sign of fiction: unlike his other art-critical essays, it is addressed to an individual, "M****," "Directeur de la *Revue Française,*" and the pseudo-dialogue that often results reveals the personality of the writer (and the reader) to a greater extent than do the forms of the other essays.[11] Perhaps because his visit was short, Baudelaire describes at length works

[10] This is, of course, the critical gestures Keats makes in his "Ode on a Grecian Urn."

[11] Pichois indicates that in the version of the essay published in the *Revue Française,* the word "Morel," referring to Jean Morel, is found every time "M****" (or "M***") is found in subsequent editions. The epistolary conventions, he writes, are explained by the fact that Baudelaire wrote the *Salon* in Honfleur, where he was staying with his mother. See Pichois, ed., *Œuvres,* II, 1383-4.

not visible at the salon, notably those of Boudin, Meryon and Christophe; four of the nine chapters engage general considerations on the nature of art; the use of citation (of Crowe, Chateaubriand, Hugo and Baudelaire) is much greater here than elsewhere. All of these aspects imply an essay less concerned with descriptive accuracy than earlier efforts.

Perhaps the best place to start such an analysis would be the description of Delacroix's *Ovide chez les Scythes*. The extravagant use of citation, coming as it does just before Baudelaire's denunciation of Ingres's recourse to a *poésie du passé*, invites close reading: how is the writer going to justify his own use of a "poetry from the past?" The passage is long, but Baudelaire attenuates that length by constructing the passage with layers of citation:

> Le voilà couché sur des verdures étranges, avec une mollesse et une tristesse féminines, le poète illustre qui enseigna l'*art d'aimer*. Ses grands amis de Rome sauront-ils vaincre la rancune impériale? Retrouvera-t-il un jour les somptueuses voluptés de la prodigieuse cité? Non, de ces pays sans gloire s'épanchera vainement le long et mélancolique fleuve des *Tristes;* ici, il vivra, ici il mourra.
>
> 'Un jour, ayant passé l'Ister vers son embouchure et étant un peu écarté de la troupe des chasseurs, je me trouvai à la vue des flots du Pont-Euxin. Je découvris un tombeau de pierre, sur lequel croissait un laurier. J'arrachai les herbes qui couvraient quelques lettres latines, et bientôt je parvins à lire ce premier vers des élégies d'un poète infortuné:
>
> "Mon livre, vous irez à Rome, et vous irez à Rome sans moi."
>
> 'Je ne saurais vous peindre ce que j'éprouvai en retrouvant au fond de ce désert le tombeau d'Ovide. Quelles tristes réflexions ne fis-je point sur les peines de l'exil, qui étaient aussi les miennes, et sur l'inutilité des talents pour le bonheur! Rome, qui jouit aujourd'hui des tableaux du plus ingénieux de ses poètes, Rome a vu couler vingt ans, d'un œil sec, les larmes d'Ovide. Ah! moins ingrats que les peuples d'Ausonie, les sauvages habitants des bords de l'Ister se souviennent encore de l'Orphée qui parut dans leurs forêts! Ils viennent danser autour de ses cendres; ils ont même retenu quelque chose de son langage: tant leur est douce la mémoire de ce Romain qui s'accusait d'être le barbare, parce qu'il n'était pas entendu du Sarmate!'

> Ce n'est pas sans motif que j'ai cité, à propos d'Ovide, ces réflexions d'Eudore. Le ton mélancolique du poète des *Martyrs* s'adapte à ce tableau, et la tristesse languissante du prisonnier chrétien s'y réfléchit heureusement. Il y a là l'ampleur de touche et de sentiments qui caractérisait la plume qui a écrit *Les Natchez;* et je reconnais, dans la sauvage idylle d'Eugène Delacroix une *histoire parfaitement belle,* parce qu'il y a mis la *fleur du désert, la grâce de la cabane et une simplicité à conter la douleur que je ne me flatte pas d'avoir conservées.* Certes je n'essayerai pas de traduire avec ma plume la volupté si triste qui s'exhale de ce verdoyant *exil.* Le catalogue, parlant ici la langue si nette et si brève de Delacroix, nous dit simplement, et cela vaut mieux: 'Les un l'examinent avec curiosité, les autres lui font acceuil à leur manière, et lui offrent des fruits sauvages et du lait de jument.' Si triste qu'il soit, le poète des élégances n'est pas insensible à cette grâce barbare, au charme de cette hospitalité rustique. Tout ce qu'il y a dans Ovide de délicatesse et de fertilité a passé dans la peinture de Delacroix; et, comme l'exil a donné au brillant poète la tristesse qui lui manquait, la mélancolie a revêtu de son vernis enchanteur le plantureux paysage du peintre. (II, 635-6)

Baudelaire uses the word *tristesse* to qualify the figure's attitude in the first sentence, and echos it in citation and direct discourse throughout the text: he cites the title of the book Ovid is to write, *Tristia,* as he does the sad reflections of Eudore, whom Chateaubriand put on the scene three centuries later. Baudelaire underlines Eudore's sadness, and attributes that emotion to the atmosphere of Delacroix's painting; finally, he analogizes Ovid's evolution to Delacroix's: both become sad. The echoes of the term sketch a progression across the centuries; aligning these echoes in chronological sequence, Baudelaire implies that the poet's sadness is to continue, beyond his death, communicating itself to his readers, to Chateaubriand's readers, and to Delacroix's viewers. Such a device in literature is the analog of a winding road in landscape painting, which links the planes of the picture by forcing calculation of their respective distances from the viewer. At each moment of the inferred narrative, one becomes aware of a loss: Ovid's loss of favor, Eudore's loss of faith in Rome, France's loss of Chateaubriand and of its first romantics. The question of future compensation naturally arises, but Baudelaire denies that hope: ". . . ici il vivra, ici il mourra."

Baudelaire thus imposes temporality on what can only be an idyllic painting, as he admits himself. It is a wide verdant vista under pleasant skies, where all the needs of the viewer are satisfied: here one finds food, company, and no hint of danger. Baudelaire's gloss is not so much a description of the painting as an answer to Balzac's question – "Quels sont leurs chagrins?" –, and it functions like the tomb and its inscription in Poussin's painting, *Les Bergers d'Arcadie*. Baudelaire introduces temporality, regret, and mortality in a painting which depicts a perpetual present. Further, discovering pathos in a "voluptuous" and "fertile" "idyll," one turns back all the more eagerly to the painting.

It is a landscape, about three feet by four feet in size, a rectangle divided horizontally into four bands. In the foreground, the largest band, the poet reclines on the left; he is greeted by shepherds, another shepherd milks a mare. The ground on which these figures stand must be elevated, for the heads and bodies only of two men, one on foot, the other horseback, rise above the ground, in the middle of the picture, as they climb the hill to Ovid's location. Behind these men, a wide landscape spreads, blocked on the left by a small, chalky hill, but open on the right. In the middle distance, a bay; beyond the bay mountains rise on either side, but between them recedes, zigzag, a valley which the eye follows to the far horizon. A blue sky, partly obscured by clouds, covers the upper quarter of the canvas.

Pleasure dominates Baudelaire's, and any, reaction to the picture: its viewer is afforded a distant view; signs of protection – a small thatched hut, an area closed off by hill, hut and picture plane, – are in evidence; the environment is not hostile: Ovid is approached with reverence by the shepherds who kneel; the climate is pleasant: temperate and fertile. Needs are provided for: there is food, water, shelter, companionship. Such iconography calls for reference to the prospect/refuge theory of landscape; this theory holds that landscape is pleasing to the eye when it offers the viewer (symbols of) security, while at the same time providing him with a wide range of courses of action.[12] Such a theory, which

---

[12] Jay Appleton proposes this idea in his *The Experience of Landscape* (New York: John Wiley & Sons, 1975), pp. 70-120. In large part, he develops this theory because of what he perceives as the limitations of aesthetic interpretations of landscape: "As long as we have to ask 'what is beauty in landscape?' there is

Delacroix's painting illustrates perfectly, poses a large problem, however: it implies that a picture is pleasing when it satisfies imaginary needs. Baudelaire himself corroborates this reading:

> L'artiste qui a produit cela peut se dire un homme heureux, et heureux aussi se dira celui qui pourra tous les jours en rassassier son regard. L'esprit s'y enfonce avec une lente et gourmande volupté, comme dans le ciel, dans l'horizon de la mer, dans les yeux pleins de pensée. (II, 636)

A theme of satisfaction – *heureux, rassassier, volupté,* – comes to the fore, even as Baudelaire sketches a narrative of loss and regret. This theme can easily be explained as that of the "happiness of sadness": the narrative offers a formal pleasure even as it tells a story of pain. But what remains to be explained is how to read the notion of satisfaction itself in an essay which has until now argued so consistently against manifestations of interest: prizes, privileges, narcissism, and eroticism. It is as though the theme of loss, so stressed by the commentary, required some compensation, even if that compensation comes in the form of a theme of satisfaction, the very notion Baudelaire repudiates in his introduction: such autonomy would imply that description obeys laws different from the theory it claims to illustrate.

A logical place to examine this claim more closely would be the chapter on landscape; Delacroix's painting is a landscape, but most landscape painters, Baudelaire claims, do not employ their imagination to explicate nature:

> J'avouerai, avec tout le monde, que l'école moderne des paysagistes est singulièrement forte et habile; mais dans ce triomphe et cette prédominance d'un genre inférieur, dans ce culte niais de la nature, non épurée, non expliquée par l'imagination, je vois un signe évident d'abaissement général. (II, 660)

---

a presupposition that it must be the same as beauty in sculpture or in dancing, otherwise we should not describe it by the same word. But as soon as we re-phrase the question as 'What is the source of that pleasure we derive from the contemplation of landscape?' we are perfectly free to postulate that it may be different from the source of pleasure to be derived from any other experience." (p. 15) Seeking a "source" rather than a definition does free one from systematic thought, but it also tends to define pleasure as the mark of satisfaction of a need.

If landscape painters fail to supplement nature with imagination, one would expect this chapter especially to exemplify imaginative criticism. This expectation is all the more justified as the metaphors used to describe the effects of imagination come back again to explain the problem of landscape. The metaphor of the dictionary, for example, illustrates the lack of imagination:

> . . . ils peignent tous fort bien, et presque tous oublient qu'un site naturel n'a de valeur que le sentiment actuel que l'artiste y sait mettre. La plupart tombent dans le défaut que je signalais au commencement de cette étude: ils prennent le dictionnaire de l'art pour l'art lui-même; ils copient un mot du dictionnaire, croyant copier un poème. Or un poème ne se copie jamais: il veut être composé. (II, 661)

Imagination relates, it does not repeat; it arranges disordered nature. Imagination is thus like grammar: ordering elements nature provides, it produces a signifying totality. By contrast, landscape painting is a mere vocabulary list.

I showed earlier (Chapter 2) how Baudelaire imposed a narrative structure on his description of Boudin's seascapes; he uses the same procedure to explicate the engraver Charles Meryon's cityscapes, whose commentary immediately follows. A text by Victor Hugo is embedded in this description, which thus serves as prolog and epilog to that citation. The commentary of Meryon's etchings runs thus:

> Il y a quelques années, un homme puissant et singulier, un officier de marine, dit-on, avait commencé une série d'études à l'eau-forte d'après les points de vue les plus pittoresques de Paris. Par l'âpreté, la finesse et la certitude de son dessin, M. Meryon rappelait les vieux et excellents aquafortistes. J'ai rarement vu représenté avec plus de poésie la solennité naturelle d'une ville immense. Les majestés de la pierre accumulée, les clochers *montrant du doigt le ciel*, les obélisques de l'industrie vomissant contre le firmament leurs coalitions de fumée, les prodigieux échafaudages des monuments en réparation, appliquant sur le corps solide de l'architecture leur architecture à jour d'une beauté si paradoxale, le ciel tumultueux, chargé de colère et de racune, la profondeur des perspectives augmentée par la pensée de tous les drames qui y sont contenus, aucun des

éléments complexes dont se compose le douleuruex et glorieux décor de la civilisation n'était oublié. Si Victor Hugo a vu ces excellents estampes, il a dû être content; il a retrouvé, dignement représenté, sa

> Morne Isis, couverte d'un voile!
> Araignée à l'immense toile,
> Où se prennent les nations!
> Fontaine d'urnes obsédée!
> Mamelle sans cesse inondée,
> Où, pour se nourrir de l'idée,
> Viennent les générations!
> . . . .
> Ville qu'un orage enveloppe!

Mais un démon a touché le cerveau de M. Meryon; un délire mystérieux a brouillé ces facultés qui semblaient aussi solides que brillantes. Sa gloire naisante et ses travaux ont été interrompus. Et depuis lors nous attendons toujours avec anxiété des nouvelles consolantes de ce singulier officier, qui était devenu en un jour un puissant artiste, et qui avait dit adieu aux solennelles aventures de l'Océan pour peindre la noire majesté de la plus inquiétante des capitales. (II, 666)

As he did in the Boudin passage, Baudelaire employs echo here: the words *puissant, singulier,* and *solennelles* occur before and after the description of the studies. A minimal biography also frames it: Meryon's early life as a sailor, his initial success as an artist, precede description; the madness which cut his activity short follows it. This biography traces the outline of a minor tragedy: from strength, Meryon falls into imbecility through the intervention of a superhuman force. His story is an allegory of the story of Babel (mentioned by Hugo in "A l'Arc de Triomphe"), where work was also interrupted by divine intervention. The more speculative aspects of the description also repeat the notion of decline: Paris is menaced with destruction. The sky, for example, is "chargé de colère et de racune." The lines quoted from "A l'Arc de Triomphe" insist on industry, but their coda suggests that this very activity will lead to the city's disappearance. Twelve lines later, in fact, Hugo does write: "Il se taira pourtant."[13] A storm

---

[13] See Hugo, I, 939.

promises to break. Further, any reference to Hugo's poem must suggest "Paris à l'état de ville morte" (II, 151), and thus predict the city's death. The periphery of the actual description tells a story which attributes Meryon's fall (and Paris's decline) to his (its) very success.

The citation from Hugo is at the apex of this tragedy: the early elements of Meryon's biography announce the Hugo passage, and that passage in turn announces Meryon's fall. The citation is an apostrophe in the present tense, as though exempted from the temporality surrounding it. The story of "A l'Arc de Triomphe," that of the decline of a great city and of the recollection of its past glory, corresponds to the biography of Meryon.

But, as though to differentiate itself from that story, the description is enumerative, not narrative. The list of Meryon's etchings ("les majestés de la pierre accumulée, etc.") echoes the phrase Baudelaire uses to describe the cityscape: "une agglomération d'hommes et de monuments." Each of its items names an element from Meryon's studies: *pierre, obélisques de l'industrie, monuments en réparation, ciel,* and *perspectives.* Baudelaire then adds a human element, a subjective dimension, to each object: *majesté, beauté si paradoxale, rancune et colère, la pensée de tous les drames.* Each object serves as the foundation for an interpretation.[14] The description thus mimicks what it describes: it is agglomerative and accumulative, and this tendency appears in words like *accumulée, coalitions, appliquer, charger,* and *augmenter.* In short, the phrase "agglomération d'hommes et de monuments" is repeatedly transformed to produce the description, in a perfect example of Riffaterre's "transformation of the matrix." Unlike the narrative, which establishes causal relations, the description is only enumerative; each element repeats a previous element: sequence does not imply consequence. Further, such repetition, compulsively rephrasing the matrix of the phrase, bears

---

[14] The procedure employed here should be compared to the thought from *Fusées:* "– *Ciel tragique.* Epithète d'un ordre abstrait appliqué à un être matériel." (I, 653) As Claude Pichois aptly notes, the phrase describes most of Baudelaire's poetics. (*Œuvres,* I, 1476) It should also be noted that the thought bears a striking resemblance to the very example of the poetry so despised by Joseph Delorme: "Au lieu du mot vaguement abstrait, métaphysique et sentimental, employer le mot propre et pittoresque; ainsi, par exemple, au lieu de *ciel en courroux,* mettre *ciel noir et brumeux . . .*" (Sainte-Beuve, *Vie,* p. 147.)

every indication of serving the pleasure principle.[15] The description does not illustrate, but complements its frame.

This tension between description and fiction is strongly in evidence in the poem "Danse macabre" of 1859, quoted in part in the chapter on sculpture of that year's *Salon.* Beyond the immediate link afforded by the citation, many parallels can be found between the poem and the *Salon.* Baudelaire wrote the poem after a visit to the studio of the sculptor Ernest Christophe, where a statuette, *Le Squelette,* caught his eye,[16] and the poem retains a reference to that visit in its dedication to the sculptor. The *Salon* treats the first 22 verses of the poem as an "illustration" of the figure Baudelaire describes: their evocative power is such that he may insert them to "abridge" his description. He claims thus that the poem is interchangeable with prose description, and the play between description and the more elaborate poem is particularly revealing of the nature of imaginative criticism.

The poem starts with a description, only to end with an apostrophe to the viewer to adopt a more sensible attitude.

> Fière, autant qu'un vivant, de sa noble stature,
> Avec son gros bouquet, son mouchoir et ses gants,
> Elle a la nonchalance et la désinvolture
> D'une coquette maigre aux airs extravagants.
>
> Vit-on jamais au bal une taille plus mince?
> Sa robe exagérée, en sa royale ampleur,
> S'écroule abondamment sur un pied sec que pince
> Un soulier pomponné, joli comme une fleur.

---

[15] The "repetition compulsion" causes the subject to repeat "des expériences anciennes sans se souvenir du prototype et avec au contraire l'impression très vive qu'il s'agit de quelque chose qui est pleinement motivé dans l'actuel." J. Laplanche and J. B. Pontalis, *Vocabulaire de la psychanalyse* (Paris: Press Universitaires de France, 1967), p. 86. Baudelaire's repetition of a single phrase, and his simultaneous insistence that he is describing a present object, allow comparison of his behavior to that described by Laplanche and Pontalis.

[16] A letter from Christophe to Baudelaire, the 10th of February, 1859, accompanying the study, indicates that Baudelaire had visited the former's studio sometime earlier and admired the figure. Since the poem was sent to Calonne January 1st, 1859, one would assume that Baudelaire visited Christophe's studio before that date. See Pichois, ed., *Œuvres,* I, 1030.

La ruche qui se joue au bord des clavicules,
Comme un ruisseau lascif qui se frotte au rocher,
Défend pudiquement des lazzi ridicules
Les funèbres appas qu'elle tient à cacher.

Ses yeux profonds sont faits de vide et de ténèbres,
Et son crâne, de fleurs artistement coiffé,
Oscille mollement sur ses frêles vertèbres.
O charme d'un néant follement attifé!

Aucuns t'appeleront une caricature,
Qui ne comprennent pas, amants ivres de chair,
L'élégance sans nom de l'humaine armature.
Tu réponds, grand squelette, à mon goût le plus cher!

Viens-tu troubler, avec ta puissante grimace,
La fête de la vie? ou quelque vieux désir,
Eperonnant encor ta vivante carcasse,
Te pousse-t-il, crédule, au sabbat du Plaisir?

Au chant des violons, aux flammes des bougies,
Espères-tu chasser ton cauchemar moqueur,
Et viens-tu demander au torrent des orgies
De rafraîchir l'enfer allumé dans ton cœur?

Inépuisable puits de sottise et de fautes!
De l'antique douleur éternel alambic!
A travers le treillis recourbé de tes côtes
Je vois, errant encor, l'insatiable aspic.

Pour dire vrai, je crains que ta coquetterie
Ne trouve pas un prix digne de ses efforts;
Qui, de ces cœurs mortels, entend la raillerie?
Les charmes de l'horreur n'enivrent que les forts!

Le gouffre de tes yeux, plein d'horribles pensées,
Exhale le vertige, et les danseurs prudents
Ne contempleront pas sans d'amères nausées
Le sourire éternel de tes trente-deux dents.

Pourtant, qui n'a serré dans ses bras un squelette,
Et qui ne s'est nourri des choses du tombeau?

Qu'importe le parfum, l'habit ou la toilette?
Qui fait le dégoûté montre qu'il se croit beau.

Bayadère sans nez, irrésistible gouge,
Dis donc à ces danseurs qui font les offusqués:
'Fiers mignons, malgré l'art des poudres et du rouge
Vous sentez tous la mort! O squelettes musqués,

'Antinoüs flétris, dandys à face glabre,
Cadavres vernissés, lovelaces chenus,
Le branle universel de la danse macabre
Vous entraîne en des lieux qui ne sont pas connus!

'Des quais froids de la Seine aux bords brûlants du Gange,
Le troupeau mortel saute et se pâme, sans voir
Dans un trou du plafond la trompette de l'Ange
Sinistrement béant ainsi qu'un tromblon noir.

'En tout climat, sous tout soleil, la Mort t'admire
En tes contorsions, risible Humanité,
Et souvent, comme toi, se parfumant de myrrhe,
Mêle son ironie à ton insanite!' (I, pp. 96-8)

The poem hyperbolizes sexual desire (a form of interest): that desire could continue beyond death implies that it is present even when it is denied, in polite gatherings, in humour, and yes, even in aesthetics. Further, if the skeleton represents such permanent desire, the rhetorical question ". . . qui n'a serré dans ses bras un squelette?" argues that just as the skeleton is present in any body, just as death is present in any sexuality, so also is desire present in any personal relation, and so is interest present in any appreciation.

Baudelaire exemplifies the existence of such a hard "armature" throughout the poem: its movement from aesthetic to ethical, from description to fiction, and from assertion to irony flesh out this thesis. The first four stanzas of the poem are descriptive; the last three are reported disourse, attributed to the figure described. The poem moves from description to exhortation, and this move requires justification. The first verses describe a figure, *elle,* who remains unnamed until verse 20. The figure combines attributes of death and of life; of the latter, the accessories of social pleasures predominate. Several ambiguous epithets – *stature, maigre, sec, fu-*

nèbre – intimate that the figure is not a living woman, but only with the words *grand squelette* does the ambiguity cease. The description treats the figure as an aesthetic object, referring to it with third person pronouns and appending to it the epithets of aesthetic judgment: *joli, charme, élégance.* No particularized individual steps forward to assume the description: it is addressed to no one and to everyone, as are all aesthetic propositions. It is also true it is uttered by no one: the exclamation "O charme . . ." is left suspended in mid air. The vagueness of the enunciation, its source, its aim, its object prevents the reader from understanding who is speaking, about what and to whom.

With verse 20 this state of affairs changes: the figure is named, the skeleton is referred to as *tu,* and a speaker steps forward to assume the pronoun *je.* Now that it has become a *tu* for the narrator's *je,* it also acquires the attributes implied by the personal pronoun:[17] desires, hopes, resentments. Such personification is entirely compatible with Baudelaire's explicit theory; in accord with his definition of the imagination, he has replaced neutral, omniscient, aesthetic discourse with a set of fictions: personifications, narratives of desire and of vengeance; disparities between statement and intention.

The narrator interrogates the skeleton, demanding to know the motives for her appearance. Two are suggested: a desire on the figure's part to satisfy herself through participation in social pleasures, and, conversely, an intention to affect others through her presence. These motives are in turn doubled: the motive of desire is either a desire to "chasser un cauchemar moqueur" or to "rafraîchir l'enfer allumé dans son cœur": either lucidity or satisfaction. The motive of affecting others is also double: the skeleton will

[17] The attribution of speech to a figure who represents death is the same as the attribution of speech to a dead person; the former is however more general in its implications. This subspecies of personification is a recognized figure: prosopopoeia. Pierre Fontanier defines the figure thus: "La *Prosopopée,* qu'il ne faut confondre ni avec la *Personnification* ni avec l'*Apostrophe,* ni avec le *Dialogisme,* qui l'accompagnent presque toujours, consiste à mettre en quelque sorte en scène, les absens, les morts, les êtres surnaturels, ou même les êtres inanimés; à les faire agir, parler, répondre, ainsi qu'on l'entend; ou tout au moins à les prendre pour confidens, pour témoins, pour garans, pour accusateurs, pour vengeurs, pour juges, etc., et cela, ou par feinte, ou sérieusement. . . ." *Les Figures du discours,* Gérard Genette, ed. (Paris: Flammarion, 1968), pp. 404-5.

either revolt them, producing *amères nausées,* or teach them a lesson: "Vous sentez tous la mort!"

The last desire – to teach a lesson – is different from the first three. Those could be subsumed as part of the "descriptive system"[18] of the skeleton-in-love: she wants to live, to love, to touch others, and these desires remain fictions. The apostrophe she directs to her viewer or to her reader – it cannot be decided – implies interest: she tells "us" something for our own good. There is some beneficial effect – negative knowledge, perhaps – in understanding one's own mortality. Put differently, until line 46, the poem is a fiction, and its aim is undecidable; after line 47, it is a parable, and its aim is didactic.

The very fictions that were supposed to free aesthetic discourse from interest reintroduce interest into description, and it returns, so to speak, with a vengeance. Producing laughter, asserting power, teaching lessons, the poem follows the dictates of interest more than aesthetic renunciations. More generally, whether interest is defined as the Good (as in "Danse Macabre") or narcissism (as in the description of Boudin's works) or as sensual satisfaction (the description of *Ovide en exil*), it is indissociable from aesthetic appreciation, and this secret union is revealed by description.

[18] See note 24, Chapter 3.

8

RECOGNIZING MODERN BEAUTY: *LE PEINTRE DE LA VIE MODERNE*

> ... whereas we have traditionally been accustomed to reading literature by analogy with the plastic arts, and with music, we now have to recognize the necessity of a non-perceptual, linguistic moment in painting and in music, and learn to *read* pictures rather than to *imagine* meaning.[1]

In 1845, Baudelaire inaugurated a search for the "painter of modern life": "Celui-là sera le *peintre,* la vrai peintre, qui saura arracher à la vie actuelle son côté épique, et nous faire voir et comprendre, avec de la couleur ou du dessin, combien nous somme grands et poétiques dans nos cravates et nos bottes vernies." (II, 407) The following year, he reiterated this desire: "La vie parisienne est féconde en sujets poétiques et merveilleux. Le merveilleux nous enveloppe et nous abreuve comme l'atmosphère; mais nous ne le voyons pas." (II, 496) Thus when *Le Peintre de la vie moderne* was finally published in *Le Figaro* in 1863 Baudelaire accomplished an old ambition. However, it was only with the republication of the essay in 1869, in *L'Art romantique,* that the *peintre* was identified: Constantin Guys, a professional illustrator working for the *Univers illustré* and the *Illustrated London News.* The surprise of this choice is echoed even now: why did Baudelaire choose Guys as his painter of modern life, rather than Manet or even Delacroix? why did he choose drawing over painting? why

---

[1] Paul de Man, "The Resistance to Theory," *Yale French Studies* 63 (1982), p. 10.

did he choose a minor art over a major art?[2] In short, why did Baudelaire fail to recognize some great artist as the heroic painter of modern life?

It is with respect to such questions that the impact of *Le Peintre de la vie moderne* must be assessed, for such questions alone indicate the unexpectedness of Baudelaire's choice: Constantin Guys, despite efforts to circulate his works, remains an artist who emerges from obscurity under the light projected by Baudelaire's article.[3] Baudelaire correctly foretold Delacroix's, Corot's, Meryon's, Boudin's and Manet's future acceptance, and just as correctly foretold Vernet's and Scheffer's obscurity. Why then did he select Guys to celebrate in his longest monograph? To admirers and critics of Baudelaire alike, the question is embarrassing as long as they consider aesthetic judgment a matter of recognition. For them, the value of Baudelaire's criticism stands or falls on his recognition of talent and here, Baudelaire's judgment is faulty: it fails to gain universal assent.

I stress the point, for I believe that Baudelaire made this choice as a provocation, an effort to unsettle received notions of beauty,

---

[2] Henri Lemaître: "Constantin Guys (1805-1892) semble aujourd'hui bien oublié . . .," from *Curiosité esthétiques – l'Art romantique,* by Charles Baudelaire (Paris: Garnier, 1962), p. 458; Jonathan Mayne: "Whether or not we agree that Baudelaire was justified in glorifying Guys to this extent . . . ," from *The Painter of Modern Life and Other Essays,* by Charles Baudelaire (London: Phaidon Publishers Inc., 1964), p. xiv; Pierre-Georges Castex: "Le peintre complet de la vie moderne ne saurait s'identifier à un interprète de la mode, même heureusement inspiré. Sans doute Baudelaire aurait-il pu trouver une matière plus riche, sinon pour une analyse de la modernité au sens où il entendait cette notion, du moins pour une analyse du génie moderne en peinture, dans les œuvres d'Edouard Manet," from *Baudelaire critique d'art* (Paris: SEDES, 1969), p. 74; and Anne Coffin Hanson: "Despite the brevity of his remarks Baudelaire seems to have seen in Manet the potential to meet his aims for an artist of modern life." (p. 22)

[3] For example, Karen Smith writes in the introduction of the Cleveland Museum's catalogue *Constantin Guys: Crimean War Drawings 1854-1856:* "Throughout his career Guys avoided public notice. However, he enjoyed the friendship of many of the major artists, writers, and critics of his time. Among his friends and avid collectors of his work were such members of the avant-garde as Gavarni, Théophile Gautier, the Goncourt brothers, Champfleury, Edouard Manet and Emile Zola. His greatest champions, however, were Charles Baudelaire, whose essay *Le Peintre de la vie moderne* was about Guys, and the photographer Nadar, who assisted Guys throughout his life and owned the drawings which make up this exhibition." The Cleveland Museum of Art, *Constantin Guys: Crimean War Drawings 1854-1856,* by Karen W. Smith (Cleveland: The Cleveland Museum of Art, 1978), p. 9.

and first among them, the notion that beauty is recognized. To choose a recognized artist, or even a to-be-recognized artist, would only confirm some readers in their error. Choosing Guys, by contrast, Baudelaire left generations of readers asking uneasy questions of the type just mentioned, and searching for a notion of beauty based not on authority but on play. No canon or authority corroborates Baudelaire's choice of Guys, and it was precisely to free himself from such criteria that he made that choice. The beauty Baudelaire finds in Guy's works can only be a matter of taste, and beyond Constantin Guys or *modernité, Le Peintre de la vie moderne* celebrates the freedom of taste.

In the first paragraphs of the essay, Baudelaire mocks those who consider beauty a figure to be recognized; such persons seek beauty in museums, not the world; in names, not paintings; in memory, not perception:

> Il y a dans le monde, et même dans le monde des artistes, des gens qui vont au musée du Louvre, passent rapidement, et sans leur accorder un regard, devant une foule de tableaux très intéressants quoique de *second ordre,* et se plantent rêveurs devant un Titien ou un Raphaël, un de ceux que la gravure a le plus popularisés; puis sortent satisfaits, plus d'un se disant: 'Je connais mon musée.' Il existe aussi des gens qui, ayant lu jadis Bossuet et Racine, croient posséder l'histoire de la littérature.
>
> Par bonheur se présentent de temps en temps des redresseurs de torts, des critiques, des amateurs, des curieux qui affirment que tout n'est pas dans Raphaël, que tout n'est pas dans Racine, que les *poetæ minores* ont du bon, du solide et du délicieux . . . (II, 683)

In short, the museum-goer is simply recognizing masterpieces, not judging beauty: he recognizes a name, the original of a familiar copy, the place where masterpieces are found. Baptizing his experience with the name of knowledge – "Je connais mon musée" – his activity resembles reading signs more than it does judging beauty; such appreciation resembles nothing more than the school-study of classic authors. By contrast, Baudelaire will find beauty in works that are not masterpieces, by an unknown (and, in 1863, unnamed) artist, and will go, as it were, into the streets to find that beauty.

When Baudelaire disparages the museum-goer, he takes part in a critique of learning which had been on-going since Hegel's time, and whose chief exponent, at the moment of *Le Peintre de la vie moderne,* was Hippolyte Taine, appointed in 1864 to the Ecole des Beaux-Arts. That year, Taine gave a series of courses which he published the following year under the title *Philosophie de l'art.* There, he criticizes contemporary culture for having sacrificed the ability to feel in favor of the ability to know:

> Le propre de l'extrême culture est d'effacer de plus en plus les images au profit des idées. Sous l'effort incessant de l'éducation, de la conversation, de la réflexion et de la science, la vision primitive se déforme, se décompose et s'évanouit pour faire place à des idées nues, à des mots bien classés, à une sorte d'algèbre. Le train courant de l'esprit est désormais le raisonnement pur. S'il revient aux images, c'est avec effort, par soubresaut maladif et violent, par une espèce d'hallucination désordonnée et dangereuse. – Tel est aujourd'hui notre état d'esprit.[4]

Taine opposes a conceptual mode of understanding to an imagistic mode; the latter, he claims, is immediate and complete. When Baudelaire repudiates the museum-goer's recognition of masterpieces, he makes the same argument: aesthetic appreciation is opposed to recognition; doing so, he makes an explicit claim for the power of images.

However, Baudelaire seeks also to reappraise the "minor arts," such a reappraisal must not be underestimated. To find "du bon, du solide et du délicieux" in the works of the *poetæ minores* is to say

---

[4] Hippolyte Taine, *Philosophie de l'art* (Paris: Hachette, 1882), I, 151-2. Such justifications of criticism of modern art are common; Baudelaire's passage resembles one by Sainte-Beuve from thirty years earlier: "Cette critique-là (academic criticism) sans doute a droit à nos respects; elle est grave, savante, définitive; elle explique, elle pénètre, elle fixe et consacre des admirations confuses, des beautés en partie voilées, des conceptions difficiles à atteindre. . . . Mais outre cette critique réfléchie et lente . . . qui s'assied dans une silencieuse bibliothèque, en présence de quelques bustes à demi obscurs, il en est une autre plus alerte, plus mêlée au bruit du jour et à la question vivante . . ." Just as Sainte-Beuve sought to present contemporary poets, Baudelaire sought to draw attention to "un homme singulier" (II, 687), and both renounce the discourse of knowledge in order to discuss their contemporaries. Charles-Augustin Sainte-Beuve, "Victor Hugo," in *Portraits Contemporains* (Paris: Calmann-Lévy, 1868), I, 416-7.

that these are not *poetæ minores,* for if they merit the consideration given to Raphael, Bossuet, and Racine, they might also merit the epithets bestowed on the classics. If so, beauty does not reside in books or paintings but in judgment.

To exemplify this freedom of judgment, Baudelaire asserts that beauty can be found in a set of engravings representing costumes from the last decade of the eighteenth century:

> J'ai sous les yeux une série de gravures de modes commençant avec la Révolution et finissant à peu près au Consulat. Ces costumes, qui font rire bien des gens irréfléchis, de ces gens graves sans vraie gravité, présentent un charme d'une nature double, artistique et historique. (II, 684)

The alternative Baudelaire proposes is thus provocative: to the museum he opposes the popular reproduction; to the painting, engraving; to Titian and Raphael, Debucourt and Saint-Aubin; to the human form he opposes its clothing. There is hardly a concept one can invoke – prestige, authority, canon, seriousness – to justify this choice, and there lies the thesis of Baudelaire's essay.

For these works are nevertheless beautiful. Appealing to the timehonored metaphor for the effect of artistic beauty on its viewer – resurrection – Baudelaire writes that these costumes can be made to "come to life" in the mind of the viewer or on the stage of a theater. The past will become present; the difference between presence and representation will collapse:

> L'imagination du spectateur peut encore aujourd'hui faire marcher et frémir cette *tunique* et ce *schall.* Un de ces jours, peut-être, un drame paraîtra sur un théâtre quelconque, où nous verrons la résurrection de ces costumes sous lesquels nos pères se trouvaient tout aussi enchanteurs que nous-mêmes dans nos pauvres vêtements. . . . Le passé, tout en gardant le piquant du fantôme, reprendra la lumière et le mouvement de la vie, et se fera présent. (II, 684)

This passage has elicited strong critical attention; Paul de Man has shown how the *fantôme* figures the synthesis of two temporal moments: past and present, of two modes of perception, memory and sensation.[5] The passage also combines tenses and temporal references to blur the signification of past, present and future. In this passage and elsewhere Baudelaire describes a double movement, which consists in isolating a moment in time (the past) and then, within that moment, discovering the trace of its correlate (the present). It is not more accurate to say that Baudelaire seeks modernity than that he seeks pastness: in both cases, he seeks the complement of a temporal given, and thus starts the dialectical movement that characterizes this passage. Whether he describes "history," "modernity," "art," or "mores" he discovers duality, play between rule and variation:

> Dans l'art hiératique, la dualité se fait voir au premier coup d'œil. (II, 685)
>
> La dualité de l'art est une conséquence fatale de la dualité de l'homme (II, 685-6)
>
> La modernité, c'est le transitoire, le fugitif, le contingent, la moitié de l'art, dont l'autre moitié est l'éternel et l'immuable. (II, 695)
>
> Il s'établit alors un duel entre la volonté de tout voir, de ne rien oublier, et la faculté de la mémoire qui a pris l'habitude d'absorber vivement la couleur générale et la silhouette, l'arabesque du contour. (II, 698)

Why are these oppositions so frequent? Baudelaire asserts that such dualities are defining characteristics of beauty: ". . . le beau est toujours, inévitablement, d'une composition double, bien que l'impression qu'il produit soit une . . ." (II, 685) Pursuing this thought, I would argue that Baudelaire's insistence on duality, opposition, and struggle in this essay translates a proverbial requirement of aesthetic judgment: that, when judging beauty, one seek play, not knowledge.

Here as elsewhere, Baudelaire advances propositions argued seventy years earlier by Kant. Again, I do not claim to discern Kantian influence in Baudelaire's aesthetic thought: I am arguing

[5] de Man, "Literary History," p. 156.

however that, as a consequent and perceptive thinker, Baudelaire recognized the paradoxes of aesthetic propositions and adopted Kantian solutions in order to safeguard his freedom of judgment. In its deepest theses, *Le Peintre de la vie moderne* is undeniably Kantian: Baudelaire proposes the decorative arts as an example of beauty; he refuses to admit that beauty is recognized; he offers instead a notion of play. Indeed, in Baudelaire's formulation of beauty as a composite of the eternal and the transitory, of rule and of variation, one can read an allegory of the "*free conformity to law* of the imagination" of the third *Critique.*[6]

Even if the characteristics of Baudelaire's aesthetic judgment had been formulated much earlier, his formulations were innovative. The year of *Le Peintre de la vie moderne*'s publication was also that of the French translation of Goethe's conversations with Eckermann, and there one finds an example of the aesthetic thought against which Baudelaire argues. Specifically, the word "composition" which Baudelaire inherited from Poe, is in question:

> C'est avec autant d'impropriété dans les termes que les Français, en parlant des œuvres de la nature, emploient le mot de composition. L'expression convient quand il s'agit des différents fragments d'une machine faite morceau à morceau, mais non pas quand j'ai dans l'esprit les parties d'un tout organisé, parties qui vivent par elles-mêmes et qui sont animées d'une même âme . . .
>
> . . . C'est un mot d'une bassesse extrême que nous devons aux Français, et dont nous devrions tâcher de nous débarrasser et le plus tôt possible, dit Goethe. Comment peut-on dire que Mozart a *composé* son *Don Juan.* Composition! comme si c'était un gâteau ou un biscuit, que l'on fabrique avec des œufs, de la farine, et du sucre. Une création intellectuelle, c'est ce qui, dans le détail comme dans l'ensemble, est pénétre d'un seul esprit, conçu d'un seul jet, animé d'un souffle de vie unique . . .[7]

---

[6] ". . . although in the apprehension of a given object of sense it (the imagination) is tied down to a definite form of this Object and, to that extent, does not enjoy free play . . . , still it is easy to conceive that the object may supply ready-made to the imagination just such a form of the arrangement of the manifold, as the imagination, if it were left to itself, would freely project in harmony with the general *conformity of law to the understanding.*" Kant, p. 86.

[7] Johann. P. Eckermann, *Conversations de Goethe,* trans. E. Delerot (Paris: Charpentier, 1863), II, 302.

The procreative metaphors – *jet, souffle, création* and especially *conçu* – translate an expressive aesthetic which was not Baudelaire's. For Goethe, the artist is dominated by an idea which he expresses and the recognition of which is essential to the appreciation of the work. Baudelaire's view of art is radically different; it is against a background such as this that one must read his definition of poetry from the *Salon de 1859:* ". . . un poème ne se copie jamais; il veut être composé." (II, 661) The word *composition* occurs at least seven times in *Le Peintre de la vie moderne* to qualify Guys's drawings or beauty generally. "Composition" implies not unity but multiple elements, elements between which there is play, as there is in the machine Goethe so detests. Indeed, Guy's compositions resemble more the "machine faite morceau à morceau" than the "création intellectuelle." They are literally assembled at night from raw materials gathered during the preceding day's wanderings: "La fantasmagorie a été extraite de la nature. Tous les matériaux dont la mémoire s'est encombrée se classent, se rangent, s'harmonisent et subissent cette idéalisation forcée . . ."[8] (II, 694) Guys "fences" with his pen, and the result of this play is the "rebirth" of the images observed during the day:

> Maintenant, à l'heure où les autres dorment, celui-ci est penché sur sa table, dardant sur une feuille de papier le même regard qu'il attachait tout à l'heure sur les choses, s'escrimant avec son crayon, sa plume, son pinceau, faisant jaillir l'eau du verre au plafond, essuyant sa plume sur sa chemise, pressé, violent, actif, comme s'il craignait que les images ne lui échappent, querelleur quoique seul, et bousculant lui-même.
>
> Et les choses renaissent sur le papier, naturelles et plus que naturelles, belles et plus que belles, singulières et douées d'une vie enthousiaste comme l'âme de l'auteur. (II, 693-4)

Guys composes his images, and this composition produces an image more intense than does ordinary sensation. In other words, the interplay of memory and perception, characteristic of Guys's compositions but also of aesthetic experience, produces beauty not

[8] For a definitive commentary on this passage, one that underlines the dialectical aspect of Guys's composition, see de Man, "Literary History," pp. 157-61.

present in the original sensation. Beauty does not reside in the object, a quality to be recognized; it is an effect which arises from play, play which "extracts" it from ordinary life as one "extracts" energy from matter or meaning from nature.

In large part, this play arises from the unfinished nature of the drawings: ". . . à n'importe quel point de son progrès, chaque dessin a l'air suffisamment fini; vous nommerez cela une ébauche si vous voulez, mais ébauche parfaite." (II, 700) The sketch or *ébauche*, unfinished, requires imaginary completion, and such completion is often read as beauty. Here again, Baudelaire is entering a vigorous nineteenth-century debate: to finish or not to finish? During his brief acquaintance with Delacroix, he could have heard the painter elaborate on the question; the theme is found several times in Delacroix's *Journal.*[9] The entry of April 20, 1853, for example, contrasts the two points of view:

> . . . nous avons parlé de Chopin. Il me contait que ses improvisations étaient beaucoup plus hardies que ses compositions achevées. Il en était pour cela, sans doute, comme de l'esquisse du tableau comparée au tableau fini. Non, on ne gâte pas le tableau en le finissant. Peut-être y a-t-il moins de carrière pour l'imagination que dans un ouvrage ébauché. On éprouve des impressions différentes devant un édifice qui s'élève et dont les détails ne sont pas encore indiqués, et devant le même édifice quand il a reçu son complément d'ornements et de fini. Il en est de même d'une ruine qui acquiert quelque chose de plus frappant par les parties qui manquent. Les détails en sont effacées ou mutilées, de même que dans le bâtiment qui s'élève on ne voit encore que les rudiments et l'indication vague des moulures et des parties ornées. L'édifice achevé enferme l'imagination dans un cercle et lui défend d'aller au-delà. Peut-être que l'ébauche d'un ouvrage ne plaît tant que parce que chacun l'achève à son gré.[10]

---

[9] Armand Moss, in his *Baudelaire et Delacroix* (Paris: Nizet, 1973), has argued that Baudelaire overstates his friendship with the painter, who seems not to have reciprocated the poet's admiration. Whether Baudelaire formulated his notion of finish in response to Delacroix or to another painter is of little consequence: the question was one widely debated at the period, and any critic had to have an opinion on the subject. For other examples of Delacroix's thought on finish, see Eugène Delacroix, *Journal: 1822-1863* (Paris: Plon, 1980), pp. 138, 341, 621.

[10] Delacroix, p. 330.

For Delacroix, the question of finish is a question of freedom: finished works enclose the imagination, forbid movement, compel recognition. Unfinished works elicit the activity of the imagination, which finishes them at will. Although more understanding than many of his contemporaries of the attractions of the sketch, Delacroix prefers the finished work: it limits meaning, as does syntax, and if so, he assimilates beauty to understanding. Baudelaire prefers the sketch, because it elicits the free play of imagination.

Extraire is the verb Baudelaire uses to describe this free play; the artist's perception of beauty in the world is called "extraction." Perceiving a form not present in raw sensation, the artist intuits the object's beauty:

> Le passé est intéressant non seulement par la beauté qu'ont su en extraire les artistes pour qui il était le présent, mais aussi comme passé, pour sa valeur historique, (II, 684)
>
> La fantasmagorie a été extraite de la nature. (II, 694)
>
> . . . pour que toute *modernité* soit digne de devenir antiquité, il faut que la beauté mystérieuse que la vie humaine y met involontairement en ait été extraite. (II, 695)

It is possible, Baudelaire maintains, to communicate an original impression through layers of signifiers; he calls this communication "translation." Further, "translation" can be repeated without loss of the original impression: describing the experience of seeing Guys's drawings, he writes: "Le spectateur est ici le traducteur d'une traduction toujours claire et enivrante." (II, 698) Similar effect, similar means: in order to achieve this continuity of effect, Baudelaire adopts literary procedures which resemble Guys's devices in drawing. He suggests, he does not state; he narrates, he does not describe; he proposes accounts as ephemeral as Guys's drawings:

> Les considérations et les rêveries morales qui surgissent des dessins d'un artiste sont, dans beaucoup de cas, la meilleure traduction que le critique en puisse faire; les suggestions font partie d'une idée mère, et, en les montrant successivement, on peut la faire deviner. (II, 712)

To be able to communicate something one does not recognize is of course a paradox, and the proposal of beauty which differs from the beauty one "knows" requires Baudelaire to confront this difficulty. His descriptions of Guys's drawings thus bear a large burden: they must communicate beauty without communicating knowledge; they must present beauty without representing it. In the remainder of this chapter, I propose to show how Baudelaire's descriptions inevitably assume an informative responsibility.

The chapter entitled "Le Militaire" offers a promising example of this ambition: Baudelaire describes the soldier in terms of play, and substitutes a narrative of long travels for an enumeration of the drawing's elements. The *militaire* is defined as a combination of calm and daring, of indifference and enthusiasm, of the adult who is about to die and the child who has just started life:

> Le signe particulier de la beauté sera donc, ici, une insouciance martiale, un mélange singulier de placidité et d'audace; c'est une beauté qui dérive de la nécessité d'être prêt à mourir à chaque minute. Mais le visage du militaire idéal devra être marqué d'une grande simplicité; car, vivant en commun comme les moines et les écoliers, accoutumés à se décharger des soucis journaliers de la vie sur une paternité abstraite, les soldats sont, en beaucoup de choses, aussi simples que les enfants; et, comme les enfants, le devoir étant accompli, ils sont faciles à amuser et portés aux divertissements violents. (II, 707-8)

The soldier is an oxymoron defying comprehension; he combines oppositions, and thus compostion serves to prevent recognition. His beauty results from the play of antithetical elements, and the notion of play *(divertissement)* appears in the passage to confirm this reading.

Even if in theory the soldier is an unrecognizable composite, the individual examples Baudelaire describes are specimens of a uniform type: all resemble one another; all wear the same expression; all have had the same adventure, and most importantly, their collective character is fully intelligible:

> J'ai actuellement sous les yeux une de ces compositions d'une physionomie générale vraiment héroïque, qui représente une tête de colonne d'infanterie; peut-être ces hommes reviennent-ils d'Italie et font-ils halte sur les boulevards devant l'enthou-

siasme de la multitude; peut-être viennent-ils d'accomplir une longue étape sur les routes de la Lombardie; je ne sais. Ce qui est visible, pleinement intelligible, c'est le caractère ferme, audacieux, même dans sa tranquillité, de tous ces visages hâlés par le soleil, la pluie et le vent.

Voilà bien l'uniformité d'expression créée par l'obéissance et les douleurs supportées en commun, l'air résigné du courage éprouvé par les longues fatigues. Les pantalons retroussés et emprisonnés dans les guêtres, les capotes flétries par la poussière, vaguement décolorées, tout l'équipement enfin a pris lui-même l'indestructible physionomie des êtres qui reviennent de loin et qui ont couru d'étranges aventures. On dirait que tous ces hommes sont plus solidement appuyés sur leurs reins, plus carrément installés sur leurs pieds, plus d'aplomb que ne peuvent l'être les autres hommes. (II, 708)

While the discussion of the general type stressed the soldier's compositeness, the description seeks only unity: Baudelaire distills *une physionomie, l'uniformité d'expression* and an *indestructible physionomie* from the "composition" he claims to have before his eyes. If oxymoron and antithesis characterized the former, repetition governs the latter: dialectic has given way to stereotypes; play has given way to certainty. A vocabulary of cruelty – *douleur, fatigues, emprisonné, flétri* – allegorizes the triumph of knowledge over aesthetic pleasure. In short, theory has been betrayed by description.

An entirely similar passage from uncertainty to certainty occurs in the chapter "Le Dandy." Like the *militaire,* the *dandy* is defined first in general terms, only later to be illustrated with reference to Guys's drawings. "Le dandysme," Baudelaire writes, "est une institution vague . . ." (II, 709) It is vague because it cannot be categorized: it belongs neither to the past nor to the present, because it is found in both; it is from neither the Old World nor the New for the same reason. The dandy is both frivolous and Spartan, hedonistic and ascetic. Paradoxically, the result is *distinction:* "Aussi, à ses yeux, épris avant tout de *distinction,* la perfection de la toilette consiste-t-elle dans la simplicité absolue, qui est, en effet, la meilleure manière de se distinguer."[11] (II, 710) In other

[11] I would stress that Baudelaire's category, *distinction,* is entirely empty and thus is different from a conception of *distinction* such as that advanced by Goblot: "Ce n'est pas pour être belle, c'est pour n'être pas confondue que la bourgeoisie s'applique à être distinguée dans sa tenue, ses manières, son langage, les objets

words, indeterminacy produces distinction: what could not be categorized can be categorized as uncategorizable. This is what is meant, I believe, by Baudelaire's qualification of dandysme: "Le dandysme, qui est une institution en dehors des lois, a des lois rigoureuses auxquelles sont strictement soumis tous ses sujets . . ." (II, 708) Such a conclusion is entirely assimilable to Kantian aesthetics which qualifies beauty as the sensation resulting from the free conformity to law of the imagination: beauty results from our inability to formulate a law (which we are nevertheless sure is there) which would account for the pleasure we feel. Like beauty, the dandy exemplifies "conformity to law without a law."[12]

However, Baudelaire's description closes on a much less ambiguous note:

> Le caractère de beauté du dandy consiste surtout dans l'air froid qui vient de l'inébranlable résolution de ne pas être ému; on dirait un feu latent qui se fait deviner, qui pourrait mais qui ne veut pas rayonner. C'est ce qui est, dans ces images, parfaitement exprimé. (II, 712)

Of the characteristics of the dandy, Baudelaire chooses one – his coldness, interestingly enough, for it could stand as a metaphor for the loss of free play – and brings that to prominence.

In other words, in an essay which both argues and exemplifies the freedom of aesthetic judgment, there are examples of renunciation of that freedom in favor of a kind of cognitive security: instead of saying "this drawing is beautiful," Baudelaire says "here is a soldier, here is a dandy"; instead of saying "this is beautiful," Baudelaire says "this is beautiful because . . ." Baudelaire substitutes knowledge for aesthetic judgment.

This should not be surprising, for the paradoxes of aesthetic judgment are demanding ones, leaving the judge in a state of suspense. The aesthetic judgment in effect dares its audience to disagree, but cannot, should such disagreement arise or even be suspected, offer support without losing its status as aesthetic

---

dont elle s'entoure. L'opposé de distingué est 'commun': est commun ce qui ne distingue pas, 'vulgaire' ce qui distingue mal et traduit une infériorité." See E. Goblot, *La Barrière et le niveau* (Paris: Alcan, 1925), p. 42.

[12] Kant, p. 86.

judgment. The example of Baudelaire is not isolated; the tendency of aesthetic judgments to become identifications is widespread, and is exemplified also by . . . Kant.

After discussing the various aspects of the aesthetic judgment – its universality, its refusal to refer to interest, purpose, or perfection – Kant admits that examples of such judgments are rare, and refer to a limited category of objects: "free beauties": ". . . designs *à la grecque,* foliage for framework or on wall-papers, &c., have no intrinsic meaning; they represent nothing – no Object under a definite concept – and are free beauties." There exists however another beauty, "appendant beauty," which is much more familiar: ". . . the beauty of a man . . . the beauty of a horse, or of a building . . . , presupposes a concept of the end that defines what the thing has to be, and consequently a concept of its perfection; and is therefore merely appendant beauty."[13] Kant also calls this beauty "Ideal Beauty": it must be judged with reference to a concept, according to rules; it is not true beauty, but it is the stock-in-trade of traditional aesthetics, a temptation even for the writer of the *Critique of Judgment.*

In the case of Baudelaire, there is no explicit apology for what could be called "Ideal Beauty": whenever he writes about beauty in general terms, he insists on his freedom of judgment and insists, consequently, on the notion of play. He is nevertheless tempted by a more powerful discourse, one of logic and demonstration, and this temptation surfaces in his descriptions.

The most extended analysis of a single subject is that of feminine beauty; it is comprised of the chapters "La Femme," "Eloge du Maquillage," and "Des Femmes et des Filles." As elsewhere, Baudelaire's initial considerations are general and theoretical; as elsewhere in the essay, he defines beauty as the product of play, between body and dress, face and make-up, nature and artifice. Beauty results when these poles are combined:

> Quel poète oserait, dans la peinture du plaisir causé par l'apparition d'une beauté, séparer la femme de son costume? Quel est l'homme qui, dans la rue, au théâtre, au bois, n'a pas joui, de la manière la plus désintéressée, d'une toilette savamment composée . . . ? (II, 714)

---

[13] Kant, pp. 72-3.

> ... qui ne voit que l'usage de la poudre de riz, si niaisement anathématisé par les philosophes candides, a pour but et pour résultat de faire disparaître du teint toutes les taches que la nature y a outrageusement semées, et de créer une unité ... (qui) ... rapproche immédiatament l'être humain de la statue ... ? (II, 717)

The long description of Guys's drawings, "Des Femmes et des Filles," falls then under the sign of play; play also pervades its title, which opposes woman to girl, wife to unmarried woman, "respectable" women to prostitutes. Baudelaire organizes the drawings he discusses in a "descending" order ("Nous sommes descendus jusqu'au dernier degré de la spirale ..." (II, 721)); given this order, one would expect that the word *femme* be found in the first descriptions, and *fille* in the last, but this is not the case. Curiously, the examples chosen of socially-accepted women are *petites filles,* while the later examples of the *filles* are all *femmes:* "la femme errante," "la femme révoltée," "la femme galante." (II, 720) *Fille* occurs only in a family context; in the context of prostitution, *femme* is used.

Beyond the theory of beauty Baudelaire advances, play characterizes another element of the discussion: that of the name of the women he discusses. If *filles* are *femmes,* and *femmes, filles,* the subject itself is generating play. In his *The Painting of Modern Life,* Timothy Clark offers an insight which corroborates this interpretation; he argues that at the time of Manet's *Olympia* (and Baudelaire's *Peintre*), the *prostitute* herself was uncategorizable by bourgeois society: she had no fixed place of work, no definite position in the social hierarchy, no sure meaning for art, and it was necessary for bourgeois society to invent the *courtisane* in order to achieve even limited representation of the institution.

> The *courtisane* was a category, that is my argument: one which depended not just on a distinction made between *courtisane* and *femme honnête* – though this was the dominant theme of the myth – but also on one between *courtisane* and prostitute proper. The category *courtisane* was all that could be *represented* of prostitution, and for this to take place, she had to be extracted

from the swarn of mere sexual commodities that could be seen making use of the streets.[14]

If only the *courtisane* could be represented, the prostitute proper was unrepresentable and inconceivable, a perfect example of free beauty.

Perversely, though, Baudelaire's descriptions of women of standing insist on play; the descriptions of prostitutes do not. Not surprisingly, play is found at the theater. Some "jeunes filles du meilleur monde" watch the show, "recevant et renvoyant la lumière avec leurs yeux, avec leurs bijoux . . ." (II, 718) As they do so, they are acting as much as the actors before them: ". . . elles sont théâtrales et solennelles comme le drame ou l'opéra qu'elles font semblant d'écouter." (II, 718) The actors themselves emulate poet and prostitute: "Si par un côté la comédienne touche à la courtisane, par l'autre elle confine au poète." (II, 720) In these examples, Baudelaire stresses an inability to conceptualize an object – a particular light, pretentious *jeunes filles,* the *comédienne* – and indicates this inability as the source of their beauty.

Even the evocation of the *beauté interlope* follows this pattern: she owes allegiance to the *bourgoises* just mentioned, but also participates in the activities of the *demi-monde;* while "aiming" at the elegance of *un meilleur monde,* she is nonetheless "savage" and "barbarous"; her backdrop is both heavenly and infernal. She is not, however, as uncategorizable as other women: for the first time in this description, Baudelaire drops the claim that beauty is ambiguous: "Elle a sa beauté qui lui vient du mal . . ." (II, 719) The origin of beauty is clear and unequivocal.

Appropriately, with his description of the *fœmina simplex* – the unrepresentable prostitute – Baudelaire abandons his project of exemplifying modernity, and lapses into the depiction of stereotypes. If the *petites filles* and the *femme interlope* were women who somehow tested powers of comprehension, that difficulty is no longer the case here. A language of prejudice and preconception furnishes an abundance of ready-made definitions which enable the *fœmina simplex* to be recognized:[15]

---

[14] Clark, p. 109.

[15] Baudelaire's description of prostitutes bears a strong resemblance to an entry from that storehouse of knowledge, Pierre Larousse's *Grand Dictionnaire*

> Parfois elles trouvent, sans les chercher, des poses d'une audace et d'une noblesse qui enchanteraient le statuaire le plus délicat, si le statuaire moderne avait le courage et l'esprit de ramasser la noblesse partout, même dans la fange: d'autres fois elles se montrent prostrées dans des attitudes désespérées d'ennui, dans des indolences d'estaminet, d'un cynisme masculin, fumant des cigarettes pour tuer le temps, avec la résignation du fatalisme oriental; étalées, vautrées sur des canapés, la jupe arrondie par-derrière et par-devant en un double éventail, ou accrochées en équilibre sur des tabourets et des chaises; lourdes, mornes, stupides, extravagantes, avec des yeux vernis par l'eau-de-vie et de fronts bombés par l'entêtement. Nous sommes descendus jusqu'au dernier degré de la spirale, jusqu'à la *fœmina simplex* du satirique latin. Tantôt nous voyons se dessiner, sur le fond d'une atmosphère où l'alcool et le tabac ont mêlé leurs vapeurs, la maigreur enflammée de la phtisie ou les rondeurs de l'adiposité, cette hideuse santé de la fainéantise. Dans un chaos brumeux et doré, non soupçonné par les chastetés indigentes, s'agitent et se convulsent des nymphes macabres et des poupées vivantes dont l'œil enfantin laisse échapper une clarté sinistre; cependant que derrière un comptoir chargé de bouteilles de liqueurs se prélasse une grosse mégère dont la tête, serrée dans un sale foulard qui dessine sur le mur l'ombre de ses pointes sataniques, fait penser que tout ce qui est voué au Mal est condamné à porter des cornes. (II, 721)

Statues, men, members of a harem, alcoholics, dolls, devils: the women of these drawings resemble anything but what they are. In this sense, Baudelaire exemplifies Clark's contention that the prostitute is unrepresentable: she must be analogized to something else in order to be described. He is even all too willing to supply such analogons. Although the paragraph starts with an opposition of *parfois* to *d'autres fois,* the basic structure of the passage is not binary but enumerative: verbs disappear and adjectives replace them, as though the narrator's primary burden were to qualify the prostitutes. These qualifiers are arranged in the simplest of orders:

---

universelle du XIXème siècle (Paris: Administration du Grand Dictionnaire Universelle, 1875), XIII, 289-298, and thus betrays a comparable will to power. There, in order to know the unmanageable subject of "Prostitution," Larousse distributes French prostitutes into 8 categories, and arranges these categories in descending order, ending with "la catégorie la plus vile et la plus abjecte," the *pierreuses* (XIII, 294).

a crescendo: *lourdes, mornes, stupides, extravagantes.* Further, the narrator speaks with the inclusive *nous,* as though he wished to hide behind another's corroboration of his opinion. Hysteria can be detected in this rhetoric: the narrator seems to be trying to master a perceived danger by naming it, and to reduce that fear by attributing it to another. As elsewhere, one could attribute this sympton to repressed desire: the *fœmina simples* is emminently available. All the other women Baudelaire has mentioned in the passage are elements of couples: father/daughter, husband/wife, lover/mistress. Now, when no man is present, the narrator calls the figures names which simultaneously betray his desire and his anxiety: Messalina, *mégère,* etc. In other words, not simply does recognition replace free judgment, that recognition is in the service of a desire for mastery.

That desire should be tied up with recognition is not obvious: theoretically, the drive to know is disinterested. Baudelaire intimates that it is not, however; his "Rêve parisien," dedicated to Constantin Guys, advances this argument by opposing a dream world to a real world, and suggesting that the latter offers satisfactions not available in the former.

I

De ce terrible paysage,
Tel que jamais mortel n'en vit,
Ce matin encore l'image,
Vague et lointaine, me ravit.

Le sommeil est plein de miracles!
Par un caprice singulier,
J'avais banni de ces spectacles
Le végétal irrégulier,

Et, peintre fier de mon génie,
Je savourais dans mon tableau
L'enivrante monotonie
Du métal, du marbre et de l'eau.

Babel d'escaliers et d'arcades,
C'était un palais infini,
Plein de bassins et de cascades
Tombant dans l'or mat ou bruni;

Et des cataractes pesantes,
Comme des rideaux de cristal,
Se suspendaient, éblouissantes,
A des murailles de métal.

Non d'arbres, mais de colonnades
Les étangs dormants s'entouraient,
Où de gigantesques naïades,
Comme des femmes, se miraient.

Des nappes d'eau s'épanchaient, bleues,
Entre des quais roses et verts,
Pendant des millions de lieues,
Vers les confins de l'univers;

C'étaient des pierres inouïes
Et des flots magiques; c'étaient
D'immenses glaces éblouïes
Par tout ce qu'elles reflétaient!

Insouciants et taciturnes,
Des Ganges, dans le firmament,
Versaient le trésor de leurs urnes
Dans des gouffres de diamant.

Architecte de mes féeries,
Je faisais, à ma volonté,
Sous un tunnel de pierreries
Passer un océan dompté;

Et tout, même la couleur noire,
Semblait fourbi, clair, irisé;
Le liquide enchâssait sa gloire
Dans le rayon cristallisé.

Nul astre d'ailleurs, nuls vestiges
De soleil, même au bas du ciel,
Pour illuminer ces prodiges,
Qui brillaient d'un feu personnel!

Et sur ces mouvantes merveilles
Planait (terrible nouveauté!
Tout pour l'œil, rien pour les oreilles!)
Un silence d'éternité.

II

Et rouvrant mes yeux pleins de flamme
J'ai vu l'horreur de mon taudis,
Et senti, rentrant dans mon âme,
La pointe des soucis maudits;

La pendule aux accents funèbres
Sonnait brutalement midi,
Et le ciel versait des ténèbres
Sur le triste monde engourdi. (I, 101-3)

The poem has been considered the expression of a characteristic fantasy, brought to an untimely end by the striking of a clock; the reader is asked to appreciate the fantasy as a product of the author's imagination. The dream expresses Baudelaire's "aesthetics": a world of stone, order, light and silence illustrates his "concept" of beauty. Such an interpretation is offered by Antoine Adam.[16]

In more comprehensive analyses, the title and structure of the poem attract critical attention: the poet's dream of a better, beautiful world is shattered by his awakening when he returns to worries and misery. Sartre proposes an interpretation of this type: "Au milieu des villes, au contraire, entouré d'objets précis dont l'existence est déterminée par leur rôle et qui sont tous auréolés d'une valeur et d'un prix, il se rassure: ils lui renvoient le reflet de ce qu'il souhaite être: une réalité *justifiée.*"[17] To existence Baudelaire opposes a world of artifice in which all things are part of a grand design, a design which serves ultimately to reassure the poet of his place: an ordered world allows one to deny one's own freedom. In support of such an interpretation, one could offer the imagery of the poem, which, insisting on architecture while refusing the vegetal, gives precedence to system over life. The tense struc-

---

[16] Antoine Adam, *Les Fleurs du mal,* by Charles Baudelaire (Paris: Garnier, 1961), pp. 396-8.

[17] Jean-Paul Sartre, *Baudelaire* (Paris: Gallimard, 1963), p. 133. Strictly speaking, the citation does not gloss "Rêve parisien." However, given Sartre's method (discussion of characteristic imagery rather than specific texts) and the thematic proximity of the texts under discussion to "Rêve parisien," I believe the use of the citation is legitimate.

ture – imperfect in part I, *passé composé* in part II – defines the former as descriptive, the latter as narrative. The poet is aware of time, and consequently, of choice, in part II. The fantasy of omnipotence is reduced to awareness of obligation. In short, Baudelaire embraces a concept of beauty the better to evade the anxieties of existence.

Such an interpretation is tempting, but fails to explain the dedication, which first appeared in the second edition of *Les Fleurs du mal,* to Constantin Guys. Why was Guys named? Jacques Crépet and Georges Blin have pointed out that Baudelaire offered an explanation of the dedication: "... la pièce ne présente, avec Constantin Guys, 'd'autre rapport *positif* et *matériel* que celui-ci: c'est que comme le poète de la pièce, il se lève généralement à midi.'"[18] If so, it would be appropriate to consider these lines descriptive of Guys's awakening at the end of "Rêve parisien": "'Quel ordre impérieux! quelle fanfare de lumière! Depuis plusieurs heures déjà, de la lumière partout! de la lumière perdue par mon sommeil! Que de choses *éclairées* j'aurais pu voir et que je n'ai pas vues!" (II, 692) Here Baudelaire writes the melody of "Rêve parisien" in a major key: not simply is an hour of awakening common to Guys and to the poet, but a sense of regret and a consequent longing to make up for lost time are too.

Secondly, although the last part is only two stanzas long, it possesses narrative weight at least equal to that of the first part, which describes fantasy. There is an unhappy urgency about the second part of the poem – in the *soucis maudits,* in the "brutal" striking of the clock – which drives the poet to consciousness. The poet abandons his dreaming for more pressing concerns, and although this abandonment is stated in a mood of regret, one must say that the shift from aesthetic appreciation to consciousness implies a desire for knowledge. The poem thus ends with questions, not with answers, questions which exemplify the drive for knowledge it illustrates. The poet's *soucis maudits* require response, just as the reader's desire to know more about them requires an answer. The desire for knowledge outweighs the pleasures of aesthetic appreciation.

---

[18] Crépet and Blin, eds., p. 481.

9

BEYOND FORM: *L'ŒUVRE ET LA VIE D'EUGÈNE DELACROIX*

Je résolus de m'informer du pourquoi, et de transformer ma volupté en connaissance . . . (II, 786)

Eugène Delacroix died on August 13, 1863; four days later, Baudelaire attended the painter's funeral, and over the course of the autumn, published *l'Œuvre et la vie d'Eugène Delacroix* in *L'Opinion nationale.* The essay, the second of only two monographs he was to write, shows signs of fatigue, and indeed, Baudelaire was to fall stricken in Namur only two years later. The poet reproduces passages from two earlier essays, and the obituary bears resemblance in places to the *Exposition universelle* article of 1855.[1] In it, Baudelaire, quoting Emerson, insists on the "concentration" of Delacroix's work.[2] The echoes of earlier essays, the references to "concentration," the "ultimate" character of this obituary article all invite consideration of the monograph as a distillation of Baudelaire's thoughts on painting, a summit of his aesthetic inquiry.

This meditation was of course prompted by death, and that motivation leaves its trace in the essay. Baudelaire stresses the possibility of compensation for Delacroix's loss, the possibility of

---

[1] Baudelaire quotes from his 1859 theory of the imagination (II, 624-5), and from a short 1861 article "Peintures murales d'Eugène Delacroix à Saint-Sulpice" (II, 729-31). See Pichois, ed., *Œuvres,* II, 1442-3.

[2] "The hero is he who is immovably centered" (II, 755) and "The one prudence in life is concentration; the one evil is dissipation." (II, 761) The citations are taken from *The Conduct of Life, Nature and Other Things* (Boston: Houghton and Mifflin, 1860). See Pichois, ed., *Œuvres,* I, 1488-9.

refurbishing the splendor of Delacroix's name, the possibility of spirit continuing despite the death of the body. In short, the obituary form itself requires an idealism, an assertion of the enduring over the transitory, of spirit over matter, of content over form. Nevertheless, I would argue that this essay accurately summarizes Baudelaire's solutions to the dilemmas of aesthetic judgment: faced with the impossibility of justifying a purely formal judgment, he paraphrases the works' contents in order to support his claim that Delacroix is the rival of Rubens, Raphael and Veronese.

Not surprisingly, the metaphor of translation occurs frequently in the obituary: translation presupposes a meaning independent of signifiers, capable of being represented by other signifiers. Thus, Delacroix "translates" the mysterious;[3] he "translates" words into plastic images;[4] most importantly, Delacroix needs, now more than ever, a "translator" who would transfer his works from their vulnerable oil-on-canvas support to the security of the printed medium:[5]

> Une des grandes préoccupations de notre peintre dans ses dernières années, était le jugement de la postérité et la solidité incertaine de ses œuvres. Tantôt son imagination si sensible s'enflammait à l'idée d'une gloire immortelle, tantôt il parlait amèrement de la fragilité des toiles et des couleurs. D'autres fois il citait avec envie les anciens maîtres, qui ont eu presque tous le bonheur d'être traduits par des graveurs habiles, dont la pointe ou le burin a su s'adapter à la nature de leur talent, et il regrettait ardemment de n'avoir pas trouvé son traducteur. (II, 769)

Of course, Baudelaire is explicitly suggesting a Meryon or a Gavarni, but he is implicitly suggesting himself: he hopes to

[3] ". . . quel est donc ce je ne sais quoi de mystérieux que Delacroix, pour la gloire de notre siècle, a mieux traduit qu'aucun autre?" (II, 744)

[4] ". . . il a pu traduire la *parole* par des images plastiques plus vives et plus approximantes que celles d'aucun créateur de même profession . . . " (II, 743)

[5] It bears recalling that "translation" means also "to transfer to heaven or to a nontemporal condition without death." *(Webster's Seventh New Collegiate Dictionary* Springfield: G. & C. Merriam Company, 1961) Baudelaire's explicit aim cannot be better described than to "translate" Delacroix in this sense.

"translate" Delacroix's forms, just as Delacroix translated Dante, Shakespeare and Goethe.

It can be objected that "translations," especially good ones, involve play of the signifier just as much as they ensure the communication of a message. Baudelaire makes it plain however that by "translation" he means communication, not play, and that such communication of content is the hallmark of beauty. The issue is that of the copy: Delacroix, a complete artist, employs two distinct methods of copying, one of which is playful, the other of which is faithful:

> Il avait deux manières très distinctes de copier. L'une, libre et large, faite moitié de fidélité, moitié de trahison, et où il mettait beaucoup de lui-même. De cette méthode résultait un composé bâtard et charmant, jetant l'esprit dans une incertitude agréable . . . Dans l'autre manière, Delacroix se faisait l'esclave le plus obéissant et le plus humble de son modèle, et il arrivait à une exactitude d'imitation dont peuvent douter ceux qui n'ont pas vu ces miracles. (II, 762)

It would be hard to find an example corresponding better to "free beauty" than the first manner: it is "free," "uncertain," "composite." And yet, it is only "charming" and "agreeable": the second method is "miraculous."[6] If Delacroix only achieves "miracles" through servile imitation, one can infer that, Poe and Baudelaire's allegiance to him to the contrary, free play is not a sufficient condition for Baudelairian beauty: he insists on content, the transmission of some kind of knowledge. This is, I believe, the sense of the famous definition of beauty from *Fusées:*

---

[6] It should be noted, in support of Armand Moss's thesis (that Baudelaire overstates the extent and the warmth of this friendship with Delacroix), that this formulation of the notion of copy is practically the contrary of Delacroix's:

> La gravure est une véritable traduction, c'est-à-dire l'art de transporter une idée d'un art dans un autre comme le traducteur le fait à l'égard d'un livre écrit dans une langue et qu'il transporte dans la sienne. La langue du graveur, et c'est ici que se montre son génie, ne consiste pas seulement à imiter par le moyen de son art les effets de la peinture, qui est comme une autre langue. Il a, si l'on peut parler ainsi, sa langue à lui qui marque d'un cachet particulier ses ouvrages, et qui, dans une traduction fidèle de l'ouvrage qu'il imite, laisse éclater son génie. (*Journal,* pp. 619-20)

> J'ai trouvé la définition du Beau, – de mon Beau. C'est quelque chose d'ardent et de triste, quelque chose d'un peu vague, laissant carrière à la conjecture. . . . Le mystère, le regret sont aussi des caractères du Beau. . . . Je ne prétends pas que la Joie ne puisse pas s'associer avec la Beauté, mais je dis que la Joie (en) est un des ornements les plus vulgaires; – tandis que la Mélancolie en est pour ainsi dire l'illustre compagne, à ce point que je ne conçois guère (mon cerveau serait-il un miroir ensorcelé?) un type de Beauté où il n'y ait du *Malheur.* (I, 657-8)

Baudelaire cannot conceive of an aesthetics distinct from ethics; moral considerations (necessarily arising from notions of happiness and unhappiness) cannot be dissociated from questions of beauty.

When Delacroix "translated" the *Inferno, Hamlet,* or *Faust,* he did what is commonly understood by "translation": he represented a moment or scene of the narrative in pictorial terms: figures can be identified by decoding their attributes; moment and movement can be inferred from context. However, when Baudelaire translates Delacroix, something else must be understood: the translation of form, not of anecdote. Not surprisingly, figures of pure form (things that Kant would qualify as "free beauties") abound in the essay. Delacroix is a bouquet-covered volcano, or a tiger: "On eût dit un cratère de volcan artistement caché par des bouquets de fleurs." (II, 758) ". . . le tigre, attentif à sa proie, a moins de lumière dans les yeux et de frémissements impatients dans les muscles que n'en laissait voir notre grand peintre . . ." (II, 759) He is shrouded in ice (II, 757); his savage nature is belied by an appearance of courtesy and obedience to convention. Thus, any "translation" of Delacroix worthy of the name would account not simply for the subject matter but for the surfaces of his works; it would derive meaning from form, not from language. Beneath these surfaces a meaning waits to be laid bare.

In these respects, Baudelaire resembles Heinrich Heine, whose *Salon de 1831* he quoted in 1846. There, Heine defines the critic as an interpreter who brings a message hidden from the artist to consciousness, and significantly, that message is found in a bouquet of flowers:

> L'artiste resemble à cette princesse somnambule qui, la nuit dans les jardins de Bagdad, cueillait avec la science la plus profonde de l'amour et disposait en sélam les fleurs les plus rares et n'en

> savait plus la signification quand elle se réveillait. Puis elle s'asseyait le matin dans son harem, regardait son bouquet de la nuit, se perdait en réflexions comme à propos d'un songe oublié et finissait par l'envoyer au calife bien-aimé. Le gras eunuque qui le portait, tout ravi qu'il était à la vue de ces belles fleurs, n'en soupçonnait pas le sens. Mais Haroun-el-Radschid, chef des Croyants, successeur du prophète, possesseur de l'anneau de Salomon, comprenait tout de suite le langage du bouquet; son cœur bondissait de joie; il baisait chaque fleur et il riait en sentant ses larmes tomber sur sa longue barbe.
>
> Je ne suis ni successeur du prophète ni possesseur de l'anneau de Salomon, je n'ai pas non plus de barbe longue, mais je puis assurer pourtant que j'ai compris le beau sélam que Decamps nous a rapporté de l'Orient . . .[7]

"Science," "signification," "comprehension": the bouquet Heine describes is more important for its content than for its arrangement, a curious state of affairs for a decorative object. For Heine, beauty can please without being understood (as the eunuch shows), but there *is* something to be understood. I would argue that the same holds true for Baudelaire: beauty begs to be understood, and rewards efforts to do so.

Both the personality and the works of Delacroix exemplify this movement: the poet initially reacts to the beauty of "surfaces," but that beauty in turn demands a more convincing demonstration and Baudelaire thus seeks its reasons in the surfaces he appreciates. Delacroix's personality comprises two registers, a "dualité de la nature" (II, 743); there is on one hand an appearance and on the other a secret truth. The former, presented to the world, and indeed defined by the world, causes pleasure: ". . . Eugène Delacroix apparaissait simplement comme un homme *éclairé,* dans le sens honorable du mot, comme un parfait *gentleman* sans préjugés et sans passions." (II, 757) Delacroix is a dandy (II, 759). More significantly, Baudelaire appreciates Delacroix's "manners": "Il y avait en lui beaucoup de l'homme du monde; cette partie-là était destinée à

[7] Heinrich Heine, *De la France,* ed. Paul Laveau, in *Werke* (Berlin: Akademie-Verlag, 1977), XVIII, 123. Jean-Jacques Rousseau cites the "sélam" as a means of non-verbal communication in his *Essai sur l'origine des langues,* Charles Porset, ed. (Paris: A. G. Nizet, 1970), p. 37. For further references on this subject, see Peter Brooks, *The Melodramatic Imagination* (New Haven: Yale University Press: 1976), p. 212.

voiler la première et à la faire pardonner." (II, 758) "Il tirait aussi de lui-même, . . . une certitude, une aisance de manières merveilleuse, avec une politesse qui admettait, comme un prisme, toutes les nuances, depuis la bonhomie la plus cordiale jusqu'à l'impertinence la plus irréprochable." (II, 759) The pleasure Baudelaire takes in admiring Delacroix can only be aesthetic: disinterested, demanding the assent of his audience, he refers to conceptions of decorum admired only in the breaking.

Delacroix's conduct occasions delectation in Baudelaire, but what must be noted is that the painter's courtesy and politesse can only imply a rebellious nature requiring restraint, and thus the very beauty of Delacroix's manners is founded on something that is not beautiful. Politeness hides egotism; calm conceals violence. Delacroix's *dandysme* defines him as a resident of a certain country at a certain moment, but closer inspection reveals traits which suggest different times and places, and a savage who refuses the conventions the "gentleman" willingly accepts:

> Le tigre, attentif à sa proie, a moins de lumière dans les yeux et de frémissements impatients dans les muscles que n'en laissait voir notre grand peintre, quand toute son âme était dardée sur une idée ou voulait s'emparer d'un rêve. Le caractère physique même de sa physionomie, son teint de Péruvien ou de Malais, ses yeux grands et noirs, mais rapetissés par les clignotements de l'attention, et qui semblaient déguster la lumière, ses cheveux abondants et lustrés, son front entêté, ses lèvres serrées, auxquelles une tension perpétuelle de volonté communiquait une expression cruelle, toute sa personne enfin suggérait l'idée d'une origine exotique. Il m'est arrivé plus d'une fois, en le regardant, de rêver des anciens souverains du Mexique, de ce Moctézuma dont la main habile aux sacrifices pouvait immoler en un seul jour trois mille créatures humaines sur l'autel pyramidal du Soleil, ou bien de ces princes hindous qui, dans les splendeurs des plus glorieuses fêtes, portent au fond de leurs yeux une sorte d'avidité insatisfaite et une nostalgie inexplicable, quelque chose comme le souvenir et le regret de choses non connues. (II, 759-60)

"Regret for things never known": the phrase sums up Baudelaire's conception of beauty. Beauty is an incitement to learn, a promise of knowledge which can never be fulfilled; it seems as though it even consists in knowledge *(regret)*, but such knowledge is only an illusion *(non connues)*. Beauty is thus an illusion of knowledge which hopes to become certainty. In the case of Delacroix, the beauty of the painter's personality overlies violence; beneath the surface which may be enjoyed lies a mystery which must be known. Baudelaire exchanges an appearance for a mystery, trades pleasure for knowledge.

It is relatively easy to show how Baudelaire's appreciation of Delacroix's manners gives way to a more insistent demand to know the painter's origins: manners are not a common subject of aesthetic appreciation. However, when formal analysis becomes content analysis, one can be sure that there is some instability in the aesthetic judgment; this is precisely what occurs in *L'Œuvre et la vie d'Eugène Delacroix*. Moreover, this movement happens at the very moment Baudelaire argues for the autonomy of formal appreciation of Delacroix's paintings.

As a colorist, Baudelaire maintains, Delacroix suffered from the common prejudice: that color, more material than line, was less capable of awakening noble thoughts. Those who hold this opinion are in error, he argues:

> J'ai souvent entendu des personnes de cette espèce établir une hiérarchie des qualités, absolument inintelligible pour moi; affirmer, par exemple, que la faculté qui permet à celui-ci de créer un contour exact, ou à celui-là un contour d'une beauté surnaturelle, est supérieure à la faculté qui sait assembler des couleurs d'une manière enchanteresse. Selon ces gens-là, la couleur ne rêve pas, ne pense pas, ne parle pas. (II, 752)

Rather, color *and* line dream, think, and speak, and should be opposed in this respect to subject: form can transmit a message just as Decamps' bouquet spoke to Heine; the proof of such communication is the existence of messages vehicled by form and entirely different from the message vehicled by the content of the work:

> La ligne et la couleur font penser et rêver toutes les deux; les plaisirs qui en dérivent sont d'une nature différente mais parfaitement égale et absolument indépendante du sujet du tableau. (II, 753)

This contention is entirely assimilable to Kantian aesthetics, and Poe too would be happy with it: form – color or line – can be appreciated without reference to content, in a free play which relieves the viewer of any need to compare form with a referent. The verbs *penser* and *parler* might give room for pause, but in general terms, Baudelaire is pleading for the autonomous appreciation of form.

What one can say however about form once content has been abstracted from it is uncertain, and Baudelaire thus offers an example of such an independent reading:

> Un tableau de Delacroix, placé à une trop grande distance pour que vous puissiez juger de l'agrément des contours ou de la qualité plus ou moins dramatique du sujet, vous pénètre déjà d'une volupté surnaturelle. Il vous semble qu'une atmosphère magique a marché vers vous et vous enveloppe. Sombre, délicieuse pourtant, lumineuse, mais tranquille, cette impression, qui prend pour toujours sa place dans votre mémoire, prouve le vrai, le parfait coloriste. Et l'analyse du sujet, quand vous vous approchez, n'enlèvera rien et n'ajoutera rien à ce plaisir primitif, dont la source est ailleurs et loin de toute pensée concrète.
>
> Je puis inverser l'exemple. Une figure bien dessinée vous pénètre d'un plaisir tout à fait étranger au sujet. Voluptueuse ou terrible, cette figure ne doit son charme qu'à l'arabesque qu'elle découpe dans l'espace. Les membres d'un martyr qu'on écorche, le corps d'une nymphe pâmée, s'ils sont savamment dessinés, comportent un genre de plaisir dans les éléments duquel le sujet n'entre pour rien; si pour vous il en est autrement, je serai forcé de croire que vous êtes un bourreau ou un libertin. (II, 753)

It is possible to appreciate color even when line and subject cannot be discerned; the pleasure of color is thus autonomous and the most immediate of visual pleasures. Further, those who confuse the appreciation of subject and that of form can only be projecting the desires aroused by the subject into their reading of form.

Again, the explicit statement is entirely orthodox: the pleasure of form is distinct from recognition of content, and because it is not based on recognition, it alone is aesthetic. And yet, Baudelaire's analysis of form is heavily endebted to his description of content. The paintings he evokes represent scenes of violence and of love: "un martyr qu'on écorche, le corps d'une nymphe pâmée . . .,"subjects whose gravitational pull, as it were, is strong enough to elicit the projections of *bourreaux* and *libertins*. Further, the words supposedly descriptive of the autonomous (and disinterested) pleasures of form echo these subjects: the sadistic *découper,* the sexually-suggestive *volupté* and *pénétrer*. In other words, what Baudelaire has promised as an example of the autonomy of formal pleasure is a restatement of content, as though form could only echo content, as though content's demand for statement had always to be met.

Such movements or slippages are significant, for they indicate that Baudelaire conceived of beauty as more than formal, and thus, that his attachment to content was strong enough overstep his allegiance to free beauty. Just as significantly, however, such shifts in aesthetic thought are starting points for poetic reflection: "Hymne à la Beauté," "Les Phares," "Danse Macabre," and "Rêve Parisien" show how poetic language employs and inflects notions of universality, purposiveness, disinterestedness and recognition. "Horreur Sympathique," from 1860 and ostensibly a transposition of Delacroix's *Ovide en exil chez les Scythes,* suggests, beauty's freedom to the contrary, that knowledge generally can be gleaned from aesthetic experience:

De ce ciel bizarre et livide,
Tourmenté comme ton destin,
Quels pensers dans ton âme vide
4 Descendent? réponds, libertin.

– Insatiablement avide
De l'obscur et de l'incertain,
Je ne geindrai pas comme Ovide
8 Chassé du paradis latin.

Cieux déchirés comme des grèves,
En vous se mire mon orgueil;
11 Vos vastes nuages en deuil

Sont les corbillards de mes rêves,
Et vos lueurs sont le reflet
14 De l'Enfer où mon cœur se plaît. (II, 77-8)

The poem is about the relation of pleasure to knowledge: on the one hand, its basic question is "Do the pleasant forms of clouds transmit any knowledge?" On the other, it asks whether pleasure generally implies knowledge: does pleasure turn to regret, as it did for Ovid? Is aesthetic pleasure the vehicle of some content? A debate surrounding the poem echoes these questions and tends to confirm their relevance: what painting is the poem about? In 1942, Crépet and Blin argued that "Horreur sympathique" was the transposition into verse of Boudin's pastels, already transposed into prose in the *Salon de 1859*.[8] In 1961, Adam argued that Delacroix's *Ovide en exil chez les Scythes* was the true pretext for the poem.[9] In 1976, Pichois indicated both Boudin's and Delacroix's works as the origins of the poem.[10] All agree that despite the poem's dialogue structure and insistence on subjective state, it is about a painting; that a fixed form must be assigned to "ce ciel bizarre et livide" to "cieux déchirés," that knowledge of a referent is essential to appreciation of the poem. These reactions are perfectly appropriate to the poem, and are, perhaps, the only appropriate response to it. However, it should be pointed out that they cannot be proved any more than an aesthetic judgment can.

Initially, the poet seems to assert that pleasure and knowledge are distinct. The poem, an exchange between a first person (whom

---

[8] Jacques Crépet and Georges Blin write:

> On sait que Baudelaire a célébré maintes fois la magie des nuages . . .: ici dans *Bénédiction* . . . et dans *Le Voyage* . . . – dans les *PPP* . . ., où on le voit se baptiser le 'marchand de nuages' . . . et surtout dans *CE* à propos des pastels de Boudin 'le roi des ceils', comme l'appelait Corot. Boudin habitait à Honfleur le 'pavillion des Trente-Six-Marches' et se trouvait ainsi le voisin de Mme. Aupick. Baudelaire est allé visiter son atelier et en avait gardé une impression que la page des *CE* rend en termes assez proches de ceux qu'on trouve aux v. 1, 9 et 11 de notre pièce . . .

Crépet and Blin, eds., p. 430.

[9] Antoine Adam writes "Si l'on observe que Baudelaire va dans la deuxième strophe parle d'Ovide exilé, que le libertin du vers 4 est certainement Ovide, on est amené à conclure, à la suite de Jean Prévost, que ce *'ciel bizarre et livide'*, c'est le ciel du tableau de Delacroix. Adam, p. 367.

[10] Claude Pichois agrees with Crépet, Blin and Adam: "C'est à la fois en marge d'*Un mangeur d'opium* . . . et par référence au tableau de Delacroix, *Ovide en exil chez les Scythes* . . ., comme en souvenir des œuvres de Boudin qu'il a vues à Honfleur en 1859 . . . que Baudelaire compose ce sonnet." See Pichois, ed., *Œuvres*, I, 983.

I will call the narrator) and a second (whom I will call the poet), reveals the existence of pleasure where one would have expected regret: asked what associations the clouds bring to mind, the poet responds with an appreciation of their forms, describing their light, contour, and shading; the question is rude ("ton âme vide," "réponds libertin") and the narrator's tone indicates that he is seeking to hurt the poet with it. If so, the thoughts demanded are of a moral order, regrets and reflections on the causes of present unhappiness. Explicitly, the poet refuses to regret "je ne geindrai pas," and one can take the appreciation of form as his mode of evasion. This difference accounts for the curiously oblique dialogue that takes place; where *vous* responds to *tu,* where the narrator addresses the poet, while the poet addresses nature. Finally, the poet asserts that even though he is in Hell, he is pleased to be there: the aesthetic contemplation of one's state produces a pleasure greater than the pain of that state. The formal perfection of the poem – it is as sonnet – supports readings which assert the primacy of form. The poem thus exemplifies the claim that aesthetic enjoyment lies in the free play of the imagination: the poet is sufficiently disinterested in his condition to find its correspondance to exterior nature a subject of aesthetic pleasure.

If so, the poem represents a modification of the typical Romantic schema: ordinarily, the poet complains of a lack of harmony between self and nature, and aspires to some union with nature; happiness would lie in such harmony. This is the case of "Le Lac," for example, or "Tristesse d'Olympio." Here, by contrast, the poet is in harmony with nature, but only because nature reflects his unhappiness. And yet, that harmony is a source of pleasure: while Olympio was unhappy because he was out of step with nature, Baudelaire's poet is happy despite the fact he is in step with nature. In other words, the homology between self and nature is beautiful, even if it is not symbolic.

A few elements still need elucidating, however; for a poem about the sky (or about a painting), it is singularly abstract: the vocabulary of theology *(orgueil, Enfer)* tends to take away from the sensual character of an apology of pleasure. Each form the poet contemplates is translated into subjective terms: *cieux* becomes *orgueil, nuages* becomes *rêves,* and *lueurs* resembles the poet's heart. Further, each concrete element is not allowed to stand alone, but is compared to another element, and one could even label the analogies obsessive. The sky resembles destiny; the clouds resemble beaches which in turn mirror the poet's pride; the clouds resemble the poet's dreams; and the light resembles the Hell of his soul. The poet seeks repeatedly to define his perceptions, but no comparison is satisfactory. Like a debtor trying to pay a debt with borrowed money, the poet moves further from the definition he seeks with each analogy he makes. In other words, even before the poet translates the outer world into an inner vocabulary, that outer world has undergone a transformation which implies that it has already been conceptualized, and if one takes pleasure in something because it is like something else, that enjoyment is not aesthetic but cognitive.

More so perhaps than any other poet, Baudelaire was aware of the sensory basis of aesthetic judgment: such judgments refer only to subjective pleasure, and consequently should give primacy to formal elements. At every turn, however, Baudelaire, like any critic, encounters what could be called the temptation of knowledge: the tendency to supply logic and reference where only judgment is demanded. This temptation becomes all the stronger when mortality is in question, as though knowledge were inherently more important than judgment. It would be impossible to argue this point; what can be said however is that while aesthetic judgment refers only to its source, knowledge appears to exist independently of such sources, and when death eliminates judges, knowledge endures.

CONCLUSION

"La poésie . . . n'a pas d'autre but qu'elle-même." (II, 333) Baudelaire's paraphrase of Poe's "Poetic Principle" has often been taken as the theory of beauty to which he adhered, and there is a certain wisdom to this: strictly speaking, beauty can only be defined as distinct from any content – science, morals, truth –, and reference to such content in aesthetic judgment can only diminish the force of such judgments. To this extent, Baudelaire's rehearsal of Poe's credo is perfectly logical, and his aesthetics is correspondingly Kantian. Baudelaire would seem to be an advocate of "free beauty": his evaluations are free from interest, refer to no purpose or concept, and exemplify a beauty which can only be asserted, never proved.

What makes Baudelaire's aesthetics genuinely Kantian however is the force with which he asserts his judgments: he does not propose his essays as expression of individual taste; these essays, from 1846 onwards, are much more emphatic and apodictic. Baudelaire demands that his audience agree with his judgments, and such demands, made on behalf of unprovable assertions, make his criticism simultaneously unacceptable and aesthetic, for he requires agreement and yet can furnish no support.

This paradox exists in any aesthetics, and elicits a response of the type Kant himself provided: to redefine beauty as possessing a content, and hence, provable. Kant's substitution of "ideal beauty" for "free beauty" serves this purpose; Hugo, Ruskin, and Proust all develop comparable solutions. Baudelaire uses theory and description to support his judgments; theories which justify judgments through logical argument, descriptions which do so through reference.

If aesthetic judgment cannot be proved in the first place, however, the theory that defends it can only be a fiction, and if so, the status of description in art criticism is essentially that of description in narrative: description there is a figure; its function is to stop demands for further explanation by referring to inarticulate reality. In Baudelaire's art criticism, and, I believe, in art criticism generally, the function of description is identical to its function in narrative: description is the last trope of argument; it is a device which, producing the celebrated *effet de réel,* hopes to put an end to logical interrogation. Intentions and effects are not one, however, and here there is a divergence: although description's job is to stop the search for meaning, its effect is to continue that search. This is what Barthes and Riffaterre discovered in their analyses of the *effet de réel,* where the apparent failure of an element to signify is in turn significant. In art-criticism, the trope that ends argument in turn generates meanings.

If so, one conclusion to be derived from this analysis is that the distinction between narrative and art criticism is even more difficult to maintain than has been suggested. The "arguments" of both discourses are more similar than has been thought: both are radically fictitious. Both employ description, and further, the relation of description to argument is identical in the two cases.

What is also apparent in Baudelaire's art-criticism is that description is the less reliable of the two supports of aesthetic judgment. While in his theory, Baudelaire tends to elaborate the characteristic freedoms and ambition of aesthetic judgment, in his description, he speaks a language of system and determinism. Where theory speaks of universal assent, description speaks of individual preference; where the former advocates freedom from purpose, the latter acknowledges ultimate aims; where disinterest is proposed, desire emerges, and where newness is sought, one discovers what one already knew. A second conclusion then would be that the figural status of description precludes its use in the service of argument.

Subjectivity, purpose, desire, recognition: these are so many reasons for aesthetic preference, but precisely because they are reasons, they have nothing to do with aesthetics. And yet, knowledge is what aesthetic judgment is fated to seek: reasons for its claim to universal assent, arguments to stop "rude dismissal of its claim," references to deflect attention from its own apodictic character. If as I argue in the first chapter, criticism assumes aesthetic judgment to its benefit, what is also true is that such judgment demands the certainties of scientific discourse. Thus a third conclusion would be that in art criticism, the discourse of science and subjective discourse are inextricably interwoven, each one appealing to the other for its justification.

Finally, the case of Baudelaire's art-criticism has implications for criticism more generally. If aesthetic judgment tends to generate a search for knowledge, can one fail to conclude that behind authoritative discourses may lie an aesthetic impulse, which, because it is paradoxical and profoundly irrational, would color its assertions of authority? A case in point would be Baudelaire's defense of Delacroix, a cause already won in 1845, when the poet's critical life began, but which he nonetheless pleads in most of his essays, using comparison, demonstration, description and poetry to make the point that Delacroix's knowledge, abilities, and fame are universal. And yet, it would be difficult to say that such imposition of an already-accepted opinion detracts from the interest of his essays; rather, one should say that the efforts Baudelaire makes to resurrect Delacroix's battles and victories is at the basis of his criticism's literary merit. This is of course just one example, but others can be adduced; suffice it to say that it is in the tension between its transmission of knowledge and its imposition of judgment that the poetry of Baudelaire's art criticism is most evident.

BIBLIOGRAPHY

The bibliography is divided into two parts, corresponding to the major divisions of the book. When a book or article has been referred to in both Parts I and II, it is included in the bibliography of the part where it is cited most often.

PART I: A POETICS OF ART CRITICISM

Abrams, Meyer H. *The Mirror and the Lamp.* New York: Oxford University Press, 1953.

Aristotle. *Aristotle's Poetics.* Trans. Leon Golden. Tallahassee: University Presses of Florida, 1981.

Barthes, Roland. *Système de la mode.* Paris: Editions du Seuil, 1971.

Bois, Y.-A. et al., eds. *Histoire/Théorie de l'Art.* In *Critique,* 315/316 (1973).

Bonnefis, Philippe, and Pierre Reboul, eds. *Des Mots et des couleurs.* Lille: Publications de l'Université de Lille, 1979.

Bonnefoy, Yves. *Le Nuage rouge.* Paris: Mercure de France, 1977.

———. *L'Improbable,* suivi de *Un Rêve fait à Mantoue.* Paris: Gallimard, 1980.

Bouverot, Danielle. "La Rhétorique dans le discours sur la peinture, ou la métonymie généralisée, d'après la critique romantique." In *Rhétoriques, Sémiotiques, Revue d'Esthétique,* 1-2 (1979), 55-74.

Breton, André. *Le Surréalisme et la peinture.* Paris: Gallimard, 1965.

Butlin, Martin and E. Joll. *The Paintings of J. M. W. Turner.* 2 vols. New Haven: Yale University Press, 1975.

Chateaubriand, François-René de. *Œuvres romanesques et voyages.* Ed. M. Regard. Paris: Gallimard (Bibliothèque de la Pléiade), 1969.

Claudel, Paul. *L'Œil écoute.* Paris: Gallimard, 1946.

Culler, Jonathan. *The Pursuit of Signs.* Ithaca: Cornell University Press, 1981.

Damisch, Hubert. *Théorie du nuage.* Paris: Editions du Seuil, 1972.

Derrida, Jacques. *La Vérité en peinture.* Paris: Flammarion, 1978.

Dumarsais, César C. *Les Tropes avec un commentaire raisonné par M. Fontanier.* 1818; rpt. Genève: Slatkine, 1967.

Frye, Northrop. *Anatomy of Criticism: Four Essays.* Princeton: Princeton University Press, 1957.

Gaudon, Jean. *Le Temps de la contemplation.* Paris: Flammarion, 1969.

———. "Vers une rhétorique de la démesure: *William Shakespeare.*" *Romantisme,* 3 (1972), 78-85.

Gaudon, Jean. "Victor Hugo: Mesure et démesure." *Revue d'Histoire Littéraire de la France,* LXXX (1980), 222-230.

———, ed. *Le Rhin.* By Victor Hugo. 2 vols. Paris: Imprimerie Nationale, 1984.

Gaudon, Sheila. "James Pradier, Victor Hugo et l'arc de triomphe de l'Etoile." *Revue d'Histoire Littéraire de la France,* 68, No. 5 (1968), 713-25.

Genette, Gérard. *Figures II.* Paris: Editions du Seuil, 1969.

Gilpin, William. *Essays on Picturesque Beauty.* 1791; rpt. Wemstead, Gregg International Publishers Limited, 1972.

Gombrich, Ernst. *Art and Illusion.* Princeton: Princeton University Press, 1960.

———. *The Sense of Order.* Ithaca: Cornell University Press, 1979.

Hermeren, Goran. *Representation and Meaning in the Visual Arts.* Stockholm: Laromedels-Forlaget, 1969.

Jean-Aubry, Georges. *Eugène Boudin d'après des documents inédits.* Paris: Editions Bernheim-Jeune, 1922.

Kittay, Jeffrey, ed. *Towards a Theory of Description.* No. 61 of *Yale French Studies,* 1981.

de Knyff, G. *Eugène Boudin raconté par lui-même.* Paris: Editions Mayer, 1976.

Krieger, Murray. "The Ekphrastic Principle and the Still Movement of Poetry." In *The Play and the Place of Criticism.* Baltimore: The Johns Hopkins University Press, 1967, 105-28.

Lamy, Bernard. *La Rhétorique ou l'art de parler.* 1699; rpt. Brighton: The University of Sussex Library, 1969.

Leroux, Pierre. *Œuvres.* 1850-1; rpt. Genève: Slatkine, 1978.

Mallarmé, Stéphane. *Œuvres complètes.* Eds. H. Mondor and G. Jean-Aubry. Paris: Gallimard (Bibliothèque de la Pléiade), 1945.

Mallion, Jean. *Victor Hugo et l'art architectural.* Paris: Presses Universitaires de France, 1962.

de Man, Paul. "Intentional Structure of the Romantic Image." In *Wordsworth.* Ed. M. H. Abrams. Englewood Cliffs: Prentice Hall, 1972.

———. "The Rhetoric of Temporality." In *Interpretation.* Ed. C. Singleton. Baltimore: The Johns Hopkins University Press, 1969.

———. "The Epistemology of Metaphor." In *On Metaphor.* Ed. S. Sacks. Chicago: University of Chicago Press, 1979.

———. "The Resistance to Theory." *Yale French Studies,* 63 (1982), 3-20.

Marin, Louis. *Etudes sémiologiques: écritures, peintures.* Paris: Klincksieck, 1971.

Mitchell, W. J. T., ed. *The Language of Images,* Vol. 6, No. 3 of *Critical Inquiry,* 1980.

Pascal, Blaise. *Œuvres complètes.* Paris: Editions du Seuil, 1963.

Pater, Walter. *The Renaissance.* Chicago: Pandora Books, 1978.

Paulson, Ronald. "Turner's Graffiti: The Sun and its Glosses." In *Images of Romanticism.* Ed. Karl Kroeber. New Haven: Yale University Press, 1982.

———. *Literary Landscape: Turner and Constable.* New Haven: Yale University Press, 1982.

Philostratus. *Imagines.* Trans. Fairbanks. Cambridge: Loeb, 1931.

Planche, Gustave. "*Les Voix intérieures* de M. V. Hugo." *La Revue des Deux Mondes,* 11, 4ème série (1837), 161-84.

Plutarch. *Plutarch's Moralia.* Trans. F. C. Babbit. Cambridge: Harvard University Press, 1957.

Poulet, Georges, ed. *Les Chemins actuels de la critique.* Paris: Plon, 1967.

Praz, Mario. *Mnemosyne.* Princeton: Princeton University Press, 1970.

Proust, Marcel. *Contre Sainte-Beuve.* Ed. Pierre Clarac. Paris: Gallimard (Bibliothèque de la Pléiade), 1971.

Riffaterre, Michael. "Système d'un genre descriptif." *Poétique,* 9 (1972), 15-30.
———. *La Production du texte.* Paris: Editions du Seuil. 1979.
———. "Descriptive imagery." *Yale French Studies,* 61 (1981), 107-25.
———. "Interpretation and Undecidability." *New Literary History* (1981), 227-42.
Ruskin, John. *The Works of John Ruskin* (Library Edition). 39 vols. Eds. E. T. Cook and A. Wedderburn. London: George Allen and Sons, 1903-12.
———. *La Bible d'Amiens.* Trans. Marcel Proust. Paris: Mercure de France, 1947.
Sacks, Sheldon, ed. *On Metaphor.* Chicago: University of Chicago Press, 1979.
Saint-Lambert, Jean-François de. *Les Saisons.* 3ème éd. Amsterdam: 1771.
Scheffer, Jean-Louis. *Scénographie d'un tableau.* Paris: Editions du Seuil, 1969.
Spitzer, Leo. "The Ode on a Grecian Urn." In *Essays on English and American Literature.* Ed. Hatcher. Princeton: Princeton University Press, 1962.
Todorov, Tsvetan. *Théories du symbole.* Paris: Editions du Seuil, 1977.
Wimsatt, W. K. *The Verbal Icon.* Lexington: The University of Kentucky Press, 1954.

PART II: THE POETRY OF BAUDELAIRE'S ART CRITICISM

MODERN EDITIONS OF WORKS BY CHARLES BAUDELAIRE
(Chronological Order)

Ferran, André, ed. *Le* Salon de 1845 *de Charles Baudelaire.* By Charles Baudelaire. Toulouse: Aux Editions de l'Archer, 1933.
Crépet, Jacques, and Georges Blin, eds. *Les Fleurs du mal.* By Charles Baudelaire. Paris: José Corti, 1942.
Baudelaire, Charles, trans. *Œuvres en prose.* By Edgar Allan Poe. Paris: Gallimard (Bibliothèque de la Pléiade), 1951.
Mayne, Jonathan, trans. *The Mirror of Art.* By Charles Baudelaire. London: Phaidon, 1955.
Pommier, Jean, and Claude Pichois, eds. *Les Fleurs du mal.* By Charles Baudelaire. Paris: Club des Libraires de France, 1959.
Adam, Antoine, ed. *Les Fleurs du mal.* By Charles Baudelaire. Paris: Garnier, 1961.
Lemaître, Henri, ed. *Curiosités esthétiques – l'Art romantique.* By Charles Baudelaire. Paris: Garnier, 1962.
———. *Petits poèmes en prose.* By Charles Baudelaire. Paris: Garnier, 1962.
Mayne, Jonathan, trans. *The Painter of Modern Life.* By Charles Baudelaire. London, Phaidon, 1964.
Pichois, Claude, ed. *Correspondance.* By Charles Baudelaire. 2 vols. Paris: Gallimard (Bibliothèque de la Pléiade), 1973.
———. *Œuvres complètes.* By Charles Baudelaire. 2 vols. Paris: Gallimard (Bibliothèque de la Pléiade), 1975.
Kelley, David, ed. *Salon de 1846.* By Charles Baudelaire. Oxford: The Clarendon Press, 1975.

OTHER WORKS

Abel, Elizabeth. "Redefining the Sister Arts: Baudelaire's Response to the Art of Delacroix." *Critical Inquiry,* 6 (1980), 363-384.
About, Edmond. *Voyage à travers l'exposition des beaux-arts.* Paris: Hachette, 1855.
Appleton, Jay. *The Experience of Landscape.* New York: John Wiley & Sons, 1975.
Austin, Lloyd James. *L'Univers poétique de Baudelaire.* Paris: Mercure de France, 1956.

Austin, Lloyd James. "Baudelaire et Delacroix." In *Baudelaire.* Actes du Colloque de Nice. 25-7 May, 1967. Nice: Minard. 1968, 13-25.

Babinet, M. "De la lumière artificielle." *La Revue des Deux Mondes.* 25ème année, seconde série, nouvelle période, vol. 1212 (1855).

Barbey d'Aurevilly, Jules-Amédée. *Du dandysme et de Georges Brummel.* (Paris: Emile-Paul Frères, 1918).

Barthes, Roland. *La Chambre claire.* Paris: Edition du Seuil, 1980.

———. "Rhétorique de l'image." In *L'Obvie et l'obtus.* Paris: Editions du Seuil, 1982, 25-42.

———. "L'Effet de réel." In *Le Bruissement de la Langue.* Paris: Editions du Seuil, 1984, 167-74.

Batteux, Charles. *Les Beaux-Arts réduits à un même principe.* 1773; rpt. Genève: Slatkine, 1969.

Becq, Annie. "Baudelaire et 'l'Amour de l'art': La dédicace 'aux bourgeois' du *Salon de 1846.*" *Romantisme,* 17-18 (1977), 71-8.

Benjamin Walter. *Illuminations.* Trans. H. Zohn. Ed. H. Arendt. New York: Schocken Books, 1969.

———. *A Lyric Poet in the Age of High Capitalism.* Trans. H. Zohn. London: New Left Books, 1973.

———. *Reflections.* Trans. E. Jephcott. Ed. Peter Demetz. New York: Harcourt Brace Jovanovich, 1978.

———. "A Short History of Photography." Trans. P. Patton. In *Classic Essays on Photography.* Ed. Alan Trachtenberg. New Haven: Leete's Island Books, Inc., 1980.

Bersani, Leo. *Baudelaire and Freud.* Berkeley: University of California Press, 1977.

Blanc, Charles. "Eugène Delacroix," *La Gazette des Beaux-Arts* XVI (1885), 5-27 and 97-129.

Boime, Albert. *The Academy and French Painting in the Nineteenth Century.* London: Phaidon, 1971.

Bonnefoy, Yves. "Baudelaire contre Rubens." In *Le Nuage rouge.* Paris: Mercure de France, 1977, 9-80.

du Bos, Jean-Baptiste. *Réflexions critiques sur la poésie et sur la peinture.* 1770; rpt. Genève: Slatkine, 1982.

Boschenstein, Bernard. "Les Muses Tardives. Une lecture des 'Phares'." In *Mouvements premiers: Etudes critiques offertes à Georges Poulet.* Paris: José Corti, 1972.

Brooks, Peter. *The Melodramatic Imagination.* New Haven: Yale University Press: 1976.

Burke, James. *Charles Meryon: Prints and Drawings.* New Haven: Yale University Art Gallery, 1974.

Burty, Philippe. *Maîtres et petits-maîtres.* Paris: G. Charpentier, 1877.

Cargo, Robert T. *A Concordance to Baudelaire's* Les Fleurs du mal. Chapel Hill: University of North Carolina Press, 1965.

———, *Concordance to Baudelaire's* Petits poèmes en prose. (University: University of Alabama Press, 1971.

Castex, P.-G. *La Critique d'art en France au XIXème siècle.* Paris: Centre de Documentation Universitaire, 1959.

———. *Baudelaire critique d'art.* Paris: SEDES, 1969.

Cellier, Léon. "Les 'Phares' de Baudelaire, étude de structure." *Revue des sciences humaines,* NS 121 (1966), 97-105.

———. "Baudelaire et Hugo." In Victor Hugo, *Œuvres complètes,* Edition chronologique publiée sous la direction de Jean Massin. Paris: Club Français du Livre, 1967-70, vol. 13, I-LXVIII.

Chambers, Ross. "Baudelaire et l'espace poétique." In *Le Lieu et la formule: Hommage à Marc Eigeldinger.* Neuchâtel: La Baconnière, 1978.
Clark, Timothy. *The Painting of Modern Life.* New York: Knopf, 1984.
Cleveland Museum of Art. *Constantin Guys: Crimean War Drawings 1854-1856.* By Karen W. Smith. Cleveland: The Cleveland Museum of Art, 1978.
Cousin, Victor. *Du vrai, du beau, et du bien.* Paris: Didier, 1853.
Crépet, Jacques and Blin, Georges, eds. *Les Fleurs du mal.* By Charles Baudelaire. Paris: Corti, 1942.
Delaborde, Henri. *Ingres, sa vie, ses travaux, sa doctrine.* Paris: Plon, 1870.
Delacroix, Eugène. *Journal 1822-1863.* Paris: Plon, 1980.
———. *Hamlet; treize sujets dessinés par Eug. Delacroix.* Paris: Gihaut Frères, 1843.
———. *Eugène Delacroix, sa vie et ses œuvres.* Paris: Imprimerie de J. Claie, 1865.
Diderot, Denis. *Salons.* 4 vols. Eds. Jean Seznec and Jean Adhémar. Oxford: Oxford University Press, 1957.
———. *Œuvres esthétiques.* Ed. P. Vernière. Paris: Garnier Frères, 1968.
Drost, Wolfgang. "De la critique d'art Baudelairienne." In *Baudelaire.* Actes du Colloque de Nice. 24-7 May, 1967. Nice: Minard, 1967, 79-87.
Eckermann, Johann P. *Conversations de Goethe.* Trans. E. Delerot. Paris: Charpentier, 1863.
Eder, Joseph Maria. *History of Photography.* Trans. Edward Epstean. New York: Columbia University Press, 1945.
Emerson, Ralph Waldo. *The Conduct of Life, Nature and other Essays.* Boston: Houghton and Mifflin, 1860.
Fairlie, Alison. "Aspects of Expression in Baudelaire's Art Criticism." In *French 19th Century Painting and Literature.* Ed. U. Finke. Manchester: Manchester University Press, 1972, 40-64.
Fénelon, François de Salignac de la Motte–. *Les Aventures de Télémaque.* Paris: Bélin-Leprieure, 1844.
Ferran, André. *L'Esthétique de Baudelaire.* Paris: Hachette, 1933.
Fontanier, Pierre. *Les Figures du discours.* Ed. Gérard Genette. Paris: Flammarion, 1968.
Fried, Michael. "Painting Memories: On the Containment of the Past in Baudelaire and Manet." *Critical Inquiry,* 10, No. 3 (March, 1984), 510-42.
Fromentin, Eugène. *Les Maîtres d'autrefois.* Ed. P. Moisy. Paris: Garnier, 1972.
Gautier, Théophile. *Les Beaux-Arts en Europe.* Paris: Levy, 1855.
———. *Guide de l'amateur au Musée du Louvre.* Paris: 1882.
———. *Poésies complètes.* 3 vols. Ed. R. Jasinski. Paris: Nizet, 1970.
Gide, André. "Théophile Gautier et Charles Baudelaire." *Les Ecrits nouveaux,* 1, No. 1 (1917), 6-14.
Goblot, E. *La Barrière et le niveau.* Paris: Alcan, 1925
Halpin, M. ed. *North American Indians.* By George Catlin. 2 vols. New York: Dover Publications, 1973.
Hamilton, George Heard. *Manet and his Critics.* New Haven: Yale University Press, 1954.
Hanson, Anne Coffin. *Manet and the Modern Tradition.* New Haven: Yale University Press, 1977.
Hartman, Geoffrey. "Literary Commentary as Literature." In *Criticism in the Wilderness.* New Haven: Yale University Press, 1980.
Hegel, Georg Wilhelm Friedrich. *Hegel's Aesthetics.* 2 vols. Trans. T. M. Knox. Oxford: The Clarendon Press, 1975.
Heine, Heinrich. *De la France.* Ed. Paul Laveau. In *Werke.* Berlin: Akademie-Verlag, 1977.
Herbert, Judd David. *L'Esthétique des* Fleurs du mal. Genève: P. Caillier, 1953.

Herbert, Judd David. "Les Premiers *Tableaux parisiens*." *Kentucky Romance Quarterly*, 13 (1968), 195-219.
Horner, Lucie. *Baudelaire critique de Delacroix*. Geneva: Droz, 1956.
Hugo, Victor. *Œuvres poétiques*. Ed. P. Albouy. 3 vols. Paris: Gallimard (Bibliothèque de la Pléiade), 1964.
Huyghe, René. *L'Esthétique de l'individualisme à travers Delacroix et Baudelaire*. Oxford: Oxford University Press, 1955.
Goncourt, Jules et Edmond de. *Etudes d'art*. Paris: Librairie des Bibliophiles, 1893.
Gore, Keith. "Ernest Renan et l'art." *Revue d'Histoire Littéraire de la France*, 81, No. 3 (1981), 391-412.
Johnson, Barbara. *Défigurations du langage poétique*. Paris: Flammarion, 1979.
Johnson, Lee. *Eugène Delacroix*. London: Weidenfeld and Nicholson, 1963.
Kant, Immanuel. *Critique du jugement*. Trans. J. Barni. Paris: Ladrange, 1846.
———. *Kant's Critique of Judgement*. Trans. J. H. Bernard. London: Macmillan and Co., 1931.
———. *The Critique of Judgement*. Trans. James Creed Meredith. New York: Oxford University Press, 1952.
Kelley, David. "Delacroix, Ingres et Poe: Valeurs picturales et valeurs littéraires dans l'œuvre critique de Baudelaire." *Revue d'Histoire Littéraire de la France*, 71, 705-17.
———. "*Modernité* in Baudelaire's Art Criticism." In *Artists and Writers in France: Essays in Honor of Jean Seznec*. Eds. F. Haskell, A. Levi and R. Shackleton. London: Oxford University Press, 1974.
———. "Deux Aspects du *Salon de 1846* de Baudelaire: La dédicace et la couleur." *Forum for Modern Language Studies*, 5, 331-46.
Kermode, Frank. *The Genesis of Secrecy*. Cambridge: Harvard University Press: 1979.
Lacoue-Labarthe, Philippe. "Baudelaire *contra* Wagner." *Etudes françaises*, 17 (1980), 23-52.
Landow, George. "Baudelaire and Ruskin on Art and Artist." *University of Toronto Quarterly*, 37 (1968), 295-308.
Laplanche, J. and Pontalis, J.-B. *Vocabulaire de la psychanalyse*. Paris: Presses Universitaires de France, 1967.
Larousse, Pierre, gen. ed. *Grand Dictionnaire universelle du XIXème siècle*. Paris: Administration du Grand Dictionnaire Universel, 1875.
Lee, Rensselaer. *Ut Pictura poesis: The Humanistic Theory of Painting*. New York: W. W. Norton, Inc., 1967.
Lessing, Gotthold Ephraïm. *Laocoön: An Essay on the Limits of Painting and Poetry*. Trans. Edward Allen McCormick. Baltimore: The Johns Hopkins University Press, 1984.
Littré, Emile. *Dictionnaire de la langue française*. 7 vols. Paris: Gallimard/Hachette, 1967.
Malraux, André. *Les Voix du silence*. Paris: Gallimard, 1951.
de Man, Paul. "The Literary Self as Origin: The Work of Georges Poulet." In *Blindness and Insight*. New York: Oxford University Press, 1971, 79-101.
———. "Literary History and Literary Modernity." In *Blindness and Insight*. New York: Oxford University Press, 1971, 142-65.
———. "Anthropomorphism and Trope in the Lyric." In *The Rhetoric of Romanticism*. New York: Columbia University Press, 1984, 239-62.
Miller, Christopher. *Blank Darkness*. Chicago: University of Chicago Press, 1986.
Moss, Armand. *Baudelaire et Delacroix*. Paris: Nizet, 1973.

Mras, George. *Eugène Delacroix's Theory of Art.* Princeton: Princeton University Press, 1966.

Paris, City of. *Salon de 1846.* Paris: Vinchon, 1846.

Paris, Palais des Beaux-Arts. *Baudelaire.* Catalogue of an exposition from November 23, 1968 to March 17, 1969. Paris: Réunion des Musées Nationaux, 1968.

de Piles, Roger. *Conversations sur la Connoissance de la Peinture.* Paris: Langlois, 1677.

Poulet, Georges. "Baudelaire." In *Etudes sur le temps humain.* Edinburgh: At the University Press, 1949, 334-53.

———. "Baudelaire." In *Les Métamorphoses du cercle.* Paris: Plon, 1961, 397-432.

———. "Baudelaire et la critique d'identification." *Paragone,* XVIII, No. 213/4, 18-36.

———. "Baudelaire précurseur de la critique moderne." In *Journées Baudelaire.* Actes du Colloque Namur-Bruxelles. 10-13 octobre, 1967. Bruxelles: Académie Royale, 1968, 232-45.

———. *Qui était Baudelaire?* Genève: Skira, 1969.

Prévost, Jean. *Baudelaire, essai sur l'inspiration et la création poétiques.* Paris: Mercure de France, 1953.

Prideaux, Tom. *The World of Delacroix.* New York: Time-Life Books, 1966.

Quatremère de Quincy, Antoine-Chrysostome. *Considérations sur les arts du dessin en France.* Paris: Devaux, 1791.

———. *De l'imitation.* Eds. Léon Krier and Demetri Porphyrios. 1823; rpt. Bruxelles: Archives d'Architecture Moderne, 1980.

Raser, Timothy. "The Fate of Beauty in Romantic Criticism," *Nineteenth-Century French Studies,* 14 (1986), Nos. 3&4, 251-259.

Raymond, Marcel. "Baudelaire et la sculpture." *Preuves,* No. 207 (1968), 48-53.

Rewald, John. *History of Impressionism.* New York: The Museum of Modern Art, 1973.

Rieupeyrout, J. L. "Quand George Catlin vint à Paris." *French American Review,* 1 (1977), 198-204.

Riffaterre, Michael. *Semiotics of Poetry.* Bloomington: Indiana University Press, 1978.

Rosenblum, Robert. *Jean-August-Dominique Ingres.* New York: Abrams, no date.

Rousseau, Jean-Jacques. *Essai sur l'origine des langues.* Ed. Charles Porset. Paris: A. G. Nizet, 1970.

Sainte-Beuve, Charles-Augustin. "Victor Hugo." In *Portraits Contemporains.* Paris: Calmann-Lévy, 1968.

———. *Vie, poésie et pensées de Joseph Delorme.* Ed. Gérard Antoine. Paris: Nouvelles Editions Latines, 1956.

Sartre, Jean-Paul. *L'Imagination.* Paris: Presses Universitaires de France, 1936.

———. *Baudelaire.* Paris: Gallimard, 1963.

———. *Situations, IV.* Paris: Gallimard, 1964.

Schlegel, Friedrich. *Dialogue on Poetry* and *Literary Aphorisms.* Trans. E. Behler and R. Struc. University Park, Pennsylvania: The Pennsylvania State University Press, 1968.

Sérullaz, Maurice. *Delacroix.* New York: Abrams, no date.

———. *Les Peintures Murales de Delacroix.* Paris: Editions du Temps, 1963.

Signac, Paul. *D'Eugène Delacroix au néo-impressionnisme.* Paris: Hermann, 1978.

Sloane, Joseph. *French Painting between Past and Present.* Princeton: Princeton University Press, 1951.

———. "Baudelaire as Art Critic." *Bulletin Baudelairien,* 5 (1969).

Sontag, Susan. *On Photography.* New York: Farrar, Straus and Giroux, 1977.

Spector, Jack. *The Murals of Eugène Delacroix at Saint Sulpice.* New York: The College Art Association of America, 1967.

———. *Delacroix: The Death of Sardanapalus.* New York: Viking, 1974.

Starkie, Enid. *Baudelaire.* Middlesex: Penguin Books, 1957.

Starobinski, Jean. "De la critique à la poésie." *Preuves.* No. 207 (1968) 43-8.

———. "Les Rimes du vide." *Nouvelle revue de psychanalyse,* No. 11 (1975). 133, 143.

Stendhal. *Histoire de la peinture en Italie.* Ed. H. Martineau. Paris: 1929.

Tabarant, A. *La Vie artistique en France au temps de Baudelaire.* Paris: Mercure de France, 1942.

Taine, Hippolyte. *Philosophie de l'art.* Paris: Hachette, 1882.

Ternois, Daniel. "Baudelaire et l'ingrisme." In *French 19th Century French Painting and Literature.* Ed. U. Finke. Manchester: Manchester University Press, 1972, 17-39.

Trapp, Frank Anderson. "The Universal Exposition of 1855." *The Burlington Magazine.* June, 1965, 300-305.

———. *The Attainment of Delacroix.* Baltimore: The Johns Hopkins University Press, 1971.

Trottein, Serge. "La Théorie du jeu: lecture de la Critique de la Faculté de Juger Esthétique de Kant." Paris: PENS, in press.

Webster's Seventh New Collegiate Dictionary. Springfield: G. & C. Merriam Company, 1961.

Wilcox, John. "The Beginnings of *l'Art pour l'Art.*" *Journal of Aesthetics and Art Criticism,* XI (1953), 360-77.

Ziegler, Jean. "Emile Deroy (1820-1846) et l'esthétique de Baudelaire." *Gazette des Beaux-Arts,* 87, Nos. 1288 and 1289, 143-59.

———. "Baudelaire et Meryon." *Bulletin Baudelairien,* 11, 3-14.

NORTH CAROLINA STUDIES IN THE ROMANCE LANGUAGES AND LITERATURES

I.S.B.N. Prefix 0-8078-

Recent Titles

LANGUAGE IN GIOVANNI VERGA'S EARLY NOVELS, by Nicholas Patruno. 1977. (No. 188). *-9188-6.*

BLAS DE OTERO EN SU POESÍA, by Moraima de Semprún Donahue. 1977. (No. 189). *-9189-4.*

LA ANATOMÍA DE "EL DIABLO COJUELO": DESLINDES DEL GÉNERO ANATOMÍSTICO, por C. George Peale. 1977. (No. 191). *-9191-6.*

RICHARD SANS PEUR, EDITED FROM "LE ROMANT DE RICHART" AND FROM GILLES CORROZET'S "RICHART SANS PAOUR", by Denis Joseph Conlon. 1977. (No. 192). *-9192-4.*

MARCEL PROUST'S GRASSET PROOFS. *Commentary and Variants,* by Douglas Alden. 1978. (No. 193). *-9193-2.*

MONTAIGNE AND FEMINISM, by Cecile Insdorf. 1977. (No. 194). *-9194-0.*

SANTIAGO F. PUGLIA, AN EARLY PHILADELPHIA PROPAGANDIST FOR SPANISH AMERICAN INDEPENDENCE, by Merle S. Simmons. 1977. (No. 195). *-9195-9.*

BAROQUE FICTION-MAKING. A STUDY OF GOMBERVILLE'S "POLEXANDRE", by Edward Baron Turk. 1978. (No. 196). *-9196-7.*

THE TRAGIC FALL: DON ÁLVARO DE LUNA AND OTHER FAVORITES IN SPANISH GOLDEN AGE DRAMA, by Raymond R. MacCurdy. 1978. (No. 197). *-9197-5.*

A BAHIAN HERITAGE. An Ethnolinguistic Study of African Influences on Bahian Portuguese, by William W. Megenney. 1978. (No. 198). *-9198-3.*

"LA QUERELLE DE LA ROSE": Letters and Documents, by Joseph L. Baird and John R. Kane. 1978. (No. 199). *-9199-1.*

TWO AGAINST TIME. *A Study of the Very Present Worlds of Paul Claudel and Charles Péguy,* by Joy Nachod Humes. 1978. (No. 200). *-9200-9.*

TECHNIQUES OF IRONY IN ANATOLE FRANCE. Essay on *Les Sept Femmes de la Barbe-Bleue,* by Diane Wolfe Levy. 1978. (No. 201). *-9201-7.*

THE PERIPHRASTIC FUTURES FORMED BY THE ROMANCE REFLEXES OF "VADO (AD)" PLUS INFINITIVE, by James Joseph Champion. 1978. (No. 202). *-9202-5.*

THE EVOLUTION OF THE LATIN /b/-/u̯/ MERGER: A Quantitative and Comparative Analysis of the *B-V* Alternation in Latin Inscriptions, by Joseph Louis Barbarino. 1978. (No. 203). *-9203-3.*

METAPHORIC NARRATION: THE STRUCTURE AND FUNCTION OF METAPHORS IN "A LA RECHERCHE DU TEMPS PERDU", by Inge Karalus Crosman. 1978. (No. 204). *-9204-1.*

LE VAIN SIECLE GUERPIR. A Literary Approach to Sainthood through Old French Hagiography of the Twelfth Century, by Phyllis Johnson and Brigitte Cazelles. 1979. (No. 205). *-9205-X.*

THE POETRY OF CHANGE: A STUDY OF THE SURREALIST WORKS OF BENJAMIN PÉRET, by Julia Field Costich. 1979. (No. 206). *-9206-8.*

NARRATIVE PERSPECTIVE IN THE POST-CIVIL WAR NOVELS OF FRANCISCO AYALA "MUERTES DE PERRO" AND "EL FONDO DEL VASO", by Maryellen Bieder. 1979. (No. 207). *-9207-6.*

RABELAIS: HOMO LOGOS, by Alice Fiola Berry. 1979. (No. 208). *-9208-4.*

"DUEÑAS" AND "DONCELLAS": A STUDY OF THE "DOÑA RODRÍGUEZ" EPISODE IN "DON QUIJOTE", by Conchita Herdman Marianella. 1979. (No. 209). *-9209-2.*

PIERRE BOAISTUAU'S "HISTOIRES TRAGIQUES": A STUDY OF NARRATIVE FORM AND TRAGIC VISION, by Richard A. Carr. 1979. (No. 210). *-9210-6.*

REALITY AND EXPRESSION IN THE POETRY OF CARLOS PELLICER, by George Melnykovich. 1979. (No. 211). *-9211-4.*

When ordering please cite the *ISBN Prefix* plus the last four digits for each title.

Send orders to: University of North Carolina Press
P.O. Box 2288
CB# 6215
Chapel Hill, NC 27515-2288
U.S.A.

NORTH CAROLINA STUDIES IN THE ROMANCE LANGUAGES AND LITERATURES

I.S.B.N. Prefix 0-8078-

Recent Titles

MEDIEVAL MAN, HIS UNDERSTANDING OF HIMSELF, HIS SOCIETY, AND THE WORLD, by Urban T. Holmes, Jr. 1980. (No. 212). *-9212-2.*

MÉMOIRES SUR LA LIBRAIRIE ET SUR LA LIBERTÉ DE LA PRESSE, introduction and notes by Graham E. Rodmell. 1979. (No. 213). *-9213-0.*

THE FICTIONS OF THE SELF. THE EARLY WORKS OF MAURICE BARRES, by Gordon Shenton. 1979. (No. 214). *-9214-9.*

CECCO ANGIOLIERI. A STUDY, by Gifford P. Orwen. 1979. (No. 215). *-9215-7.*

THE INSTRUCTIONS OF SAINT LOUIS: A CRITICAL TEXT, by David O'Connell. 1979. (No. 216). *-9216-5.*

ARTFUL ELOQUENCE, JEAN LEMAIRE DE BELGES AND THE RHETORICAL TRADITION, by Michael F. O. Jenkins. 1980. (No. 217). *-9217-3.*

A CONCORDANCE TO MARIVAUX'S COMEDIES IN PROSE, edited by Donald C. Spinelli. 1979. (No. 218). 4 volumes, *-9218-1* (set); *-9219-X* (v. 1); *-9220-3* (v. 2); *-9221-1* (v. 3); *-9222-X* (v. 4).

ABYSMAL GAMES IN THE NOVELS OF SAMUEL BECKETT, by Angela B. Moorjani. 1982. (No. 219). *-9223-8.*

GERMAIN NOUVEAU DIT HUMILIS: ÉTUDE BIOGRAPHIQUE, par Alexandre L. Amprimoz. 1983. (No. 220). *-9224-6.*

THE "VIE DE SAINT ALEXIS" IN THE TWELFTH AND THIRTEENTH CENTURIES: AN EDITION AND COMMENTARY, by Alison Goddard Elliot. 1983. (No. 221). *-9225-4.*

THE BROKEN ANGEL: MYTH AND METHOD IN VALÉRY, by Ursula Franklin. 1984. (No. 222). *-9226-2.*

READING VOLTAIRE'S "CONTES": A SEMIOTICS OF PHILOSOPHICAL NARRATION, by Carol Sherman. 1985. (No. 223). *-9227-0.*

THE STATUS OF THE READING SUBJECT IN THE "LIBRO DE BUEN AMOR", by Marina Scordilis Brownlee. 1985. (No. 224). *-9228-9.*

MARTORELL'S "TIRANT LO BLANCH": A PROGRAM FOR MILITARY AND SOCIAL REFORM IN FIFTEENTH-CENTURY CHRISTENDOM, by Edward T. Aylward. 1985. (No. 225). *-9229-7.*

NOVEL LIVES: THE FICTIONAL AUTOBIOGRAPHIES OF GUILLERMO CABRERA INFANTE AND MARIO VARGAS LLOSA, by Rosemary Geisdorfer Feal. 1986. (No. 226). *-9230-0.*

SOCIAL REALISM IN THE ARGENTINE NARRATIVE, by David William Foster. 1986. (No. 227). *-9231-9.*

HALF-TOLD TALES: DILEMMAS OF MEANING IN THREE FRENCH NOVELS, by Philip Stewart. 1987. (No. 228). *-9232-7.*

POLITIQUES DE L'ECRITURE BATAILLE/DERRIDA: le sens du sacré dans la pensée française du surréalisme à nos jours, par Jean-Michel Heimonet. 1987. (No. 229). *-9233-5.*

GOD, THE QUEST, THE HERO: THEMATIC STRUCTURES IN BECKETT'S FICTION, by Laura Barge. 1988. (No. 230). *-9235-1.*

THE NAME GAME. WRITING/FADING WRITER IN "DE DONDE SON LOS CANTANTES", by Oscar Montero. 1988. (No. 231). *-9236-X.*

GIL VICENTE AND THE DEVELOPMENT OF THE COMEDIA, by René Pedro Garay. 1988. (No. 232). *-9234-3.*

HACIA UNA POÉTICA DEL RELATO DIDÁCTICO: OCHO ESTUDIOS SOBRE "EL CONDE LUCANOR", por Aníbal A. Biglieri. 1989. (No. 233). *-9237-8.*

A POETICS OF ART CRITICISM: THE CASE OF BAUDELAIRE, by Timothy Raser. 1989. (No. 234). *-9238-6.*

When ordering please cite the *ISBN Prefix* plus the last four digits for each title.

Send orders to: University of North Carolina Press
P.O. Box 2288
CB# 6215
Chapel Hill, NC 27515-2288
U.S.A.

The Department of Romance Studies Digital Arts and Collaboration Lab at the University of North Carolina at Chapel Hill is proud to support the digitization of the North Carolina Studies in the Romance Languages and Literatures series.

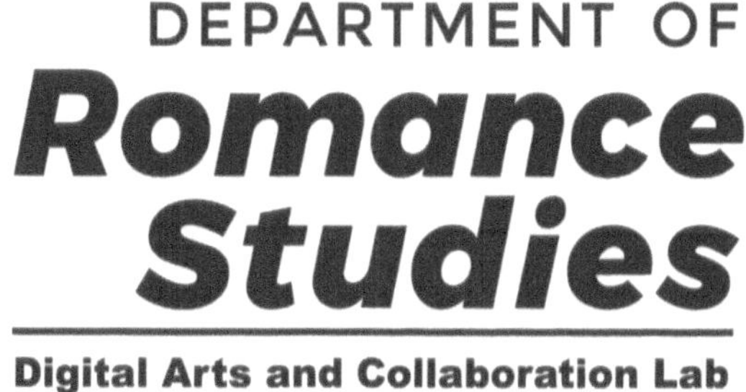

www.ingramcontent.com/pod-product-compliance
Lightning Source LLC
LaVergne TN
LVHW091145080826
845145LV00008B/2259
* 9 7 8 0 8 0 7 8 9 2 3 8 1 *